Sister's Choice

Elaine Showalter is Professor and Chair of the English
Department at Princeton University; her publications
include *A Literature of Their Own: British Women Novelists
from Brontë to Lessing, The New Feminist Criticism, The Female
Malady*, and *Sexual Anarchy: Gender and Culture at the
Fin de Siècle*.

Sister's Choice

TRADITION AND CHANGE
IN AMERICAN WOMEN'S
WRITING

The Clarendon Lectures
1989

ELAINE SHOWALTER

Oxford   New York

OXFORD UNIVERSITY PRESS

1994

Oxford University Press, Walton Street, Oxford OX2 6DP

Oxford New York
Athens Auckland Bangkok Bombay
Calcutta Cape Town Dar es Salaam Delhi
Florence Hong Kong Istanbul Karachi
Kuala Lumpur Madras Madrid Melbourne
Mexico City Nairobi Paris Singapore
Taipei Tokyo Toronto

and associated companies in
Berlin Ibadan

Oxford is a trade mark of Oxford University Press

First published 1991 by the Clarendon Press
First issued as an Oxford University Press paperback 1994

British Library Cataloguing in Publication Data

Data available

Library of Congress Cataloging in Publication Data
Showalter, Elaine.
Sister's choice : tradition and change in American women's writing
/ Elaine Showalter.
p.   cm.
'The Clarendon lectures, 1989.'
Includes index.
1. American literature—Women authors—History and criticism.
2. Women and literature—United States—History.   3. Influence
(Literary, artistic, etc.)   I. Title.
PS147.S48   1994   810.9'9287—dc20   94-18383
ISBN 0-19-282417-1

1 3 5 7 9 10 8 6 4 2

Printed in Great Britain by
Clays Ltd
Bungay, Suffolk

For Joyce Carol Oates

ACKNOWLEDGMENTS

FOUR of these Chapters (1, 2, 7, and 8) were originally delivered as the Clarendon Lectures at Oxford University in May 1989. My warmest thanks go to Kim Scott Walwyn of Oxford University Press, Stephen Gill of the English Faculty Board, and New College for their invitation and their hospitality. Among the many members of the Oxford community who made this visit so stimulating and pleasant, special thanks go to Julia Briggs, Lyndall Gordon, Elisabeth Jay, William Handley, and Kate Flint.

Gayle Wald's research assistance went far beyond the required to the inspired. I have tried to indicate in the notes the many specific intellectual debts I owe to students, colleagues, and friends over the years, especially to the members of the NEH Summer Seminar on 'Women's Writing and Women's Culture' in 1984, and the participants in the Princeton Graduate Women's Studies Colloquium in 1989. Thanks also to Roger Abrahams, Gladys-Marie Fry, Elaine Hedges, and Radka Donnell-Vogt for sharing their knowledge of quilts and quilt-makers. Michael Cadden, Larry Danson, Cathy Davidson, Joanne Dobson, Emory Elliott, Judith Fetterley, Henry Louis Gates, Jr., Daniel Goldberg, William Howarth, A. Walton Litz, Wendy Martin, Lee Mitchell, Toni Morrison, Nell Painter, Albert Raboteau, Christine Stansell, and Cornel West have been continuing sources of inspiration.

Earlier and partial versions of some of these chapters have appeared elsewhere, and I am grateful to the following for permission to reprint: 'Miranda and Cassandra,' in *Tradition and the Talents of Women*, ed. Florence Howe (University of Illinois Press, 1991), © Elaine Showalter; 'Introduction,' to *Little Women*, © 1989 Viking Penguin, Inc.; 'The Death of the Lady (Novelist): Wharton's *House of Mirth*,' *Representations*, 9 (Spring 1985), 133–49, © 1985 the Regents of the University of

California; '*The Awakening* as a Solitary Book,' in *New Essays on 'The Awakening'*, ed. Wendy Martin, © 1988 Cambridge University Press; 'Women Writers between the Wars,' in *Columbia Literary History of the United States*, ed. Emory Elliott, © 1988 Columbia University Press; and 'Piecing and Writing,' in *The Poetics of Gender*, ed. Nancy K. Miller, © 1986 Columbia University Press.

E.S.

CONTENTS

ৰ্কি

LIST OF ILLUSTRATIONS

꙰

I

American Questions

In the early 1970s, when I was living in London and doing research for a book on English women writers, I became obsessed with a line from John Stuart Mill's *Subjection of Women*: 'If women lived in a different country from men, and had never read any of their writings, they would have had a literature of their own.' Mill's sentence, from which I eventually took the title of my book, struck me as an elegant and troubling summation of the problems of nationality, originality, influence, and impossibility that must plague anyone attempting to write feminist literary history. For women, despite widespread myths of Amazon utopias, have never lived in a different country from men, and can never grow up as literate and educated beings without having read men's writings. Furthermore, women, like men, are shaped by the country they inhabit, by their nation's language, history, literary canons, cultural mythologies, ideologies, and ideals.

Could women, then, ever hope to have a criticism of their own? And could an American woman really understand the delicate and complex fretwork of English literary culture? I felt very conscious of having lived in a different country from Gaskell, Eliot, and Woolf, and thus, in my mind, calling the book *A Literature of Their Own* acknowledged my American distance from the English tradition. Yet to my relief, while many reviewers questioned the idea that *women* had a literature of their own, nobody seemed concerned that these particular women writers were British. If there were cultural nuances I had missed, local idioms I got wrong, historical details I scrambled, critics kindly refrained from pointing them out. Overtly, at least, nationality did not seem to be an issue in the 1970s.

Of course, there was nothing unusual in an American scholar studying English Victorian literature; we Americans jostled for space in the British Library Reading Room and queued together at the Brontë Parsonage Museum. And in coming to England I was not only following in the footsteps of other American scholars, but also following a path that other American women writers had taken before me. The pilgrimage to Haworth was an initiation rite for the Yankee literati. Sarah Orne Jewett went with her friend Annie Fields in 1898, and celebrated the Brontës' 'lights of genius like candles flaring in a cave.' The Alcott sisters in their shabby home read Mrs Gaskell's *Life of Charlotte Brontë* and thought hopefully of themselves as American Brontës. 'I may not be a C. B., but I shall do something yet,' wrote Louisa May Alcott in her journal; and I had some of the same aspirations with regard to Kathleen Tillotson, whose book *Novels of the 1840s* was my secret critical model in every detail down to the way the footnotes looked on the page. If I could not be a K. T., I hoped to do something yet for Victorian women writers.

The theoretical problems that preoccupied me when I worked on this book were very specific to the historical moment. In restricting myself to English women writers, rather than looking at a global 'female imagination,' or grouping American and English writers thematically, I wanted to avoid the idea that women's writing had a universal sameness that might be bio-logical or psychological. Rather, it seemed to me, women's writing had to be seen historically, in its specific national con-texts. For theoretical models, I turned to what was then a frustratingly small set of sources about the 'subcultures' of Afro-American, Canadian, Anglo-Indian, and Jewish literature. I also used the first important theories of women's culture then emerg-ing from social history, such as the work of Carroll Smith-Rosenberg; and from cultural anthropology, in the work of Edwin and Shirley Ardener on muted and dominant cultures. Applying these theories of subculture to English women writers was made easier because English women's writing, until the past few decades, was racially homogeneous and regionally compact, with little ethnic, religious, or even class diversity. It thus constituted a relatively coherent literature of its own within the larger culture of English writing. The English tradition also offered many of the great classics of feminist writing, from *Jane Eyre* to *A Room of One's Own*, as well as the subversive genres of sensation fiction and the New Woman novels.

Yet it was clear to me even then that there were few novels by English women in the nineteenth century as radical or outspoken with regard to the woman question as those by their American counterparts. 'Our new country develops faculties that young women in England were unconscious of possessing,' wrote Catherine Sedgwick in *Hope Leslie. Dora, the American Amazon* (1864), for example, rides through rebel lines disguised as a man to deliver military information to Union troops.[1] While many of the great English novels struggled with the problem of feminine vocation outside the home, American women writers took for granted the idea that women should work. In Louisa May Alcott's *Little Women*, the snobbish English visitor Kate Vaughan is rebuked for patronizing Meg March because she works as a governess: 'Young ladies in America love independence as much as their ancestors did, and are admired and respected for supporting themselves.' In Alcott's feminist novel *Work* (1873), Christie Devon takes up the various forms of employment available to women in the late nineteenth century, ending as a feminist leader and orator. When Alcott became famous, her father lectured about her at women's suffrage conferences, with the theme of 'what an American girl can do.'[2]

As soon as I had finished *A Literature of Their Own*, I began to read American women writers, a belated project, for although I grew up in Boston, I knew Haworth much better than Concord, and Lake Windermere better than Walden Pond. Homecoming metaphors, of course, are rife in American literary history. As William Carlos Williams wrote to Robert Lowell, Europe was Circe, and his trip 'another Odyssey from which I hope to see your return to your Penelope (American) much enriched in your mind and ready to join your fellows here in pushing forward the craft.'[3] For black American critics of my generation, the homecoming has often been a dramatic conversion experience. Houston Baker, Jr. and Henry Louis Gates, for example, have described not only their experience as graduate students at Edinburgh and Cambridge, but also their own 'odyssey through "Western" critical theory and their ultimate [re]turn to the black idiom.'[4] In *Afro-American Poetics*, Baker tells how he began to teach at Yale in 1968 with the ambition of becoming 'a successful critic of British Victorian literature.' One night he was accosted in the middle of a lecture on New Criticism by young black nationalists who remarked on his amazing resemblance to Malcolm X. Shaken from his Arnoldian trance by this event, Baker enlisted in the black revolutionary struggle and began his own critical journey from the Black Aesthetic to blues theory to a poetics of Afro-American women's writing.[5]

But studying American women's writing has not been a comforting return to my native idiom or an easy reclamation of a literature of my own. In recent years, while new critical developments have unsettled feminist confidence in the meaning of 'women,' the consensus on the 'Americanness' of American literature and the validity of literary history has also collapsed. American literary history, which depended on belief in the exceptionalism of a national cultural identity, is now questioning itself. As William Spengemann states the case, 'We have American things, and we have literary things, but we have nothing . . . that can be called uniquely or characteristically American.'[6] In the wake of poststructuralism, the authority of historical narrative has been questioned as well. As Emory Elliott, the editor of a new literary history of the United States, observes, 'the historian is not a truthteller but a storyteller . . . and a nation's official history is ultimately no more than a story about which there is widespread agreement.'[7] In fact, Elliott admits, 'we are not so sure we know what American literature is or what history is and whether we have the authority to explain either.'[8]

When we add to these debates arguments from within feminist criticism about race, class, subjectivity, and identity, it becomes clear that writing about American women's literature in the 1990s raises much more complicated problems even for a native daughter than did writing about English women's literature as a resident alien in the 1970s. The very enterprise of gynocriticism—the study of women's writing—is itself far from accepted in academic circles. While those on the far right still regard the study of women's writing as an insignificant or un-American undertaking, to many feminist critics it is an embarrassing remnant of pre-postmodernist humanism, an endorsement of separate canons of women's writing, as well as a tacit commitment to female subjectivity. To investigate women's writing is already, in some academic circles, to damn oneself by asking naïve or unfashionable American questions. In 1988, for example, Alice Jardine and Anne Menke asked twenty leading French women writers what they thought about their place in the canon of modern French literature, their attitudes towards women writers in French literary history, and their position on the specificity of women's writing. But Jardine and Menke admitted to feeling awkward about their task: 'We felt that these were American questions, translations of an American academic desire, projections having to do with a canon that is ultimately perhaps not as French as it is American.' Their ambivalence was met by shrugs of indifference from the French women writers they interviewed. 'Here again is this story of the "canon,"' Hélène Cixous wearily remarked, 'which is really an American notion.'[9]

In this book I ask some 'American' questions about the history, traditions, and contradictions of American women's writing, but I also question the idea that in the multi-cultural reality of the present we can continue to assume a monolithic national identity with a given relation to gender and literary production. The national stereotypes which have played a significant role in feminist metacriticism can no longer be accepted. To begin with, I don't see myself as an 'American feminist critic,' that naïve essentialist who never would be missed by the English and European critics who have her on their list. But I also doubt whether such a pestilential creature really exists. Reading the examples of the 'American feminist critic' cited in various surveys it's difficult to determine the terms of definition. Is it the stamp on your passport, the place where you teach, or your theoretical affiliation? While most definitions concede, as Maggie Humm asserts, that 'feminist literary criticism has no *single hegemonic* national identity,'[10] these distinctions tend to drop out quickly on the way to promoting some alternative nationalized perspective, whether English or French. Apparently some are born American feminist critics, some become American feminist critics, and some have American feminist critic-ness thrust upon them. The media image of the 'American feminist critic' has to be sustained by focusing on a few women and a handful of texts; in reality there are far too many internal differences of race, ethnicity, and theoretical affiliation to make the idea of a monolithic American feminist criticism meaningful. Taking refuge behind such a banner in the 1990s would be intellectually indefensible, and politically retrograde. As Naomi Schor eloquently argues,

It is in the interpenetration of different national traditions, the crossing of lesbian, black, marxist, and mainstream feminisms, in short in the multiplication of all differences—national, racial, sexual, and class— that the future of feminist literary theory and criticism should lie, and not in the perpetuation of myths of segregation and national superiority.[11]

Rather than trying to theorize an 'American feminist criticism,' I would like to expand the meaning and practice of gynocriticism with reference to American women's writing. The cross-cultural contexts I was searching for in the early 1970s when I wrote *A Literature of Their Own* are now burgeoning. The embryonic field of Afro-American literary study has developed into a full-grown discipline; Chicano and Asian-American studies have added to our sense of cultural multiplicity; gay studies has extended feminist insights and methods in the study of gender. In particular, post-colonial literary theory is extraordinarily relevant to the study of American women's writing because it both views the American literary experience as the 'model for all later post-colonial writing,' and also acknowledges many correspondences with feminist criticism and practice. All of these critical practices are asking the same fundamental questions: Does a 'muted' culture have a literature of its own, or must it always revise the conventions of the dominant? Can there be an 'authentic' and separate language, theory, and culture expressive of the soul of any group living within a hybrid culture? What is the relationship between contemporary literary theory and a non-canonical literature? How can a literature find an identity and what Wole Soyinka calls 'self-apprehension,' and still avoid national, racial, or sexual essentialism?

As critics of these various and often overlapping literatures have explored our specific textual traditions, we have begun to discover similarities, shared metaphors, phases, tropes, and myths that seem to be part of a metanarrative of countercultural aesthetics. Language is a fundamental issue. Is the dominant language adequate to express the experience and reality of muted or marginal groups? As the Indian novelist Raja Rao explains, 'The telling has not been easy. One has to convey in a language that is not one's own the spirit that is one's own.'[12] In many cultures, writers have desired or demanded a language of their own, an authentic native tongue unsullied by the language of the Other. The Female Aesthetic of the 1970s was a call for a return to the Mother Tongue, a genderlect of women's speech celebrated as more immediate than patriarchal language. More recently, however, it has been recognized that what Adrienne Rich calls 'the dream of a common language' has always been a utopian fantasy. 'All forms of culture,' the post-colonial theorist Homi Bhabha argues, 'are continually in a process of hybridity.' The languages of various groups are perpetually intersecting, translating each other; minority or post-colonial cultures appropriate and subvert the language of the dominant through the strategies of neologisms, syntactic fusion, interlanguages, substitutions, and allusion.[13] Indeed, 'interlinguistic play,' or binguality is one of the most striking features of minority literatures. Such writing is always double-voiced, what Henry Louis Gates, speaking of Afro-American literature calls 'two-toned,' or Rámon Saldívar, speaking of Chicano literature calls 'the dialectics of difference,' or Naomi Schor, speaking of women's literature, calls 'bitextual.'[14]

The acts of unnaming and self-naming have long been fundamental to cultural identity and self-assertion. For Afro-American literature, the rejection of the patronymics and languages of slavery is 'a refusal to be named [that] invokes . . . a transcendent impulse to undo all categories, all metonymies and reifications, and thrust the self beyond received patterns and relationships.'[15] For Mexican and Latin-American literature, the choice of the name 'Chicano,' 'Latino,' or 'Hispanic' carries significant meaning and designates placement in a hierarchical system. The Canadian critic Robert Kroetsch writes: 'At one time I considered it to be the task of the Canadian writer to give names to his experience, to be the namer. I now suspect, that, on the contrary, it is his task to un-name.'[16]

These themes of protest and autonomy are reflected in Ursula LeGuin's feminist fable, 'She Unnames Them.' 'She' is Eve, who decides to return to Adam all the names, taxonomies, and identities he has bestowed on the animals, and to let them name themselves. Without their labels, the cattle, pets, birds, insects, and fish also shed their mythology; Eve feels differently about them: 'They seemed far closer than when their names had stood between myself and them like a clear barrier: so close that my fear of them and their fear of me became one same fear.' Finally Eve gives her own name back to Adam, who is tinkering in the garden and scarcely listens to what she is saying or notices when she leaves. No longer named in Adam's language, no longer defined in opposition to him, she is free to discover her own new words in the new world: 'My words now must be as slow, as new, as single, as tentative as the steps I took going down the path away from the house, between the dark-branched tall dancers motion-less against the winter shining.'

Whether in unnaming; or in images of the veil in black or women's writing; or in the myth of the 'redeemer-poet,' the Black Jesus, gay Christ, or feminist Messiah who will die to save us; or in the self-mocking codes of minstrelsy, camp, or ethnic humor, we will find that many aspects of a particular literary tradition have family resemblances to the others.[17] These very different cultures are not related, as Homi Bhabha has insisted, 'because of the familiarity or similarity of "*contents*"—indeed, cultural values, glibly elided in the slogan of "gender, race, and class" are often conflicting and irreconcilable—but because all cultures are symbol-forming . . . practices.'[18] Different eth-nicities are not identical and cannot be reduced to a Rainbow Coalition on the cultural left; but as producers of literature and criticism we have a common historical trajectory, if not a common language.

How do these relationships modify a feminist literary history of American women? To begin with, they complicate its origins. American women's literature was born, most scholars have argued, with the publication of Anne Bradstreet's first book of poems, *The Tenth Muse, lately sprung up in America*, in 1650. Both Americanist and feminist critics have long claimed to find in Bradstreet's verse the voice of an American Muse who welcomes 'a new world and new manners.'[19] Yet Bradstreet's revisionary rewriting is more inflected by gender than by nationality; it is not uniquely American, but rather the first phase of a post-colonial literature, the writing of an 'elite whose primary identification is with the colonizing power.'[20] Born and educated in England, Bradstreet considered herself an English citizen although she lived in Puritan America. Her language, subject matter, and meter is still very much that of English and European literature. Like her contemporaries Anne Finch and Anne Killigrew, however, Bradstreet brings an explicitly feminine voice to poetry, describing experiences and desires very different from those of her poetic masters Sidney and DuBartas. In 'The Prologue,' she differentiates her genres and subjects from those of her male predecessors. While 'poets and historians' will sing of 'wars, of captains, and of kings,' she will choose more limited and domestic topics. Bradstreet exploits the modesty topos in such characteristic self-description as 'mean pen,' 'obscure lines,' and 'wounded brain.' Her Muse, she claims, is 'foolish, broken, blemished.' And while men compete for fame and poetic laurels, she claims contentment with her small domestic niche: 'Give thyme or parsley wreath, I ask no bayes.' Bradstreet's humble parsley-wreath is both apology and an ironic cultural substitution that has the effect of calling the privileged status of the classical symbol into question. Women may have to make do with kitchen herbs like thyme or parsley, but what makes the bay-leaf so important? Why has the laurel alone become the sign of distinction? Why not a Poet Parsleyate?

English women poets of the same period use the same devices to revise neoclassical poetic symbols. In 'The Introduction' (1680), for example, Anne Finch dispatches her Muse 'with contracted wing' into retirement: 'For groves of laurel thou wert never meant | Be dark enough thy shades, and be thou there content.' For seventeenth-century women poets, the question of competition, either with men or among themselves, is problematic. In 'The Circuit of Apollo,' Finch describes a contest for the wreath only among women; Anne Killigrew worries that her laurel will adorn another because of doubt that women can create.

These strategic defenses against anticipated attack became the conventions of the minority poet, whether working-class in England or black in the United States. The nineteenth-century Afro-American poet Paul Laurence Dunbar, for example, worries in 'Prometheus' that black Americans can never produce a bard to rival Shelley. Mocking his own poetic inadequacies in a vivid cultural image, Dunbar declares: 'We strum our banjo-strings and call them lyres.'

A specifically *American* literary identity, including that of women, did not spring up spontaneously with residence on American shores, but was developed in response to English and European sneers at our national cultural inferiority. In 1820 Sydney Smith, the editor of the *Edinburgh Review*, taunted the former colonists on their failure to do anything independent in art and literature. 'Literature the Americans have none,' he sneered, 'it is all imported.' As Smith asked, 'In the four corners of the globe, who reads an American book? or goes to an American play?'[21] As they broke away from allegiance to English traditions, American writers tended to mythologize their country's uniqueness. Attacks like those of Smith fuelled the kind of patriotic passion Emerson displayed when he dedicated his journal in 1822 to 'the Spirit of America,' 'the Genius who yet counts the tardy years of childhood, but who is increasing unawares in the twilight, and swelling into strength until the hour, when he shall break the cloud, to shew his colossal youth and cover the firmament with the shadow of his wings.'[22] This gigantic American poet-hero would create an art commensurate with the vastness of the land and the scope of its dreams.

While Emerson's Spirit of America was clearly male, women too were urged to participate as readers and writers in the formation of a national literature and were promised an equal voice in democratic institutions. The link between women's writing and women's rights is an important theme in the development of an American women's literary consciousness, and the Declaration of Independence was a formative text for American women as well as men. It was revised, appropriated, and parodied in women's texts from the 'Ladies Declaration of Independence' which complained of men who 'have undervalued our talents and disparaged our attainments,' to the 'Declaration of Sentiments' of 1848 at the first American women's rights convention in Seneca Falls. Although women were barred from participation in the public oratory which was so powerful an influence on the writing of American men, they often thought of fiction as their pulpit. Harriet Beecher Stowe heard the 'Declaration' read aloud on the Fourth of July when she was a little girl and was so inspired that she vowed someday 'to make some declaration on my own account.'[23] Louisa May Alcott's *Work* begins with the heroine announcing 'There's going to be a new Declaration of Independence!' and leaving home to find a job.

Thus rather than contesting the myth of the American spirit, American women saw their own writing as its true incarnation. By the late 1840s, when the first anthologies of American women's writing, and the first critical essays appeared, Rufus Griswold's *Female Poets of America* has an epigraph from Anne Bradstreet and takes patriotic pride in 'the increased degree in which women among us are taking a leading part in literature. . . . The proportion of female writers at this moment in America far exceeds that which the present or any other age in England exhibits.'

In an essay in the *North American Review* in 1853, Caroline Kirkland described the clamor from England for an American fiction:

American! we want something American! something distinctive; something that would not be at home anywhere else; grand as your rivers; rugged as your mountains; expansive, like your great lakes . . .

> Be grand! be grand!
> Let your lines expand!
> We'll take nothing small from so monstrous a land!

In Kirkland's view, however, attempts to meet such demands were impossible and self-defeating, because the American Sublime could only be an imitation of English epic or romanticism: 'The bigger we tried to write, the more they said we stole their thunder.' Yet she also saw a uniquely American tradition emerging in the work of women writers like Catherine Sedgwick, Harriet Beecher Stowe, and Susan Warner, whose themes were domestic, local, and vernacular. 'So, by general consent, and in a happy hour, we gave up trying to write to please or instruct anybody but ourselves; and lo and behold, an American literature!'[24]

The success of women's novels in the market soured those who had been prepared to patronize women but not to compete with them. By the 1850s, indeed, when women writers were producing most of the best-selling fiction, their work was deplored as a popular dilution of a truly virile American art. In Hawthorne's famous pronouncement of 1855, 'America is now wholly given over to a damned mob of scribbling women, and I should have no chance of success while the public taste is occupied with their trash.' 'The majority of people,' wrote Whitman in the *Brooklyn Daily Times* in 1857, 'do not want their daughters trained to become authoresses and poets.'

Along with the rise of women's writing came women's culture. In the preface to *My Opinions and Betsy Bobbet's* (1873), Marietta Holley neatly connects politics and art in the terms she uses to describe her narrator's literary project:

In the first days of our married life, I strained nearly every nerve to help my companion Josiah along and take care of his children by his former consort, the subject of black African slavery also wearin' on me, and a mortgage of 200 and 50 dollars on the farm. But as we prospered and the mortgage was cleared, and the children were off to school, the black African also bein' liberated about the same time of the mortgage, then my mind bein' free from these cares—the great subject of Wimmen's Rites kept a goarin' me, and a voice kept sayin' inside of me, "Josiah Allen's wife, write a book givin' your views on the great subject of Wimmen's Rites."

In her comic and original fiction, Holley indeed concentrates on women's rites, from courtship to quilting, documenting the everyday American women's culture of the nineteenth century, with its female friendships and networks. In her pioneering 1975 study based on women's letters and diaries, the feminist historian Carroll Smith-Rosenberg called this homosocial sphere 'the female world of love and ritual,' 'a female world of varied and yet highly structured relationships,' ranging from the supportive love of sisters, through the romantic friendships of adolescent girls, to sensual avowals of love by mature women, a world in which 'men made but a shadowy appearance.'[25] As Linda Kerber points out, 'Smith-Rosenberg's work implied that there had existed a distinctive women's culture, in which women assisted each other in childbirth, nurtured each other's children, and shared emotional and often erotic ties stronger than those with their husbands.'[26] Although premarital relationships between the sexes were subject to severe restrictions, romantic friendships between women were admired and encouraged. The nineteenth-century ideal of female 'passionlessness'—the belief that women did not have the same sexual desires as men—had advantages as well as disadvantages for women. It reinforced the notion that women were the purer and more spiritual sex, and thus were morally superior to men. Furthermore, as the historian Nancy F. Cott has argued, 'acceptance of the idea of passionlessness created sexual solidarity among women; it allowed women to consider their love relationships with one another of higher character than heterosexual relationships because they excluded (male) carnal passions.'[27] In fact the homosocial world of women's culture allowed much leeway for physical intimacy and touch; 'girls routinely slept together, kissed and hugged one another.'[28] But these caresses were not interpreted as erotic expressions. 'I do not believe that men can ever feel so pure an enthusiasm for women as we can feel for one another,' wrote the novelist Catherine Sedgwick. 'Ours is nearest to the love of angels.'[29]

Smith-Rosenberg's work enabled others to theorize the relationship of women's culture to feminist political movements and institutions. It suggested that the 'bonds of womanhood' were both enabling and imprisoning, and that a female subculture was the essential first phase of political consciousness and activism.[30] Moreover, women's culture was strongly connected to nineteenth-century women's literary production. As Nina Baym notes, 'the study of American women's writing turns our attention to the questions of what a culture is, and how writing may represent it.'[31] Feminist criticism emphasized the aesthetics of a nineteenth-century American women's culture. The code of values growing out of the 'bonds of womanhood' and 'the empire of the mother' was also sustained, reinforced, and circulated through sentimental fiction.[32] Such writers as Harriet Beecher Stowe, Susan Warner, and E. D. E. N. Southworth began to publish stories and novels in the 1850s and 1860s that reflected the dominant ideology of women's culture, such as the veneration of motherhood, intense mother–daughter bonds, and intimate female friendships. Thematically and stylistically, pre-Civil War women's fiction, variously described as 'literary domesticity' or simply the 'sentimental novel,' celebrates matriarchal institutions and idealizes the period of blissful bonding between mother and child we now call pre-Oedipal. As writers, the sentimentalists looked to motherhood for their metaphors and justifications of literary creativity. 'Creating a story is like bearing a child,' wrote Stowe, 'and it leaves me in as weak and helpless a state as when my baby was born.'[33] Their most intense representation of female sexuality in these texts was not in terms of heterosexual romance, but rather the holding or suckling of a baby; for, as the historian Mary Ryan points out, 'nursing an infant was one of the most hallowed and inviolate episodes in a woman's life. . . . Breastfeeding was sanctioned as "one of the most important duties of female life," "one of peculiar, inexpressible felicity," and "the sole occupation and pleasure" of a new mother.'[34]

This fiction is permeated by the artifacts, spaces, and images of nineteenth-century American domestic culture: the kitchen, with its worn rocking chair; the Edenic mother's garden, with its fragrant female flowers and energetic male bees; the caged song-bird, which represents the creative woman in her domestic sphere. Women writers offered a matriarchal critique of patriarchal institutions from slavery to Christianity. They advocated motherly influence—'gentle nurture,' 'sweet control,' and 'educating power,'—as an effective solution to such social problems as alcoholism, crime, and war. As Stowe proclaimed, 'The "Woman Question" of the day is: Shall MOTHERHOOD ever be felt in the public administration of the affairs of state?'[35]

Many women writers, moreover, addressed themselves to a separate audience of women readers. As Nina Baym argues,

the literary women conceptualized authorship as a profession rather than a calling, as work and not as art. Women authors tended not to think of themselves as artists or justify themselves in the language of art until the 1870s and after. . . . Often the women deliberately and even proudly disavowed membership in an artistic fraternity.[36]

Insofar as art implied a male club or circle of brothers, women felt excluded from it. Instead they claimed affiliation with a literary sorority, a society of sisters whose motives were moral rather than aesthetic, whose ambitions were to teach and to influence rather than to create. Although their books sold by the millions, they were not taken seriously by male critics.

By the end of the nineteenth century, however, patterns of gender behavior and relationship were being redefined. Women's culture was breaking down from the inside as early as the 1870s, when relationships between mothers and daughters became strained as daughters pressed for education, work, mobility, sexual autonomy, and power outside the female sphere. Women sought friendship from male classmates and co-workers as well as from women in their single-sex communities. Furthermore, the separate culture of women was being attacked from the outside as sexually unnatural and psychologically unhealthy.[37] From a literary point of view, a national culture beginning to define itself in such literary histories as Moses Coit Tyler's *History of American Literature* (1878) did not want difference but rather a literature 'single in its commanding ideas' and 'its development toward uniformity.'[38]

These historical, cultural, and social changes in attitudes towards women's culture had effects on women's writing as well. Looking from the vantage-point of the turn of the century at the progress women had made in the public world, Charlotte Perkins Gilman envisioned 'fresh fields of fiction' that would come from female emancipation. These would include the drama of the young woman 'who is called upon to give up her career . . . for marriage and who objects to it'; the story of the middle-aged woman who 'discovers that her discontent is social starvation'; 'the inter-relation of women with women'; the lifelong interaction of mothers and children, and 'the new attitude of the full-grown woman.'[39] These plots would indeed appear in twentieth-century women's fiction; but so would darker ones Gilman did not predict. As the 'bonds of womanhood' were being dissolved by cultural pressures, women's plots changed as well. In 1851, for example, Susan Warner's best-selling novel *The Wide, Wide World* tearfully recounted the history of a girl painfully separated from her mother. But in 1880, Warner's artistically superior

Diana presents an astringent and startlingly modern analysis of the psychological warfare between mother and daughter, and the mother's neurotic efforts to thwart her daughter's romance.[40] As women's culture came under attack, some of its survivors clung desperately to the past, seeing men as the interlopers in their idyllic communities. While some writers began to champion the New Woman, others took the old woman as their paradigmatic heroine. By the century's end, Josephine Donovan has argued, 'the woman-centered, matriarchal world of the Victorians is in its last throes. The preindustrial values of that world, female identified and ecologically holistic, are going down to defeat before the imperialism of masculine technology and patriarchal institutions.'[41]

In Chapter 6, 'The Other Lost Generation,' I explore some of the effects of post-war literary history on American women writers. By the turn of the century, a national culture was being defined in works of criticism and history. Attacks on the 'feminization' of American literature reflected the concern of the age 'that a truly American art . . . [should] embody the values of masculine culture.'[42] The great projects of American literary history, undertaken after the wars when nationalist feeling ran high, envisioned American literature as the expression of a virile national ethos. After World War II, the editors of the *Literary History of the United States* (1948) continued to see their task as the creation of 'a single unified story' about the literary embodiment of 'the American way of life.' They identified the essentially American characteristics as democracy, mobility, progress, and independence. Great American literature, then, should be sought in works that embodied these themes. It is hardly surprising that the fifty-four men and one woman editor of the *LHUS* found very few women writers to include among the best. Afro-American writers fared even worse; of the 1,500 pages of the *LHUS*, only two were devoted to black authors.[43]

In such classic post-World War II studies as F. O. Matthiessen's *American Renaissance*, Henry Nash Smith's *Virgin Land*, Leo Marx's *Machine in the Garden*, and Richard Poirier's *A World Elsewhere*, the special nature of American literature was variously defined as democratic individualism, pastoralism, myths and symbols, or the forging of a new language. But in the 1990s,

American literary history, which has always depended on an unspoken consensus of exceptionalism, objectivity, and uniformity, is now in a new phase. Beginning with the addition of what were initially seen as anomalous texts by writers who were black, female, regional, or popular, the anomalies have accumulated in extra-canonical space and the canon has imploded. As Annette Kolodny notes, 'Americanists in the 1980s can devote entire careers to figures whose names were not even known twenty years ago.'[44] Whether they see themselves as post-colonial or not, among Americanists everywhere the politics of writing about 'American' literature today have become extremely complex as Americanists have begun to debate exceptionalism as a critical ideology. In *Critical Inquiry* (1986) Sacvan Bercovich suggests that the debate may 'alter our very concept of "Americanness" by recontextualizing it . . . or by replacing the tautologies of exceptionalism with the transnational categories of gender, class, and race.'[45] In thinking about Afro-American literature, argues Cornel West, we must look for more internationalist perspectives, and to 'larger institutional and structural battles occurring in and across societies, cultures, and economies.'[46]

Even those scholars currently involved in the enormous task of writing and editing new multi-volume national literary histories admit that we are in what Bercovich calls 'a time of dissensus.'[47] As Emory Elliott concedes in his preface to the *Columbia Literary History of the United States*, 'There is today no unifying vision of a national identity like that shared by many scholars at the closing of the two world wars.'[48] And in an ongoing debate in the pages of the journal *American Literature* over whether such literary histories should be written at all, Annette Kolodny warns that the efforts of cultural critics in the past two decades has made us aware 'that if there was something uniquely "American" about our nation and our literary inheritance, it was not a harmonious commonality or shared traditions but diversity, division, and discord.'[49]

To write a feminist literary history in a time of dissensus presents a difficult challenge. Such a history must be critical of any single paradigm of American women's history or culture; attentive to the articulation of gender, race, and class; and aware that women's writing is produced within a complex intertextual network.[50] It cannot be defined by biological essences, stereotypes of femininity, or nationalist myths. It must avoid both over-feminization, the insistence that everything in women's writing can be explained by gender; and under-feminization, or the neglect of gender inscriptions in women's texts.[51]

The idea of a women's culture must be revised, although it still has many uses for the literary historian. First of all, this formulation has depended on a specific configuration of race and class, public and private; it needs to be rethought with regard to women of color, the urban poor, or working women. Furthermore, we are now more aware of the interdependencies of men's and women's lives. Linda Kerber sees the idea of separate spheres as a metaphor, and an ideology that has outlived its usefulness. One day, Kerber predicts, 'we will understand the idea of separate spheres as primarily a trope employed by people in the past to characterize power relations for which they had no other words and that they could not acknowledge because they could not name.'

Moreover, feminist scholars have become more aware of the epistemological and rhetorical problems of what James Clifford and George Marcus call 'writing culture.' Like history, ethnography is a narrative; the cultural anthropologist is involved in a transaction with the culture he or she describes, finds metaphors for it, invents it, and transforms it. Clifford tells a wonderful ethnographic parable about the circularity of cultural narrative. At the beginning of this century, the Abbé Raponda-Walker wrote a classic study of the customs and religious rituals of the Mpongwe, a coastal group in Gabon. A few years ago, a young anthropologist returned to do a follow-up study of the Mpongwe, and to see what customs persisted. He interviewed the chief about various practices and institutions, noting down responses and variants, but at one point the chief seemed perplexed. 'Just a moment,' he declared, and disappeared into his house to return with a well-thumbed copy of Raponda-Walker's book.

For a comparable example of the back-formation of women's culture, we might look at the contemporary Chicana poet-critic Cherríe Moraga. Moraga's poems, written in a language that is both Spanish and English, and neither Spanish nor English, seem to embody Female Aestheticist concepts of the maternal/other language. But in fact Moraga learned Spanish, not as an infant from her mother in the *barrio*, but as an adult from the Berlitz School in Boston.[52]

Thus in thinking about women's culture and American women's writing, we are looking at an invented as well as a 'natural' form, and at exchanges, translations, and intertextuality as well as indigeneity. Texts by American women writers themselves often incorporate images of this complex relation. One such model is Joyce Carol Oates's *Marriages and Infidelities* (1972). In a series of short stories, Oates reimagines famous stories by Chekhov, Kafka, James, Thoreau, Flaubert, and Joyce. As she has explained, 'These stories are meant to be autonomous stories . . . Yet they are also testaments of my love and extreme devotion to these other writers. I imagine a kind of spiritual "marriage" between myself and them.'[53] At the same time, the plots of the stories often deal with the breakdown of marriage and with rebellion against it, as within Oates's stylistic marriages with the patriarchal tradition are also the signs of feminist narrative infidelities: betrayals of theme, transgressions of form, transforming visions of perspective that come from growing up female in America. The metaphor of marriage allows Oates to explore her sense of tradition and originality, the way in which a writer works her way through a history of beloved readings to an autonomous artistic voice. 'I believe,' she has said in an interview,

that we achieve our salvation, or our ruin, by the marriages we contract. I conceived of a book of marriages. Some are conventional marriages of men and women, others are marriages in another sense—with a phase of art, with something that transcends the limitations of the self. But because people are mortal, most of the marriages they go into are mistakes of some kind, misreadings of themselves.[54]

The final story, 'The Dead,' is about a woman novelist, from Detroit instead of Dublin, whose anxiety, insomnia, and anorexia seem to signal her disillusionment and dis-ease with the patriarchal institutions of the university, marriage, and literature. In 'marrying' James Joyce, Oates becomes Joyce Carol Joyce, Joyce squared and doubly herself.

Another image for the hybridity of American women's writing comes from Alice Walker's *The Color Purple*, in which two of the female protagonists, Celie and Sophia, make a quilt together out of some torn curtains and a yellow dress: 'I work in a piece every chance I get. It a nice pattern. Call Sister's Choice.' The Sister's Choice quilt pattern is a combination of a nine-patch block and a star; the name reflects both the kinship tradition in American women's quilting, and the central image of Walker's writing: the sister's choice to stay with the black Southern community or to move into an interracial international world. For Walker, the pieced quilt is an emblem of a universalist, interracial, and intertextual tradition. It brings together elements from American and African-American history; from the farm and juke joint; from women's spaces and men's stories. In Africa, where Celie's sister Nettie becomes a missionary, 'the Olinka men make beautiful quilts which are full of animals and birds and people.' Another black missionary, Corinne, quickly learns to make a quilt that combines the Olinka style with the nine-patch Sister's Choice block.

The Color Purple is a narrative quilt pieced from the spectrum of literary and cultural texts which Walker has inherited. In her lexicon, the color purple stands for the 'feminist of color' or 'womanist,' who is to feminist 'as purple is to lavender.'[55] Within the novel, purple is the color of black royalty, identified with the regal Shug Avery. By the end of the book Celie has created a room for herself in which everything is purple and red. Like the alternating letters of Celie and Nettie which make up the text, the novel incorporates pieces from historical and literary sources, male and female precursors. Walker weaves references to three classic texts by black male writers into her narrative: Jean Toomer's *Cane*, *The Autobiography of Malcolm X*, and Alex Haley's *Roots*. Walker's invented African tribe, the Olinka, re-write Haley's Mandinka warriors. At the same time, her chorus of black women's voices responds to both a black and white American female tradition. The novel is in part an act of homage to Zora Neale Hurston, but Walker also invokes Harriet Beecher Stowe and Flannery O'Connor. Writing the womanist novel in the contemporary United States is an exercise of sister's choice within a complex cultural network.

In the chapters that follow, I look at various themes, images, genres, cultural practices, and choices in the history of American women's writing, from women's rewriting of *The Tempest* to the genre of Female Gothic to the history of the patchwork quilt itself. While the thematic chapters consider a wide range of writers, including Margaret Fuller, Harriet Beecher Stowe, Mary Wilkins Freeman, Charlotte Perkins Gilman, Zora Neale Hurston, Meridel Le Sueur, Tillie Olsen, Katherine Anne Porter, Sylvia Plath, Gloria Naylor, Diane Johnson, and Joyce Carol Oates, I also focus in depth on three classic texts of American women's literature: Louisa May Alcott's *Little Women*, Kate Chopin's *The Awakening*, and Edith Wharton's *House of Mirth*.

The stories, genres, and symbols that once came out of a separate American literary sisterhood are no longer, however, either uniquely American or uniquely a sister's choice. While women have always read *men's* writings, and thus lived in the same literary country as their brothers, only recently has the reverse been true. Indeed, as it becomes part of the common heritage of American men as well as women, as through translation and dissemination it influences readers and writers far from the United States, American women's writing ceases to be 'a literature of our own.' It is in this paradox that our new literary history begins.

2

Miranda's Story

My history presents much superficial, temporary tragedy. The
Woman in me kneels and weeps in tender rapture; the Man in
me rushes forth, but only to be baffled. Yet the time will come,
when, from the union of this tragic king and queen, shall be
born a radiant sovereign self.

Margaret Fuller

Injustice. Ridicule. What did she *do*,
it would be asked (as though that mattered).
Gave birth. Lived through a revolution.
Nursed its wounded. Saw it run aground.
Published a book or two.
And drowned.

Amy Clampitt, 'Margaret Fuller, 1847'

I n his controversial memoir *Making It* (1967), Norman
Podhoretz, then the editor of the journal *Commentary*, told the
secrets of his success as a prominent man of letters in New York.
Podhoretz explained that as a Columbia University undergradu-
ate he had dreamed of becoming a famous American literary
critic. No ambition could have been more natural, for he was
surrounded and smiled upon in Philosophy Hall, home of the
Columbia English department, by the men who ran the New
York intellectual journals and quarterlies. At home in Brooklyn
too were adoring relatives, neighbors, and former teachers who
predicted a great career for him: 'The adult world and especially

22

the female part of it,' he writes, 'was one vast congregation of worshippers at the shrine of my diminutive godhead.'

When I first read *Making It*, as a hopeful graduate student writing my dissertation in New Jersey, I skimmed very rapidly over all of this. Back home in Boston no family worshippers had gathered at my shrine, and my professors at Bryn Mawr in the early 1960s had scant encouragement for women students aspiring to be New York intellectuals. Podhoretz too offered little hope to a woman who wanted to make it, unless she could become the Dark Lady. The Dark Lady, it appeared, was the only famous woman of letters in New York. Of course the Dark Lady was actually a White Lady. She was someone clever, learned, and elegant, someone who wrote scandalous fiction, and produced 'family-type' criticism, which meant criticism imbued with the confidence and authority that came from being part of the New York intellectual family in the first place.

According to Podhoretz, Mary McCarthy had originated the role, but by the 1960s 'no longer occupied it, having recently been promoted to the more dignified status of Grande Dame as a reward for her long years of service.' The new Dark Lady was Susan Sontag, who had come along coincidentally just when there was a vacancy in this cultural position. I was struck by this information. How did you get to be a Dark Lady? Where in New York could you go to try out? Most important, how old was Susan Sontag? I read this section of *Making It* so avidly and it impressed me so deeply that I was shocked on returning to the book to find that it was less than two pages long. I had remembered a chapter at least.

As Susan Sontag herself has observed, the assumption that only one Dark Lady in a generation can make it as the token woman intellectual is misogynist and grotesque; but with regard to American intellectual culture, it seems hard to overcome. Explaining why only a few women had been asked to speak at the international PEN Congress in New York in 1986, Norman Mailer declared, 'There are not that many women, like Susan Sontag, who are intellectuals first, poets and novelists second.'[1] And even Sontag, the Dark Lady, was not immune to abuse. Attacks on her politics and writing in the past few years, a 'public scourging,' in Elizabeth Hardwick's words, may reflect what

Hardwick calls the 'inclination to punish' a 'very smart, intellectually ambitious' woman, revealing the latent hostility towards the 'femme savante' who steps out of line.[2]

The 'real ancestor' of the American Dark Lady was Margaret Fuller—member of the Transcendentalist movement, editor of its journal *The Dial*, feminist, and friend of Emerson, Alcott, and Hawthorne.[3] Fuller envisioned herself as a 'symbol of intellectual womanhood,' 'chosen among women' to 'act out her nature.'[4] Indeed, she imagined herself as a possible feminist Messiah, the redeemer of her sex. 'Will not she soon appear?' Fuller asks in *Woman in the Nineteenth Century*, 'the woman who shall claim their birthright for all women; who shall teach them what to claim and how to use what they obtain?' Her own suffering suggested to her that she might be that one, and that the chosen female saviour, like the black 'redeemer-poet' heralded in nineteenth-century black newspapers and periodicals, would be a writer and an intellectual.

As an American feminist intellectual, however, Fuller has always been a problematic figure for her contemporaries and for her critics. Descended from New England lawyers who were 'men of great energy, pushing, successful, of immense and varied information, of great self-esteem and without a particle of tact,' Margaret, in the opinion of her editor Horace Mann, 'combined the disagreableness of forty Fullers.'[5] Raised as a prodigy, a girl wonder, her problem, according to her biographer Bell Chevigny, was 'that of all American women who wanted to realize in their adult lives a concept of freedom that was intended to be simply a plaything of their youth.'[6] Another problem was that she was not pretty. 'Her extreme plainness,' Emerson recalled, ' . . . all repelled, and I said to myself, we shall never get far.' Perry Miller, the Harvard professor who edited Fuller and the Transcendentalists in the 1950s, notes in his discussion of Fuller's work that she was 'phenomenally homely'—not an observation he makes of Thoreau, for example—and that her image cannot 'be dissociated from the hyperbolically female intellectualism of the period, the slightest invocation of which invites our laughter.'[7]

But women readers have found more to weep over than to laugh about in the tragic heroism that marked Fuller's career. Having worked as a journalist in New York, she went to Italy, where she supported the Revolution, and had a child by an Italian radical ten years her junior, Angelo Ossoli. Her letters about maternity, her appreciation of Ossoli's tenderness, and her determination to give him his freedom if he should fall in love with a younger woman, are intensely moving. For three years she kept the affair a secret from her family and friends, but in 1850 she decided to brave whatever scandal might await her, and to return to the United States with her lover and their child. In July 1850, just off Fire Island in New York, their ship met a storm and was wrecked. All three were drowned and their bodies never recovered; Fuller was just forty years old.

The response to her death from her male contemporaries revealed the personality of each. The narcissist Emerson wrote, 'I have lost in her my audience.' The loyal Thoreau went to Fire Island to search for the bodies and remains. And the moralist Hawthorne, who had gossiped cruelly about her liaison with Ossoli, painted an ambivalent portrait of Fuller as Zenobia, the 'Dark Lady of Salem,' in his novel *The Blithedale Romance* (1852).[8] Zenobia speaks out in the novel about the silencing of women: 'Thus far, no woman in the world has ever once spoken out her whole heart and her whole mind. The mistrust and disapproval of the vast bulk of society throttles us, as with two gigantic hands at our throats.' But for all her sensual brilliance she is doomed, and her writing elicits the narrator's pity rather than respect. 'Her poor little stories and tracts never half did justice to her intellect,' he writes. 'Her mind was full of weeds.' When Zenobia drowns herself for unrequited love, the narrator suspects her of yet one more romantic pose.

In her major feminist treatise *Woman in the Nineteenth Century* (1845), Fuller wrote about her own experience as the Dark Lady under a literary persona borrowed from another Shakespearean character: 'I . . . proudly painted myself as Miranda,' she noted in her journal.[9] Fuller's Miranda is an American feminist intellectual, 'a woman, who, if any in the world could, might speak without heat and bitterness of the position of her sex.' She is the product of a rigorous patriarchal education:

Her father was a man who cherished no sentimental reverence for Woman, but a firm belief in the equality of the sexes . . . From the time she could speak and go alone, he addressed her not as a plaything, but as a living mind . . . He called upon her for clear judgment, for courage, for honor and fidelity . . .

Thus when Miranda grew up, 'she took her place easily, not only in the world of organized being, but in the world of mind,' where 'her mind was often the leading one, always effective.' Trained in self-respect, self-reliant, 'fortunate,' according to Fuller, in lacking the feminine charms that might attract 'bewildering flatteries,' Miranda seems to represent a feminist ideal. Yet, Fuller declares, even Miranda is oppressed by sexual stereotypes. She sees that men, despite their rhetorical esteem for feminine virtue, 'never in an extreme of despair, wished to be women,' but rather taunt each other with 'feminine' weakness, and regarded all her intellectual strengths as 'masculine' traits. The woman of genius thus does not change attitudes towards women in general; she is simply perceived as an anomaly or hybrid, a woman with a 'masculine mind,' as someone who has surpassed and even transcended her sex. Trying to compliment Miranda, a friend told her that she 'deserved in some star to be a man.' Miranda responds that 'he was very much surprised when I disclosed my view of my position and hopes, when I declared my faith that the feminine side . . . was now to have its full chance, and that, if either were better, it was better now to be a woman.'[10]

Why should Fuller have called herself 'Miranda,' and what relevance can *The Tempest* have for understanding the cultural tradition of American women writers? The play has long had special meaning for *male* intellectuals in the Third World. Following the work of George Lamming, Octave Mannoni, Philip Mason, Aimé Césaire, Roberto Fernandez Retamar, and Max Dorsinville, the idea that Caliban stands as a figure for the cultural situation of African, Latin American, Caribbean, and Quebecois writers has become familiar and accepted. What Dorsinville calls 'Calibanic literature' has come to stand for a displaced indigenous voice.[11] From the late 1950s to the early 1970s, according to Rob Nixon, groups of 'dissenting intellectuals' chose *The Tempest* as 'a way of amplifying their calls for decolonization within the bounds of the dominant cultures.'[12] For the past thirty years, productions of the play have focused on the relationship between

Prospero and Caliban as the oppressor and the oppressed, the West and the rest.[13]

Caliban has also become a figure for the Afro-American intellectual, beginning at least as early as James Baldwin's *Notes of a Native Son* (1962), and cited with increasingly personal and autobiographical fervor by such leading contemporary literary critics as Houston Baker. In an essay called 'Caliban's Triple Play' (1986), Baker turns to what he calls 'the venerable Western trope of Prospero and Caliban' to talk about the problems of Afro-American critics.[14] In this and other essays, Baker sees in the Prospero–Caliban trope the cultural struggle of black Americans for linguistic and cultural autonomy. 'When Caliban knows himself as a usurped king,' he writes, 'it is time for Prospero to depart the island.'[15]

But Baker, who has also written extensively on black women writers, has trouble making Caliban a generic black Everyman, because of his own uneasy awareness that Caliban is gender-marked. Baker attempts to slur over this difficulty by calling Caliban the 'Afro-American spokesperson.' But the terminology only emphasizes the awkwardness of making Caliban speak for women. Both in the United States and Britain, stage productions of *The Tempest* have focused on race rather than gender; 'exploration of the colonial theme has been inextricably limited to experiments in interracial casting.'[16] And more globally, Rob Nixon sees the decline of the Prospero–Caliban trope in the 1980s largely due to its inadequacy to represent the situation of women in the post-colonial period. '*The Tempest*'s value for African and Caribbean intellectuals faded,' he asserts, not only because Shakespeare doesn't show us what happens after Prospero leaves, but also because of 'the difficulty of wresting from it any role for female defiance or leadership in a period when protest is coming increasingly from that quarter.'[17]

What has gone unnoticed in these discussions, however, is that *The Tempest* has long been used by American women writers as a metaphorical account of the woman artist or feminist intellectual. Instead of looking to Caliban, American women writers from Fuller to Harriet Beecher Stowe, Louisa May Alcott, Katherine Anne Porter, Sylvia Plath, and Gloria Naylor have appropriated and revised the figure of Miranda in thinking about their relationship to patriarchal power, language, female sexuality, and creativity.

In one respect, the appropriation of *The Tempest* by American women writers is not surprising considering the long history of Americanist readings of the play. There has long been a view that 'the idea of America as Arcadia lies behind Prospero's island,' that *The Tempest* has some historical relation to the establishment of the Jamestown colony in 1607.[18] Leo Marx describes the play as 'a prologue to American literature. . . . [which] in its overall design, prefigures the design of the classic American fables.'[19] The 'Americanist reading' of *The Tempest* was especially popular at the turn of the century when the scholar Walter Raleigh argued that Prospero's enchanted island was clearly America, and that Miranda was modelled after Virginia Dare, the first English child born in the original Ralegh's 'lost colony' of Roanoke Island. The New England critic Edward Everett Hale in 1902 identified Prospero's island with patriotic if prosaic fervor as Cuttyhunk Island off Cape Cod, and boasted that 'we have the right to claim Miranda as a Massachusetts girl.'[20] Fuller, Alcott, Dickinson, and Plath would also claim Miranda autobiographically as a Massachusetts girl, but they responded more to repressed and marginal elements of Shakespeare's text than to his historical intentions. Miranda may seem at first like a strange choice. Even contemporary feminist critics such as Margery Garber have regarded Miranda as 'another figure of female self-erasure . . . eagerly accepting her father's tutelage in the Elizabethan World Picture.'[21]

American women writers, however, have been interested in Miranda's role as the motherless daughter of the Father who falls in love with his language and power. Miranda is the only woman on Prospero's island; she does not remember seeing another woman and has no memory of her mother at all:

> I do not know
> One of my sex; no woman's face remember
> Save from my glass, mine own (III. 1).

Indeed, it is one of the curiosities of the play that we don't even know what has happened to Miranda's mother. Shakespeare doesn't explain what happened to Prospero's wife, or even whether she was alive when he fled to Milan with his two-year-old daughter. As Stephen Orgel points out, Prospero presents his voyage to the island as a new beginning, 'a literal childbirth' in which he 'has conceived himself as Miranda's only parent.'[22] He is also her schoolmaster, who has educated her in her knowledge and values. Like Caliban, Miranda has learned all her language, the father tongue, from Prospero; and it is a language full of sexual slurs on women. Moreover, she has been educated within the world of Prospero's great library. She has learned to adore her father's magic, to be subject to his spells, and to believe that she has no magic of her own. If Caliban curses with his language, what should Miranda do with hers? Can she too rebel? Can she possess Prospero's book, rewrite it, or destroy it? Does she have any desires of her own? Does she have any stake in the future of the island, except to populate it or to leave it for the kingdom of another man?

Like Miranda, Fuller's education reinforced her own distance and difference from women or a female tradition; in Elizabeth Hardwick's words, 'she sprang out of the head of all the Zeuses about her.'[23] Fuller's life has a trajectory that is not unique to American women but that seems a paradigmatic portrait of the woman intellectual from Mary Wollstonecraft to Simone de Beauvoir and Adrienne Rich. All began with immersion in the father's library: 'my father's library,' writes Rich, 'I felt as the source and site of his power.'[24] Fuller's father instructed her in Latin and classical history starting at the age of six, and taught her to revere the Roman world of gladiators and the forum. He also kept her away from the novels, plays, poetry, and etiquette books deemed suitable for girls, and drilled her instead in a rigorous use of language. As Fuller recalled, her father

demanded accuracy and clearness in everything: you must not speak, unless you can make your meaning perfectly intelligible to the person addressed; must not express a thought, unless you can give a reason for it, if required; must not make a statement unless sure of all particulars—such were his rules.[25]

Held to this strict logical accountability, Fuller was also forbidden the linguistic markers of feminine apology, euphemism, circumlocution, and qualification: '"But," "if," "unless I am mistaken," and "it may be so," were words and phrases excluded from the province where he held sway.'[26] This early discipline gave her speech a force and directness unusual in nineteenth-century women, a masculine assertiveness some (without analyzing the cause) found impressive, others merely self-centered, arrogant, and freakish. 'There are three categories of human being,' wrote Edgar Allan Poe; 'men, women, and Margaret Fuller.'

Moreover, Fuller recalled, her father had no understanding or tolerance for other ways of knowing. Himself 'accurate, ready, with entire command of his resources, he had no belief in minds that listen, wait, and receive. He had no conception of the subtle and indirect motions of imagination and feeling.' She repressed her own imagination in the interests of the active intellect he desired: 'My own world sank deep within, away from the surface of my life . . . But my true life was only the dearer that it was secluded and veiled over by a thick curtain of available intellect.'[27] Much as she loved Shakespeare, she associated the theater with a private feminine world of art that had to be kept behind closed stage curtains. Fiction also was too negatively associated with the emotional and the feminine, as Fuller finally concluded in deciding not to write novels: 'I have always thought . . . that I would keep all that behind the curtain, that I would not write, like a woman, of love and hope and disappointment, but like a man, of the world of intellect and action.'[28]

Fuller identified her emotional life with her mother's garden. 'The little garden, full of choice flowers and fruit-trees . . . here I felt at home.' Her mother's garden was a place of free sensual pleasure: 'There my thoughts could lie callow in the nest, and only be fed and kept warm.'[29] While the library was the austere space of the patriarchal intellect, the garden was a warm extension of the infant's bond with the mother's body, a space where thoughts did not have to be mustered, trained, and disciplined, but rather could wait and receive.

Fuller also felt a split between the free flow of language in conversation, at which she excelled—'Conversation is my natural element,' she remarked—and the labor and restraint of writing according to patriarchal laws of rhetoric and exposition. Many of Fuller's contemporaries also believed that her particular kind of female genius was most naturally expressed in speech, especially through her role as the leader of a series of 'Conversations' for Boston women. Yet conversation was not an exclusively feminine pursuit among the Transcendentalists; indeed, 'as an organized movement, Transcendentalism can be said almost to have begun and ended as a discussion group.'[30] And Fuller's Conversations were not intimate women's rituals, but 'reduced, miniature, and homebound' versions of the speaker's platform Emerson and other male Transcendentalists had on their travels.[31] Moreover, as we have seen, Fuller's speech, what Emerson called her 'parlatorio,' was unconventionally forceful.

None the less Fuller's conversation struck her contemporaries as peculiarly and disturbingly feminine. In a metaphor of sexual difference and midwifery, the Reverend Frederic Henry Hodge observed that 'for some reason or other, she could never deliver herself in print as she did with her lips.'[32] Emerson 'found something profane' in her 'amusing gossip,' and 'fancied her too interested in personal history.' He remembered that 'she made me laugh more than I liked.'[33] Still, he wrote, 'her only adequate channel was in her conversation. Her pen was a non-conductor.' Emerson's preferred language was public, aggressive, and phallic; as he wrote in his journal in 1841, 'give me initiative, spermatic, prophesying, man-making words.'[34] But when Fuller used man-making words, Emerson claimed he could not understand her: 'There is a difference in our constitution,' he wrote to Fuller. 'We use a different rhetoric. It seems as if we had been born and bred in different nations. You say you understand me wholly. But you cannot communicate yourself to me. I hear the words sometimes but remain a stranger to your state of mind.'[35]

Writing from the doubled world of women, Fuller was indeed 'born and bred' in a different America from Emerson's; could she then write a literature of her own? The problem was that, unlike Mill's vision of women who had never read the writings of men, Fuller was steeped in Emerson's man-making words. Emerson was the Transcendental Signifier of nineteenth-century American women writers, a Prospero whose inescapable magic dominated their efforts at imaginative independence. 'My dear young sisters,' Julia Ward Howe exhorted the graduates of Elmira Female College in 1882, 'prove yourselves worthy to have lived in the age which produced Henry Wadsworth Longfellow and Ralph Waldo Emerson.'[36] When Edna Pontellier, in Kate

Chopin's *The Awakening* (1899), falls asleep reading Emerson, it can be seen either as a liberating moment for American women's literature, or another phase of its enthrallment.

Woman in the Nineteenth Century was Fuller's effort to create a woman's literature of her own. In her journal she noted: 'No old [form] suits me. If I could invent one, it seems to me the pleasure of creation would make it possible for me to write.'[37] According to Annette Kolodny, Fuller had attempted to develop a new feminist discourse closely modelled on Richard Whately's *Elements of Rhetoric* (1832). In borrowing from Whately, Fuller refused the coercive strategies of rhetoric he called 'persuasion,' including ridicule of the opponent, lurid examples, trickery, artifice, and heightened emotionalism. Rather than forcing her readers' consent, Fuller wanted them to engage in a dialog with her, to be respected rather than manipulated.[38] The book represented too her effort to invent a feminine mythology to replace the classical models.[39] As Jeffrey Steele notes,

Shakespeare's portrait of Miranda in *The Tempest* is not merely an allusion that illuminates aspects of Fuller's being, as if her being were separate from the dramatic character, but rather a life that intersects Fuller's by providing the terms that illuminate it. In this regard, Fuller's use of Miranda is not that different from Freud's use of Oedipus. In both instances, a dramatic character forms part of an intertextual network that sets the very terms of self-understanding.[40]

Yet Fuller's contemporaries, and critics ever since, have criticized the book as incoherent. Male critics saw it as lacking in rational sequence. Orestes Brownson complained that it had 'neither beginning, middle nor end, and may be read backwards as well as forwards.' Perry Miller described it as 'full of wearisome digressions and excursions into fantasy and murky dreams.' Fuller's feminist friends saw the book as a garden gone wrong, somehow inorganic, unnatural and artificial. Lydia Maria Child thought reading it was 'like walking through a grand forest, obstructed with underbrush and stones, though rich in mosses and flowers.'[41] The ideas struck her as forced; 'the stream is abundant and beautiful, but it always seems to be *pumped* rather than to flow.' Caroline Sturgis, another member of Fuller's Conversations, had a similar reaction: 'There seems to be a want of vital powers as if you had gathered flowers and planted them in a garden but left the roots in their own soil. . . . It is not a book to take to heart, and that is what a book upon women should be.'[42] Thus Fuller could not succeed in her project of uniting the father's library and the mother's garden in a new feminist form.

After Fuller's death, other American women writers turned to the figure of Miranda and *The Tempest* to explore similar problems of language, imagination, and literary form. Harriet Beecher Stowe's semi-autobiographical *Pearl of Orr's Island* (1862) has much in common with Fuller. Stowe's mother had died when she was five, and she had been educated in the classics by her father, the Calvinist minister Henry Beecher, who had called her a 'genius' but 'wished she was a boy.' Stowe remembered her father's study, 'high above all the noise of the house . . . a refuge and a sanctuary,' where she watched her father write but did not dare to interrupt his 'holy and mysterious work.'[43]

As a young girl, Stowe, prevented from reading fiction and drama, had been thrilled by discovering a tattered copy of *The Tempest* in her grandmother's attic.[44] She gave her own formative literary experiences to her heroine Mara, an orphan who lives with her fisherman grandfather on Orr Island off the coast of Maine. The only books Mara sees are her cousin's Roman histories, and she dreams endlessly of 'Roman senators and warriors.' But, offered Plutarch's *Lives*, with 'more particular accounts of the men you read about in history,' Mara asks whether there are 'any lives of women.' There is no solace in history for an ardent girl, but in the garret, Mara finds 'the play of the "Tempest," torn from an old edition of Shakespeare,' which strikes a different chord, and she turns to it to satisfy her cravings 'for a "sea-change" capable of magically transforming her world.'[45] For hours she ecstatically reads and rereads this fragment, 'from which she collected dim, delightful images of a lonely island, an old enchanter, a beautiful girl, and a spirit not quite like those in the Bible, but a very probable one to her mode of thinking.' She imagines Caliban 'with a face much like that of a large skate-fish she had seen drawn ashore in one of her grandfather's nets;' and Ferdinand as her own playmate Moses, 'and how glad she would be to pile up his wood for him, if any enchanter should set him to work!' The songs 'fixed themselves in her memory,' and she sings them as she wanders up and down the beach. In this poetic dream-world she is Miranda, the daughter and sole heir of the father. But there is no real place in her society for a woman as intellectual or artist. Her fantasies are largely private and secret; 'the wonder that this new treasure excited, the host of surmises and dreams to which it gave rise, were never mentioned to anybody.' When Mara does try to tell Moses about her dreams, as Judith Fetterley notes, 'she is met with indifference, incomprehension, and finally hostility.'[46] For a woman the options are only marriage or death, and in the novel's end, Mara chooses the role of martyr.

Like *Woman in the Nineteenth Century*, *The Pearl of Orr's Island* is a problematically fragmented narrative. Stowe wrote the first part dealing with Mara's girlhood in 1852, put it aside, and did not write the second half until ten years later. The two halves do not seem to fit; and critics find the autobiographical first part much more aesthetically successful than the sentimental conclusion. They have usually explained Stowe's delay in terms of interruptions from her other literary and domestic commitments. But Sarah Orne Jewett, who regarded the novel as potentially Stowe's greatest, was more perceptive about the internal conflicts about women, language, and writing that made it impossible for Stowe to finish as she had begun. In a letter to the editor Annie Fields, Jewett wrote:

I have been reading the beginning of 'The Pearl of Orr's Island' and finding it just as clear and perfectly organized and strong as it seemed to me in my thirteenth or fourteenth year, when I read it first. . . . Alas, that she couldn't finish it in the same noble key of simplicity and harmony; but a poor writer is at the mercy of much unconcious opposition.[47]

Judith Fetterley, the contemporary feminist critic who has written most perceptively about *The Pearl of Orr's Island*, suggests that 'Stowe may have had difficulty finishing *Pearl*, and allowed and even welcomed those interruptions, because she had difficulty connecting the idea of a heroine with the idea of story and history.'[48] In Fetterley's view, *Pearl* is the only mid-nineteenth-century American women's novel comparable in its passionate, convincing, and artful expression of women's oppression to

Uncle Tom's Cabin in its expression of the oppression of black people. But Stowe's ambivalence about women's claims to self-fulfillment made it harder for her to imagine a narrative in which her heroine would be creative and free.

Stowe's compositional difficulty may also have come from the Shakespearean Miranda's confinement to a marriage plot, and her unwillingness to commit her heroine to this traditional end. Ariel's plot, however, is about liberty, and thus Ariel appealed to such rebels as Louisa May Alcott, under her sensationalist mask as the pseudonymous author of Gothic fiction. Like Fuller and Stowe, Alcott was another dutiful daughter of the Transcendental fathers, so split as a writer between the maternal and paternal voices that she had to use different names. Her Ariel is an artist who finds herself only through submission to patriarchal power.

In 'Ariel: A Legend of the Lighthouse,' published three years after *The Pearl of Orr's Island*, Alcott used the New England seacoast to create an island setting with 'chasms, cliff, torrents, and dark seas.'[49] For Alcott, who described herself as 'stage-struck,' and who went to the theater in Boston two or three times a week, the choice of Ariel over Miranda was suggested by stage productions of the play. Miranda onstage was invariably only a pretty ingenue, with most of her speeches cut, and Ariel was by far the more exciting part.[50] Although the stage directions in the text of *The Tempest* make it explicit that Ariel is male, 'by the early eighteenth century, . . . Ariel had become exclusively a woman's role, usually taken by a singer who was also a dancer, and so it remained until the 1930s.'[51] Although Alcott's heroine is called Ariel, she lives with her 'stern, dark-browed, melancholy-looking' father and a Caliban-like lighthouse keeper on the island, and when the son of her father's old enemy happens by, he comments that 'It only needs a Miranda to make a modern version of the Tempest.' In an unpublished novel, 'The Long Love Chase,' written in 1867, Alcott returned to *The Tempest* plot with the story of a passionate young woman named Miranda living on a dismal island with her grandfather, and rescued by the seductive but satanic Philip Tempest.[52]

The twentieth-century revisions of *The Tempest* build on this tradition, but add to it a modern consciousness of sexuality,

female and poetic autonomy, and personal and aesthetic destiny.
Miranda may be the only woman on the island; she may be
perfect and a wonder; but she is not immune from the common
dangers of growing up female: incestuous desire, arranged marriage, attempted rape, the trade in women. The semi-
autobiographical stories that Katherine Anne Porter called her
'Miranda cycle' deal with female initiation into the adult world of
sexuality, knowledge, and death. Porter had been obsessed with
Shakespeare since early childhood, but she thought of the name
Miranda, 'my alter-ego name,'[53] not in Shakespeare's Latin
sense, as 'strange and wonderful,' but in the Spanish meaning,
'the seeing one.'[54] Miranda is the female witness, the one who
must see and know, whose gaze transforms the patriarchal
world. In 'The Grave,' written in 1935, the parallels to *The
Tempest* are most explicit, as Porter's Miranda confronts her new
world of knowledge with 'thrills of wonder.' The story is about a
childhood trauma of sexual difference that revolves around the
discovery of the 'facts of life,' which for women are also the facts
of death. A brother and sister, Paul and Miranda, are exploring
the grandmother's family cemetery, now a 'neglected garden of
tangled rose bushes.' Nine-year-old Miranda is dreamily thinking about growing up, about putting on the organdy dresses and
violet talcum powder of a Southern belle. Paul, already a hunter
at the age of twelve, shoots a pregnant rabbit, skins and evisce-
rates it: 'He slit again, and pulled the bag open, and there lay a
bundle of tiny rabbits, each wrapped in a thin scarlet veil . . . there
they were, dark grey, their sleek wet down lying in minute even
ripples, . . . their unbelievably small delicate ears folded close,
their little blind faces almost featureless.' At first intrigued, for
'she was accustomed to the sight of animals killed in hunting,'
Miranda sees the blood running over the babies, and 'begins to
tremble without knowing why.' As Jane DeMouy explains,
while Miranda does not remember the death of her own
mother in childbirth, she recognizes 'the blood rites of womanhood. . . . She has discovered her own mortality and own
femaleness, with its frightening, awesome burden of procrea-
tion.'[55] In the image of Miranda, Porter seems to preserve the
freedom of the daughter before the invasion of her island by sexuality and reproduction. 'I have not much interest in anyone's

personal history after the tenth year, not even my own,' she wrote.[56]

The Tempest had similar meanings for Sylvia Plath. Her relation to the play was formed in early childhood, in the idyllic experiences of the seacoast at Point Shirley she recalls in her essay 'Ocean-1212-W.' That idyll ended with the great hurricane of 1938: 'the sea molten, steely-slick, heaving at its leash like a broody animal.' The tempest destroyed the 'seaside childhood' Plath would remember as the only purely happy time of her life: 'My father died, we moved inland. Whereupon those first nine years of my life sealed themselves off like a ship in a bottle—beautiful, inaccessible, obsolete, a fine, white flying myth.'[57] A few years later, when she was in the seventh grade, Plath saw at the Colonial Theatre in Boston one of the rare productions of *The Tempest* directed by a woman: Margaret Webster's controversial and heavily-cut version with the ballerina Vera Zorina as Ariel and the young boxer Canada Lee as the first black actor to play Caliban in a professional production.[58] Both she and her brother read the play; according to Linda Wagner-Martin, her 'fascination with Ariel, Miranda, and Caliban dated from January of 1945. . . . The father–daughter relationship, the reunion, the ocean, and the androgynous powers of Ariel made the story especially germane to a young girl fashioning her adolescent self-image.'[59]

Plath's personal mythology of *The Tempest* was further mediated by W. H. Auden, who came to Smith College in 1953 when she was a student and talked, as she recorded in her journal, about 'how Caliban is the natural bestial projection, Ariel the creative imagination, and all the intricate lyrical abstrusities of their love and cleavage, art and life, the mirror and the sea.'[60] Images from *The Tempest* shape Plath's work; *The Colossus* was first called *Full Fathom Five*, as if to suggest that the father's bones and eyes have been converted into poetic coral and pearl. Yet Plath's choice of Ariel rather than Miranda as her poetic alter-ego suggests the difficulties she had accepting the daughter of the father as poet. Ted Hughes has written that Plath's 'poetry is the biology of Ariel, the ontology of Ariel—the story of Ariel's imprisonment in the pine, before Prospero opened it.'[61] Nonetheless, in the *Ariel* poems, a Miranda figure begins to speak, 'poor white foot' in Daddy's black shoe.

Despite the social and political concerns reflected in the lives and works of many of these writers, the representation of the Miranda figure has been in primarily psychological terms. The issues of race that have been so crucial to post-colonial writers revising *The Tempest* do not appear in their work. This absence is unfortunate, because Miranda, as one critic has recently noted, 'offers us a feminine trope of colonialism' that exposes the 'mutual enslavement' of natives and women. Yet instead of recognizing their kinship, Miranda 'denies that Caliban possesses any being at all,' and Caliban 'sees in Miranda only the distorted being of women as sexual receptacles and patronymic extensions.' Only when Miranda and Caliban join together, however, can they succeed in freeing themselves from Prospero's power.[62]

Gloria Naylor's *Mama Day* (1988), however, moves in this imaginative direction with a black Miranda who incorporates the identities of Prospero, Caliban, and Sycorax as well. Trained in literature, with a degree in Afro-American studies from Yale, Naylor has written previous novels which revise the classical canon, such as *Lindin Hills*, based on *The Inferno*. In *Mama Day*, she sets the story on an all-black island community, Willow Springs, hurricane-swept and connected to the mainland only by a bridge, where the conjure woman Miranda Day practices her black magic. Naylor rewrites Miranda's story within Afro-American culture, bringing together black and feminist motifs. Her island becomes the black mother's garden, the 'other place' of black female creativity celebrated in essays like Alice Walker's 'In Search of Our Mothers' Gardens.' Of the novel's many reviewers, only Bharati Mukharjee, in the *New York Times Book Review* (21 February 1988), noticed its literary sources. As Mukharjee writes,

Mama Day has its roots in *The Tempest*. The theme is reconciliation, the title character is Miranda, and Willow Springs is an isolated island where, as on Prospero's isle, magical and mysterious events come to pass. As in *The Tempest*, one story concerns the magician Miranda Day, nicknamed *Mama Day*, and her acquisition, exercise and relinquishment of magical powers.

Naylor's Miranda is created in the wake of the Third World Caliban, and is both a critique of the phallocentric Prospero–

Caliban relation, and an effort to rewrite *The Tempest* as a revolutionary text for women.

The setting of the novel is important and ingenious. Naylor places Prospero's island among the Sea Islands, barrier islands along the coast of Georgia and South Carolina, which for two centuries have been the home of black Americans, descendants of slaves from Barbados and West Africa—Nigeria, Ghana, Angola, and Liberia—who speak a dialect known as Gullah or Geechee. As the folklorist Charles Joyner explains,

By the American Revolution the slaves . . . had already created a distinct culture. During the Civil War, when white planter families fled the Sea Islands before the invading Union troops, Sea Island blacks began to cultivate the land for themselves. Hundreds of them joined the Union Army in the celebrated First South Carolina Volunteers. On January 16, 1865, General William Tecumseh Sherman's famous Special Field Order No. 15 set aside for the former slaves 'the islands from Charleston south [and] the abandoned rice fields along the rivers from thirty miles back from the sea.'

Although Andrew Johnson later nullified Sherman's order, black freedmen held on to their land and bought more. A poor market for cotton and a 'series of killer hurricanes' continued to make the Islands unappealing to white planters through the 1950s. Since then, resort development on some of the Islands such as Hilton Head has radically changed the economy, and begun to threaten the indigenous culture, which reflects both 'continuity with Africa and creativity in the New World.'[63] In addition to the creole language Gullah, kinship systems, arts and crafts, folk literature, medicine, and religious practices, have begun to disappear under the impact of modernization.

Within Afro-American culture, the Sea Islands thus occupy a special place as an enclave of positive black identity and an intact African heritage. According to some researchers, Sea Island blacks who have not 'had to interact with whites or the majority culture in the same way as Blacks in this country' have 'a fierce kind of pride and a lack of fear which is seldom seen in other places.' The Sea Islanders, 'free of the white person's gaze,' seem like the symbolic center of an autonomous Afro-American expression. During the Harlem Renaissance of the 1920s, the black educator Lucy Laney urged Afro-American writers to go down to the indigenous culture and language of the Sea Islands 'where they could study the Negro in his original purity.'[64]

Naylor makes rich use of the Sea Island culture in inventing Willow Springs, especially its beliefs in magic and hoodoo, and its medical and spiritual traditions. Mama Day is the matriarch of Willow Springs. Like Prospero, she can bring the tempest and conjure spirits. She can bring lovers together or torment them. She can break a curse, with her cane made of carved snakes and her black ledger. She can create life and she can raise the dead. Her power comes from her African heritage, and her descent from a slave conjure woman Sapphira Wade, brought to the island in 1823, who married her master and persuaded him in a thousand days to deed to his slaves all the land in Willow Springs. Although 'Sapphira Wade don't live in the part of our memory we can use to form words,' she is part of the racial memory of Willow Springs, both Sycorax and Scheherazade.

Certainly, then, the Miranda figure has a long and significant history in American women's writing. But we cannot claim it as a unique marker of an American women's literary tradition, for Miranda has also played an important, albeit different, role in the literature of English Canada, appearing in novels by Charles Roberts, Margaret Laurence, Audrey Thomas, Robertson Davies, and George Lamming. The focus on Miranda rather than Caliban in English Canadian fiction, Diana Brydon suggests, is a politically conservative one, with Miranda 'a fitting representative of Canada's aspirations as a dutiful daughter of the empire.'[65] Furthermore, according to Chantal Zabus, 'the choice of Miranda as a national symbol makes the search for an English Canadian literary identity an ironic enterprise, for Miranda is and always will be Prospero's progeny and may never rebel against Prospero's authority.'[66] In my view, Canadian critics overlook the feminist aspects of the Miranda figure, especially as she appears in the novels by women, in favor of nationalist interpretations. Morag Gunn, the Miranda of Margaret Laurence's *Diviners* (1974), is an artist-heroine who has much in common with the heroines of American fiction, as we see in the synopsis of her novel: 'It's called *Prospero's Child*, she being the young woman who marries His Excellency, the Governor of some island in some ocean very far south, and who virtually worships him and then who has to go to the opposite extreme and reject nearly everything about him, at least for a time, in order to become her own person.' In George Lamming's *Water With Berries*, the Miranda figure is split into two rebellious daughters, the white Myra and the black Randa.

But the use of Shakespeare by both Canadian and American writers has built-in contradictions that impede its revolutionary power. As Third World writers have acknowledged, their use of *The Tempest* as a cultural and political metaphor is fraught with irony, for the choice of Shakespeare, 'the gold standard of literature,' also signalled allegiance to a white European canon, and reflected 'Shakespeare's distinctive position as a measure of the relative achievements of European and non-European civilizations.'[67] Since Margaret Fuller's day, women writers and intellectuals have repeatedly envisioned a literature validated by the Dark Lady, the feminist messiah, the tenth muse. In *A Room of One's Own*, Virginia Woolf named the messiah as Shakespeare's sister, the great woman artist who might be born if 'we worked for her,' and in whose name to labor 'even in poverty and obscurity, is worth while.' 'Well, she's long about her coming,' writes Adrienne Rich in 'Snapshots of a Daughter-in-Law' (1960), but still presumably on her way.

The revision of Miranda and *The Tempest* could be seen as a strategy of legitimation which looks to Shakespeare's sister in order to validate the work of Margaret Fuller and other non-canonical American women writers. But as Henry Louis Gates writes, such strategies are self-defeating and obsolete: 'We must resist the description of the works of women and the works of persons of color as . . . shadowy fragments of a Master Text that we, somehow, have been unable to imitate precisely, or to recite correctly, or to ventriloquize eloquently enough.'[68] Perhaps it is time to say that Shakespeare's American sister is *not* going to come, any more than Shakespeare's American brother; and American women writers, at least, can no longer wait around for her like female Godots, much less in poverty and obscurity. The validity of American women's writing doesn't depend on Shakespeare's sister, and it can tolerate no more Dark Ladies. Our brave new world has many women in it, and we must make its myths together or not at all.

41

3

Little Women: The American Female Myth

In the eyes of many readers and critics, Louisa May Alcott's *Little Women* (1868) is '*the* American female myth,' and Alcott's heroine Jo March has become the most influential figure of the independent and creative American woman.[1] Ardent testimonials to Alcott have come from women writers as diverse as Gertrude Stein and Adrienne Rich. 'I read *Little Women* a thousand times,' the novelist Cynthia Ozick recalls. 'Ten thousand. I am Jo in her "vortex," not Jo exactly, but some Jo-of-the-future.' In 1989, when American governors were asked to name their favourite childhood books, two of the three women governors, Rose Mofford of Alabama and Kay Orr of Nebraska, chose *Little Women*.[2]

It should not come as a surprise, however, that none of the forty-seven male governors named *Little Women* in their response. While it has influenced the work of scores of American women writers, in male literature, such as the stories of Hemingway and Fitzgerald, *Little Women* stands as a code term for female piety and sentimentality, although it is highly unlikely that either Hemingway or Fitzgerald had read it. Indeed, there can be few other books in American literary history which have had so enormous a critical impact on half the reading population, and so minuscule a place in the libraries or criticism of the other.

In the past decade, *Little Women* has been the subject of much critical re-evaluation and debate. Alcott's literary reputation, along with that of other popular nineteenth-century women novelists, such as Stowe, has been forcefully challenged by feminist critics, who have questioned the patriarchal assumptions of American literary history, while scholarly editions of Alcott's pseudonymous sensation fiction, satiric writing, feminist novels, and letters, have shown how much her work demands serious attention and rereading. Several Americanists, including Ann Douglas, Sarah Elbert, and Anne Rose, have discussed Little Women as an important feminist critique of the Transcendentalist movement. Nina Auerbach interprets Little Women as a novel about self-sustaining communities of women, while Judith Fetterley regards it as Alcott's personal Civil War, a novel split by conflicting impulses about femininity and creativity.[3]

For some feminist critics, Alcott's lifelong effort to tailor her turbulent imagination to suit the moralism of her father, the commercialism of her publishers, and the puritanism of 'gray Concord,' kept her from fulfilling her literary promise. Alcott always regarded herself as a dutiful daughter. Her father praised her in a sonnet as 'duty's faithful child,' and Alcott herself described her highest ambition as being a 'good daughter' rather than a 'great writer.' By modern feminist standards, such capitulation to the dominant culture's image of feminine propriety is a serious flaw. In the words of Adrienne Rich, for example, the woman artist must struggle to break away from such traditional and internalized ideas, for 'the dutiful daughter of the fathers can only be a hack.'[4] Moreover, by cutting themselves off from the effort to create 'literary masterpieces,' Nina Baym has argued, Alcott and other American women writers of her generation 'foreclosed certain possibilities for themselves and others.' Their work inevitably lacked the properties of 'art': 'formal self-consciousness, attachment to or quarrel with a grand tradition, aesthetic seriousness.'[5]

For other feminist critics, however, Little Women itself stands as one of the best studies we have of the literary daughter's dilemma: the tension between feminine identity and artistic freedom, and even more important, between patriarchal models of the literary career and those more relevant to women's lives. As a citizen of 'the famous land of Emerson, Hawthorne, Thoreau, Alcott & Co.,'[6] Alcott had seen at close hand the vanities of the Transcendental prophets, and especially the self-ishness and improvidence of her own father. Bronson Alcott was one of the eccentric seers of American Transcendentalism, a social visionary, speculative philosopher, and self-styled genius. Antimaterialist in his beliefs and incapable of earning money, Bronson was unabashedly willing to be subsidized by his friends as well as his in-laws, daughters, and wife. Even Emerson thought him a 'tedious archangel,' who gave genius a bad name. Growing up in Concord, Louisa was taught to worship the great men of her father's circle: Emerson, Hawthorne, the preacher Theodore Parker, and Thoreau. Emerson in particular, she noted, was 'the god of my idolatry'; she was overjoyed to receive a picture of him from her father as a birthday gift, and thrilled to be invited as a young woman to his discussion group on 'Genius.' But as she grew older, Alcott gradually became more disen-chanted about patriarchal myths of genius, and conscious of their disadvantages for women. 'To have had Mr. Emerson as an intellectual God all one's life,' she ruefully remarked, 'is to be invested with a chain armour of propriety.'[7] Through the figure of Jo March, Alcott explored alternative models for the woman artist.

To read *Little Women* at the end of the twentieth century is thus to engage with contemporary ideas about women's literary identity, critical institutions, and the American literary canon, as well as with nineteenth-century ideas of the relationship between patriarchal culture and women's culture. Alcott was so divided between the maternal and paternal sides of her lineage that she was literally ambidextrous. Born on her father's thirty-third birthday she always felt a keen sense of both kinship and rivalry with him. To Louisa, Bronson was always the esteemed 'modern Plato,' but also a comically impractical philosopher in need of constant care and much brisk female brushing-up. 'Regards to Plato,' she writes at the end of a typical letter home. 'Don't he want new socks? Are his clothes getting shiny?'[8]

Of both parents though, the impetuous, moody Louisa, who seemed 'topsy-turvy' almost from infancy, took after her hot-tempered, imaginative mother Abba May Alcott, the beloved

'Marmee' of *Little Women*. 'The mother and daughter are part of one another and cannot be separated long at a time,' observed Bronson, whose own long absences seem to have come as a welcome break to his hard-working family.[9] Louisa dedicated many of her books to her mother, nursed her through her final illness, and told a correspondent that her finest deed had been making her mother's last years happy ones.

While Abba provided steady love, sympathy, and encouragement for Louisa's literary aspirations, however, Bronson cast her as the difficult daughter in the family and did everything he could to tame her and to teach her proper feminine decorum and self-control according to his educational principles. We can get the full allegorical flavor of their struggle in a childhood episode Madelon Bedell calls 'The Drama of the Apple.' When Louisa was two and Anna four, Bronson decided to test the children's obedience by leaving prohibited apples where the children were sure to see them. Docile Anna resisted; rebellious Louisa, declaring 'Me *must* have it,' devoured the forbidden fruit. In this domestic version of *Paradise Lost*, Bronson was Jehovah to Louisa's Eve, a stern patriarchal authority figure punishing female self-assertion.[10]

The imagery of the apple and female temptation was central to the Alcott family's personal mythology of Eden and the Fall, in which women, sexuality, and the bodily appetites stood for all the earthly obstacles to male transcendence. Louisa mockingly called her father's failed utopian commune, Fruitlands, 'Apple Slump'; in the last icy winter days of the experiment, apples and water had been their only food. But eating apples also became identified in her mind with female creativity and sexuality, with writing, knowledge, and transgression. Alcott called her drafts 'green apples,' and wrote in her garret with 'a pile of apples to eat' while she planned stories, a habit she gave Jo in *Little Women*. 'I shall be a ripe and sweet old pippin before I die,' she declared in her journal. As Helena Michie points out, 'If Eve's desire for the apple represents the decentering force of women's power, it is also deeply linked with the question of authority and, finally, of authorship.'[11]

Bronson and Abba Alcott were not only Louisa's dual models of authority, but her first models of authorship as well. Her earliest memory was of 'playing with books in my father's study—building houses and bridges of the big dictionaries and diaries, looking at pictures, pretending to read, and scribbling on blank pages whenever pen or pencil could be found.' The stories Bronson told his daughters were abstract and allegorical. He used every story to teach a moral lesson; and his favorite text was Bunyan's *Pilgrim's Progress*, which he encouraged the children to act out. In contrast, Abba told 'highly romantic' stories of 'the witchcraft days' in Salem, in which her ancestors had played a part.[12] Alcott would always associate her own most pleasurable writing with witchcraft; in a memoir, she described her imagination as 'the caldron' into which every memory and experience entered. Women's writing, in the title of one of her adolescent plays, was the 'witch's curse,' a passionate legacy that could be both magical and dangerous.

Outside of the immediate family, her major literary influences also reflected patriarchal and matriarchal traditions and styles. The young Louisa read widely in American, English, and European women's literature: Madame de Staël, Mary Wollstonecraft, Maria Edgeworth, Fanny Burney, George Sand, George Eliot, Elizabeth Barrett Browning, Charlotte Yonge, Fredrika Bremer, Lydia Maria Child, Harriet Beecher Stowe, Susan Warner, Gail Hamilton, Margaret Fuller, and Harriet Prescott Spofford. Both she and Abba avidly read Elizabeth Gaskell's biography of Charlotte Brontë, and saw themselves as an American version of the tragic Brontë family.

Louisa especially identified with the literary spinster as an American Arachne. In *The Madwoman in the Attic*, Sandra Gilbert and Susan Gubar also describe the longstanding mythic tradition that 'associates virgin women—women who spin, or spinsters— with spinning spiders.'[13] American women writers' identification with the spider as Muse is frequent during the post-Civil War period, in such texts as Rose Terry Cooke's 'Arachne':

> Poor sister of the spinster clan!
> I too from out my store within
> My daily life and living plan,
> My home, my rest, my pleasure spin.

Alcott, too, often described herself as 'spinning tales like a spider' or 'like a spider, spinning out brains for money.' As a girl she had a 'curious empathy' for spiders, frequenting a childhood spot she called 'Spiderland,' and even holding elaborate funerals for deceased specimens.[14]

But like Fuller her main sanctuary and literary resource was her father's library, where she devoured Plutarch, Dante, Shakespeare, Carlyle, Dickens, Byron, Scott, and Goldsmith. Another masculine idol of literary worship was Goethe. As an adolescent, Alcott read *Goethe's Correspondence with a Child*, letters between the fifty-year-old sage and an adoring teenager, Bettina von Arnim. In this erotic but unconsummated exchange, incestuous feelings were meshed with romantic images of female devotion to towering male genius. The book was enormously popular among the Concord and Cambridge literati; Emerson thought all young women should study it. While Abba was struck by Goethe's coldness, Louisa was impressed by Bettina's passion. When she read the story, she 'at once was fired with a desire to be a Bettine [*sic*], making my father's friend [Emerson] my Goethe. So I wrote letters to him, but never sent them, sat in a tall cherry tree at midnight . . . left wild flowers on the doorstep of my "Master" and sang Mignon's song under the window in very bad German.' When she was fifteen, Emerson gave her a copy of *Wilhelm Meister*, and from that day on, she regarded Goethe as her 'chief idol.'[15]

Yet these models of male literary genius were also inhibiting and restrictive for an ambitious young woman writer. While the gods of Concord wrote in seemingly serene indifference to financial need, Alcott found the economic stimulus to be the strongest motive for her urge to write professionally. In her teens, Alcott made a Faustian vow to save her family with her success: 'I *will* do something by-and-by. Don't care what, teach, sew, act, write, anything to help the family; and I'll be rich and famous and happy before I die, see if I won't!'[16] As she grew older, the Faust theme became increasingly compelling for Alcott's imagination. In her unpublished novel, 'The Long Love Chase' (1867), Alcott imagined a young woman who makes a pact with the Devil in order to get out of her boring and confined life. In her later novel, *A Modern Mephistopheles* (1877), a young writer bargains with the Devil in order to become a famous poet. Both stories suggest her guilty sense of having bartered her womanhood and art in the name of financial expedience, to achieve literary and commercial success.

Louisa found independence from her parents only in her writing. Whenever she could snatch the time from sewing, housework, teaching, or domestic service, she gave herself up to a 'vortex' of ecstatic creativity in which she felt neither hunger nor fatigue, 'but was perfectly happy and seemed to have no wants.' Writing for Alcott was almost a trance-state. 'While a story is underway,' she told a friend, 'I live in it, see the people more plainly than real ones round me, hear them talk, and am much interested, surprised or provoked at their actions, for I seem to have no power to rule them, and can simply record their experiences and performances.'[17]

But the vortex also brought out disturbing emotions and fantasies of sexuality, anger, rebellion, and escape. And even apart from these forbidden feelings, Bronson's disapproval of female self-consciousness as selfish and narcissistic conflicted with Alcott's need to explore her own feelings as a young woman and a budding writer. When she was seventeen, he noted disapprovingly that while Anna's journal was 'about other people, Louisa's is about herself.'[18] For several years thereafter she wrote only intermittently in her journal, and her struggle to deny the self shows up as well in her characteristic omission of the first person both in her diary entries and in Jo's speech in *Little Women*.[19]

Alcott's ideas about sexuality, love, and marriage were conflicting and ambivalent. The death of her sister Lizzie in 1858 and her confidante Anna's marriage the same year to a neighbor, John Pratt, were parallel traumas. Anna's wedding signaled the breakup of a sustaining sisterhood. 'I'd rather be a free spinster and paddle my own canoe,' Louisa wrote defiantly.[20] In an interview with the writer Louise Chandler Moulton, she later commented with pre-Freudian candor on her own feelings: 'I am more than half-persuaded that I am a man's soul, put by some freak of nature into a woman's body . . . because I have fallen in love in my life with so many pretty girls and never once the least bit with any man.'[21] Many of her essays explored the possibilities of a single life for women, or a sustaining community of women artists and professionals, and she often criticized the problems caused by early marriage and wedlock: 'Half the misery of time comes from unmated pairs trying to live their legal lie decorously to the end at any cost.'[22] Yet in other stories and novels, including *Little Women*, Alcott tried to imagine genuinely egalitarian marriages in which women could be strong and loving, and in which they could continue to work and create. It is impossible to say whether her own spinsterhood was the result of a lesbian sexual preference unfulfilled in Victorian culture, or her recognition that her needs for independence could not be satisfied in the marital opportunities she was offered.

After a decade of literary apprenticeship during which she steadily published stories, poems, and essays while supporting herself as teacher, seamstress, and even domestic servant, Alcott's professional writing life really began on her thirtieth birthday. In 1862, she made the daring decision to volunteer as a nurse in a Civil War army hospital in Washington: 'I want new experiences, and am sure to get 'em if I go.'[23] Although she lasted only six weeks before she contracted typhoid fever, the experience gave Alcott her first real separation from her family, and a chance to test herself emotionally and physically without Abba's emotional protection or Bronson's surveillance. Nursing also provided the material for her first successful book, *Hospital Sketches* (1863), a book which combined Dickensian humor and indignation with a strong and serious plot.

During the next several years, she was finally able to give up other work and to write full-time, developing her literary skills by writing in several different modes. In an age when English women writers like the Brontës and George Eliot had disguised their identities under male pseudonyms, Alcott might have done the same. Instead she first followed the American model of hyperfeminine pen names, calling herself first 'Flora Fairfield,' then self-mocking names that expressed her discomfort with the role of woman intellectual or activist, such as Minerva Moody, Oranthy Bluggage, or 'Tribulation Periwinkle,' the nurse of *Hospital Sketches*.

In the mid-1860s, however, Alcott secretly published several lurid thrillers under the sexually ambiguous pseudonym 'A. M. Barnard.' These stories gave her the opportunity to unleash her imagination in plots of seduction, incest, adultery, disguise, and violent revenge. 'I think my natural inclination is for the lurid style,' she told a Concord friend. 'I indulge in gorgeous fantasies and wish that I dared inscribe them upon my pages and set them before the public.'[24] 'Behind a Mask,' which she wrote in August 1866, is the most important and suggestive of these sensation stories. The history of Jean Muir, a disillusioned and embittered middle-aged actress who successfully masquerades as a victimized young governess, deceives all the members of the family, and finally wins herself a rich husband, seems like a metaphorical representation of Alcott's own double life as dutiful daughter and rebellious fantasist. The story can be seen as a narrative meditation on the possibilities for feminist subversion of patriarchal culture, on the ways for women to express themselves, or at least their power, through role-playing. If women are trapped within feminine scripts of childishness and victimization, Alcott suggests, they can unmask these roles only by deliberately overacting them.

In September 1867, Thomas Niles, a partner in the enterprising Boston firm of Roberts Brothers, asked Alcott to write a 'girls' story' for them, and in February 1868, Bronson Alcott, who was hoping to get Roberts Brothers to publish his book of Transcendental essays, repeated the request: 'They want a book of 200 pages or more just as you choose. Mr Niles the literary partner spoke in terms of admiration of your literary ability, thinking most highly of your rising fame and prospects. He obviously wishes to become *your* publisher and *mine*.' Louisa was dubious at first: 'I plod away, though I don't enjoy this sort of thing. Never liked girls, or knew many, except my sisters; but our queer plays and experiences may prove interesting, though I doubt it.'[25]

What was a 'girls' story'? Essentially moralistic, it was designed to bridge the gap between the schoolroom and the drawing room, to recommend docility, marriage, and obedience rather than autonomy or adventure. Writing for girls bestowed more obligations on the author too. 'Girls' literature ought to help to build up women,' wrote one nineteenth-century critic, Edward Salmon. 'If in choosing the books that boys shall read it is necessary to remember that we are choosing mental food for the future chiefs of the race, it is equally important not to forget in choosing books for girls that we are choosing mental food for the future wives and mothers of that race.'[26]

Alcott would not give in to the self-pity, the lachrymose sentiment, and the lugubrious piety that characterized so much female scribbling of the period. Her admiration for the novels of Dickens gave her a comic perspective on her characters. Furthermore, her fondness for the American idiom made her turn more to the pungency of a Caroline Kirkland or a Gail Hamilton than the mournful language of Warner or Charlotte Yonge. Having just returned from a trip to 'slow going' England, where, she writes in her letters home, everything was so 'unyankee,' orderly, and sedate, Alcott was all the more aware of her native land, where 'the very cows . . . look fast.'[27] She gave her characters, and especially Jo, the distinctive accents of American girls.

Louisa had long planned a novel, possibly satiric, about Bronson's visions and the Alcott family's hardships, to be called 'The Pathetic Family,' 'The Cost of an Idea,' or 'The Forlornites.' But when she started writing, she gave up this plan, and shifted attention from her father's experiments to herself and her sisters, sending 'Mr March' off to the Civil War, and beginning with Christmas among the March girls and their mother.

In June she sent Niles the first twelve chapters, which they both found dull. 'But work away and mean to try the experiment; for lively, simple books are very much needed for girls, and perhaps I can supply the need.'[28] Her idea was to take the family of daughters through a year, and in planning the narrative framework of *Little Women*, Alcott incorporated both patriarchal and matriarchal traditions: the allegory of *Pilgrim's Progress* and the theatrical melodrama of 'The Witch's Curse.' She wanted readers to be aware of the Bunyan model, and had decided that instead of a preface she would use an epigraph based on Part II of *Pilgrim's Progress*, in order to 'give some clue to the plan of the story.'[29] Yet Alcott also wanted to revise Bunyan to explore women's experience. Bunyan's allegory deals primarily with male pilgrimage; his Christiana has four sons 'to tell you what | It is for men to take a *Pilgrims* lot.' Alcott, however, makes the pilgrim of her epigraph a woman whose example will teach 'young damsels' and 'little tripping maids' to follow God.

Allusions to *Pilgrim's Progress* structure the story in Part I, beginning with the first chapter, 'Playing Pilgrims,' in which Marmee announces the theme of female progress towards the paradise of goodness: 'Our burdens are here, our road is before us, and the longing for goodness and happiness is the guide that leads us through many troubles and mistakes to the peace which is a true Celestial City.' The March girls receive copies of Bunyan's little book for Christmas (*not* the New Testament, as some critics have thought), and they pursue their quest, guidebooks in hand, discussing their burdens, as Beth finds the Palace Beautiful in Mr Laurence's mansion, Amy goes through the Valley of Humiliation at school, Jo meets the monster Apollyon when she lets her anger at Amy smoulder, and Meg is tempted by Vanity Fair in a visit to the wealthy Moffat family.

By mid-July Alcott had written ten more chapters, ending the manuscript with the family's Christmas reunion, when Mr March returns from the war. Beth tells that she has been reading how 'after many troubles, Christian and Hopeful came to a pleasant green meadow, where lilies bloomed all the year round, and there they rested happily, as we do now, before they went on to their journey's end.' But Niles was not content. 'I am not sure that it would not be best to add another chapter to Little Women,' he wrote to her. 'I have read the whole of it & I am sure it will "hit," which means I think it will sell well. A chapter could well be added, in which allusions might be made to something in the future.'[30] Finally Alcott wrote the twenty-third chapter about Meg's engagement, ending with the promise of more to come, and emphasizing the dramatic metaphor which along with *Pilgrim's Progress*, provided the structure for the book: 'So grouped the curtain falls upon Meg, Jo, Beth and Amy. Whether it ever rises again, depends upon the reception given to the first act of the domestic drama, called "LITTLE WOMEN."' When the proofs arrived at the end of August Niles was enthusiastic, and Alcott found her own work 'not a bit sensational, but simple and true, for we really lived most of it.'[31]

Despite her disclaimers about the book, Alcott's realism was never simplistic; she found a number of innovative ways to represent the tensions and conflicts in her characters' lives. While the *Pilgrim's Progress* drama uses Bronson Alcott's favorite moral allegory to teach female self-restraint, the melodrama of 'The Witch's Curse,' as Karen Halttunen has suggested, allows for 'passionate self-expression.' In the play, Jo can dress like a man, make love to her sister, express rage and plot murder, and practice witchcraft with impunity. Yet insofar as Alcott always thought of the female imagination as 'the witch's curse,' the play suggests the frustrating paradox of Jo's creative drives in a post-Salem New England society.[32]

In addition to balancing the novel between the attractions of moral pilgrimage and the temptations of rebellious witchcraft, Alcott incorporated a variety of literary forms into the novel's two books, making full imaginative use of her own youthful writings, including stories, plays, poems, letters, and even newspapers. The chapter called 'The P. C. and P. O.,' in which the four March girls take on the identities of Dickens's male Pickwick Club members, is another feminist revision of a male literary model. Although they have assumed male names, Meg and Beth insist that theirs is a 'ladies' club,' and resist Laurie's admission; Jo, however, insists that Laurie will 'give a tone' to their paper and 'keep us from being sentimental.' Jo even remodels her own works in imitation of Laurie's masculine tones. Yet the Victorian sentimentality of which the book is often accused by those who have never read it is belied by Alcott's naturalness, humor, and restraint even in the death scenes. When Beth's canary, Pip, dies of neglect, for example, and Amy proposes to revive him in the oven, Beth retorts, 'He's been starved and he shan't be baked.' The description of the death of the Hummel baby ('it gave a little cry and trembled and then lay very still') is equally direct. Alcott's experience in the war had given her an authority in writing about death which made sentimentality unlikely.

Little Women was published on 1 October 1868, and was a huge success, far overshadowing Bronson's simultaneous publication of his *Tablets*. By the end of October, the first edition of two thousand copies had been sold, and Niles wrote to ask her for 'corrections to make for a new edition of "Little Women,"' noting that there had been some objections from Sunday School librarians to the Christmas theatricals. 'For my part,' he wrote, 'I think it is about the best part of the whole book. Why will people be so *very good*?'[33]

Alcott resisted the suggestion to substitute something for Christmas theatricals, but immediately began a sequel, writing 'like a steam engine' at the rate of a chapter a day. 'I dont like sequels, and dont think No 2 will be as popular as No 1,' she wrote her uncle, 'but publishers are very *perwerse* & wont let authors have thier [sic] way so my little women must grow up & be married off in a very stupid style.' She was annoyed when girls wrote to her to ask 'who the little women marry, as if that was the only end and aim of a woman's life.' At first Alcott resisted the pressures of the standard marriage plot: 'I *won't* marry Jo to Laurie to please any one.' But she quickly saw the fictional possibilities in creating a different kind of marriage for Jo. 'Jo should have remained a literary spinster,' she wrote to her friend Alf Whitman, 'but so many enthusiastic young ladies wrote to me clamorously demanding that she should marry Laurie, *or* somebody, that I didn't dare refuse & out of perversity went & made a funny match for her. I expect vials of wrath to be poured out upon my head, but rather enjoy the prospect.' To Niles, she wryly suggested that the sequel might be titled 'Little Women Act Second,' 'Leaving the Nest. Sequel to Little Women,' or 'Wedding Marches,' because there was 'so much pairing off.'[34] She ended the novel with a chapter called 'Harvest Time,' in which Marmee's sixtieth birthday is celebrated by her grown-up children and grandchildren. Thus the story covers a twenty-year span, taking Jo from the age of fifteen to thirty-five.

In addition to succumbing to the requisite pairing-off, Alcott made other concessions to her publishers. In Part II, her sister May's drawings for the first edition, which had been generally criticized as amateurish by reviewers, were replaced by illustrations by the well-known American artist Hamnatt Billings, who had also illustrated the works of Tennyson and Keats. Although he first drew Laurie as a 'scrubby little boy,' and then as a 'baa lamb . . . straight out of a bandbox,' eventually Billings proved willing to follow her instructions.[35]

Despite Alcott's fears about a sequel, thirteen thousand copies of Part II were sold in the month following the publication of Part II, on 14 April 1869. By the end of the year, Louisa had made $8,500 in royalties, and the family's fortunes had turned. Even Bronson took his daughter's sudden celebrity in his stride, and began to enjoy being introduced as 'The Father of "Little Women".' 'I am riding in her chariot of glory, wherever I go.'[36] By 1870 Alcott recognized that her hard times as a writer were over. Publishers were clamoring for anything new from her pen, and in the first half of the 1870s, she accommodated publishers and readers with a steady flow of novels and short stories, including *An Old-Fashioned Girl* (1870), *Little Men* (1871), *Work* (1873), 'Transcendental Wild Oats' (1873), *Eight Cousins* (1875), and *Rose in Bloom* (1876).

But Alcott also complained that the success of *Little Women* confined her to a particular style and subject matter. In 1871 she published *A Modern Mephistopheles* anonymously in Roberts Brothers' No Name Series, and in 1879 she began *Diana and Persis*, an adult novel about two women artists, based on her sister May's career as a painter in Europe, and on her unconventional marriage to a much younger Swiss musician and businessman. In the novel, Alcott expressed her views on the combination of love and art: 'I believe a woman can & ought to have both if she has the power and courage to win them. A man expects them, and achieves them; why is not a woman's life to be as full and free as his?' But May's death in childbirth at the end of 1879 put a stop to her exploration of these new fictional territories. 'I shall try to have it unlike the others if possible,' she wrote to the children's magazine editor Mary Mapes Dodge, of a new story; 'but the dears *will* cling to the Little Women style.'[37] In 1881, having bought the copyright to her first unsuccessful novel, *Moods*, Alcott rewrote the ending to fit with middle-class ideas of morality.

It also appears that Alcott gave in around this time to her publishers' demands for a more polished and sentimentalized text of *Little Women*. In 1880, a new edition with nearly two hundred illustrations by the popular artist Frank T. Merrill appeared, which also included innumerable textual changes. Spelling errors and mistakes in French were corrected, and Alcott's vigorous slang, colloquialisms, and regionalisms were replaced by a blander, more refined and 'ladylike' prose. Jo calls her father 'Papa' rather than 'Pa,' says 'work' rather than 'grub,' 'crumpled' rather than 'crunched,' 'ways' instead of 'quirks,' 'cross' instead of 'raspy,' and 'many' instead of 'lots'. Alcott also changed many

New England regional idioms to suit her publisher's sense of a national best-seller suitable for Sunday-school libraries; 'prim as a desk' became 'prim as I can,' for example, and 'quinydingles' became 'notions.' Literary allusions were simplified for a mass audience, so that a reference to 'Garrick buying gloves of the grisette' in Chapter 26 is changed to '*Romeo and Juliet*.'[38]

More significant changes came in the descriptions of two major characters. Whereas the original Marmee was 'a stout, motherly lady, with a "can-I-help-you" look about her which was truly delightful,' explicitly *not* 'a particularly handsome person,' in the 1880 edition these details are gone, and Marmee becomes much more genteel, fashionable, and idealized: 'tall' rather than 'stout,' 'not elegantly dressed, but a noble-looking woman.'

Alcott's changed description of Laurie says even more about the dictates of gender roles in successful literary romance. In the original, when Jo sizes up Laurie at the Gardiners' party, he is both foreign and androgynous, with 'curly black hair, brown skin, big black eyes, long nose, nice teeth, little hands and feet, tall as I am.' Inviting Jo to dance, Laurie makes 'a queer little French bow.' Apparently, however, these less-than-perfect features and effeminate foreign gestures were a problem in the romantic hero. In the 1880 edition, Laurie is much improved: 'handsome nose, fine teeth, small hands and feet.' Most significantly for the belief in male superiority, Laurie is now 'taller' than Jo, and invites her to dance with 'a gallant little bow.'

Thus the 1880 edition, which is the one virtually all modern readers know, is in a sense a bowdlerized text, in which the rough edges of Alcott's imagination have been smoothed away, and the pungent originality of her voice toned way down. According to Madeleine Stern, Daniel Shealy, and Joel Myerson, the editors of Alcott's correspondence, furthermore, the changes are not discussed in her letters to Niles or her personal journals. Stern, Alcott's most distinguished biographer and literary editor, believes that 'textual alterations and variations may well have been accomplished by publishers, some careless, some over-zealous,' although we do not at this point have documentary proof that such was the case.[39] Apparently, though, Alcott went along with these changes—another sign of her loss of self-confidence and daring in the later part of her career. 'Though I do not enjoy writing "moral tales" for the young,' she wrote to an admiring correspondent, 'I do it because it pays well.'[40]

Looking at the course of Alcott's literary career, and at Jo's choice of marriage to a fatherly German professor in place of her own literary career, many feminist critics have come to the conclusion that *Little Women* was the turning point at which Alcott compromised her imaginative vision in the interests of commercial success. They see the domestic drama of *Little Women* as a capitulation to middle-class ideals of female self-sacrifice. Thus Martha Saxton finds *Little Women* 'a regression for Louisa as an artist and as a woman.' Through Jo's marriage and renunciation of her writing, Karen Halttunen maintains, 'Alcott performed literary penance for her greatest sins against the cult of domesticity: her flight to Washington, her Gothic period, her consuming literary ambition and her refusal to marry.' Judith Fetterley concludes that Jo ends in 'self-denial, renunciation, and mutilation.'[41]

But these strong negative judgments now seem overstated and extreme, demanding from Alcott's nineteenth-century female *Bildungsroman* a twentieth-century feminist ending of separation and autonomy. In my view, *Little Women* has survived because it is both convincing and inspiring. Alcott's novel of female development dramatizes the Transcendentalist dream of sexually egalitarian lives of love and work. Seen in this context, Jo's literary and emotional career is a happy one, even if it does not conform to our contemporary feminist model of a woman artist's needs. Furthermore, despite the haste with which it was written, *Little Women* is more tightly constructed and more stylistically controlled than any of Alcott's other books. In her themes as well as her style, Alcott set the escapist fantasies of sensationalism within a realistic feminist framework. In *Little Women*, she managed to do what she had never achieved in the sensation stories: create vivid, credible, and enduring characters, and write about them in a memorably American and personal voice, very different from the stilted tones of the sensation stories, or the orphic notes of her male mentors.

Critics who view the novel as the story of Jo's decline into marriage and motherhood contrast descriptions of the creative vortex in which Jo abandons herself to her art, with her apparent surrender to patriarchal values about true womanhood in marrying the professor. When 'genius burns,' young Jo gives herself up to writing with 'entire abandon,' unconscious of the ordinary cares of life and the ordinary duties of womanhood. When she goes up to the attic to write, she wears a special black 'scribbling suit,' on which she can wipe her inky pen at will (unlike the everyday dresses, the badge of her restrictive feminine role, which she invariably scorches, stains, smudges, rips, or shrinks), and a rakish cap with a red bow, 'gaily erect' when work is going well, 'plucked wholly off' when inspiration fails.

In contrast, Professor Bhaer reproaches Jo for writing sensation fiction; his library shelves hold all the patriarchal classics: Homer, Milton, Goethe, and Shakespeare. By the time he comes to court her, the novel's language suggests that sexual involvement has appropriated her creative energy; now it is his bushy hair, rather than Jo's red scribbling-bow, that is 'rampantly erect.' The literary life Jo has always desired comes to seem 'selfish, lonely, and cold.' In their life together, Bhaer will steer her into 'calmer waters,' and away from the turbulent imaginative whirlpool of the vortex.

Yet Alcott herself never idealizes the costs and effects of the vortex for the woman writer. While the surrender to 'genius' is satisfying while it lasts, it offers Jo no sustenance for her daily life; she invariably emerges from the 'divine afflatus' after a week or two, 'hungry, sleepy, cross, or despondent.' When she thinks about her future as a 'literary spinster,' Jo is realistic about the loneliness and self-denial it entails: 'a pen for a spouse, a family of stories for children, and twenty years hence a morsel of fame, perhaps.'

In exploring and comparing the artistic development of both Jo and Amy, Alcott suggests that the Romantic model of 'genius' has serious problems for women. Because it is derived from male experience and mythology, genius requires a woman artist either to sacrifice the feminine side of her personality, or to labor continually under the sense of infinite artistic inferiority. As girls, both Jo and Amy measure themselves continually against the most towering and unapproachable models of male genius: Shakespeare for Jo, Michelangelo for Amy. Amy's path takes her to Rome, where, face-to-face with the reality of her precursor's art, she decides that she is not a genius, and determines 'to be great or nothing. I won't be a common-place dauber, so I don't intend to try any more.' Instead, through Laurie's largesse, she will help other 'young women with artistic tendencies.'

Jo's trajectory is different. She too aspires to equal male literary giants, and then postpones her own literary career in the interest of educating and mothering 'poor, forlorn little lads.' None the less, Jo has learned to exchange the model of male 'genius' for a more realistic feminine model that is based on training, experimentation, professionalism, and self-fulfillment.

Alcott takes Jo through a literary progress that resembles her own pilgrimage. Beginning with fairy tales and melodramas, Jo's adolescent ambitions are vague and grand: 'I'd have a stable full of Arabian steeds, rooms piled with books, and I'd write out of a magic inkstand. . . . I want to do something splendid before I go into my castle,—something heroic, or wonderful,—that won't be forgotten after I'm dead.' The publication of her first story, 'The Rival Painters,' is both the outcome of her involvement with romance, fantasy and the foreign, and the inscription of her ongoing rivalry with Amy for the role of family artist.

Motivated by the example of 'Mrs. S. L. A. N. G. Northbury,' the successful sensationalist writer who is modelled on the best-selling American novelist of the 1850s, Mrs. E. D. E. N. Southworth, Jo then sets out to write a sensational story, 'full of desperation and despair,' for the *Blarneystone Banner*. Her first effort wins her a hundred-dollar prize, and she discovers that her pen can win comforts for the family, pay the butcher's bill, and send Beth to the seaside for a month. Her most ambitious project is a novel for which she is paid three-hundred dollars. It is criticized from all sides; but, as Jo staunchly notes, 'Not being a genius like Keats, it won't kill me.' Her writing is not the product of frail romantic genius, but of hard work: 'literary labors.' In other efforts, she produces lurid sensation fiction for the *Weekly Volcano*; didactic children's tales, and, after Beth's decline, her first commercial and critical success, a tale inspired by 'love and sorrow,' and presented in the realistic mode her father tells her is her 'true style.' Unlike Amy, Jo does not have the opportunity to travel in Europe, where every street, park, and church is saturated with literary history. Her material must come from her own experience, and Alcott intends us to believe her at the end when she vows that her writing will be all the stronger for her years as wife, mother, and teacher.

Moreover, in order to forge a complete life as a woman and writer, Jo must leave the female world of love and ritual, and discover her own sexuality and independence. Her girlhood stories often deal transparently with her feelings about her sisters: artistic rivalry with Amy, guilty responsibility for Beth, fear of losing Meg's love. 'The Rival Painters,' as Alcott notes, is written when Jo begins to realize that 'Margaret was fast getting to be a woman,' and to 'dread the separation which must surely come some time, and now seemed very near.' Alcott shows that the separation, so intensely dreaded, is none the less a necessity if Jo is to break away from the uncritical loving bonds of her family and become a mature, rather than a little, woman, as well as a serious writer. After Meg's marriage, Beth's death, and Amy's engagement, Jo acknowledges her own emotional and sexual needs. Though she 'used to be contented' with the family, she finds that she wants more. 'Mothers are the *best* lovers in the world,' she tells Marmee, 'But I'd like to try all kinds.' The horsehair pillow with which she warded off Laurie's romantic advances is sent to the garret; and she writes her story about Beth.

Within the Victorian framework of the novel, Jo's separation from her family can only be accomplished through marriage. At fifteen Jo opts to be an old maid rather than marry for money, and Marmee approves: 'better be happy old maids than unhappy wives.' Yet spinsterhood is never positively presented in the book. Miss Crocker, or 'Croaker,' as the girls call her, is a 'yellow spinster, with a sharp nose and inquisitive eyes,' a gossip and a sponger. At this stage in Alcott's writing, there are no viable alternatives to marriage, although she would explore them in her later works.

Yet Professor Bhaer proposes at the point when Jo seems to have found her literary style at last, and the marriage for which she sets aside the pen to run a school for boys has disappointed many critics. Madelon Bedell feels *Little Women* ends in 'unease and dissatisfaction' with Jo's marriage to a 'sexless, fusty middle-aged man,' sacrificing both 'romance *and* independence.' Judith

Fetterley sees Bhaer as 'the heavy authority figure necessary to offset Jo's own considerable talent and vitality. . . . In marrying Professor Bhaer, Jo's rebellion is neutralized and she proves once and for all that she is a good little woman who wishes for nothing more than to realize herself in the service of some superior male.'[42]

Some women readers have felt hostile to Bhaer because they regret the loss of the charming, sensitive, and sensual Laurie. The need to make Laurie a romantic hero, more glamorous and experienced than Jo, has also been reflected in the changes Hollywood has made in adapting the novel, both in aggrandizing Laurie and diminishing Jo. In the 1949 film directed by Mervyn LeRoy, for example, Laurie, played by Peter Lawford, is introduced as having run away from school to join the army, lying about his age, and being wounded in battle. The script by Sally Benson and Andrew Solt describes him as looking 'not unlike our idea of Edgar Allan Poe,' as if Jo's literary ambition had been displaced onto him.[43]

Yet like a number of Alcott's other works, *Little Women* represents Alcott's belief that the fullest art came from women who had fulfilled both their sexual and their intellectual needs, and her effort to imagine such a fulfillment for Jo. As Anne Hollander, alone among Alcott's contemporary critics, has argued, 'Jo can write as a true artist only later when she finally comes to terms with her own sexual self.'[44] Despite her joking complaints about pressure from her readers, Alcott intended Professor Bhaer to be much more than a 'silly match' for Jo. She portrays Bhaer as warmhearted, affectionate, and expressive, as well as unconfined by American codes of masculinity. Intellectual but unpretentious, loving and nurturant, and thoroughly dependable, Bhaer, as Sarah Elbert has noted, 'has all the qualities Bronson Alcott lacked . . . the feminine attributes Louisa admired and hoped men could acquire in a rational, feminist world.'[45] In *Jo's Boys* (1886), Alcott's continuation of the March family chronicle, Professor Bhaer hugs his sons, 'not ashamed to express by gesture or by word the fatherly emotions an American would have compressed into a slap on the shoulder and a brief "All right."'

Bhaer's courtship of Jo is unselfconscious and openhearted. He sings Mignon's song to Jo with a 'tender invitation,' reversing the roles of idol and worshipper in Alcott's Goethesque fantasy. Although in the picture of her that he cherishes, Jo is 'a severe and rigid young lady with a good deal of hair,' he responds to and encourages the warmth beneath her prim exterior, coming to her chilly doorway like 'the midnight sun.' By the time he finds the courage to propose to her, Jo has stopped comparing him with Laurie, and finds him looking 'young and handsome.' As a couple, Jo and Bhaer have both values and feelings in common; they share an interest in educational reform, in new ideas, and in practical philanthropy. Most important, he understands her need to work. 'I'm to carry my share, Friedrich, and help to earn the home,' Jo tells him. 'Make up your mind to that, or I'll never go.'

Could Alcott have imagined a satisfying life for Jo outside of marriage and motherhood? The questions of identity posed by Jo's decisions have continued to preoccupy American women writers. Joyce Carol Oates's *Bloodsmoor Romance* (1982) is a comic epic set in the nineteenth century, which brings together the plots of *Little Women* and *The Blithedale Romance* in a feminist *tour de force*. The novel traces the lives of the five Zinn sisters, who represent possibilities and fantasies for American women. Its narrative voices make brilliant parodic use of the discourses from sentimentalism to spiritualism available to women in the American culture of the period. Oates has commented that what impressed her most about the late nineteenth century was 'the *actual* lives of women . . . their physical existences, the way they must have gazed upon the world and been gazed upon in return, *without knowing the arbitrary nature of their confinement.*' In the modern novel, at least, the boundaries of this confinement can be exposed, and the women characters can be imaginatively released. Observing that 'all women *are* feminists, although not all women are in positions to speak out,' Oates used the structure of *Little Women* to explore the widest possible range of female relationships: 'The Zinn sisters, among them, covered virtually every square inch of plausible—and implausible—womanly experience of their era appropriate to their social class.'[46]

Thus the Zinn sisters find ways to assert their individuality and to fulfill all the vocational, marital, and sexual fantasies the Alcott sisters and the March sisters had to repress. The conventional Octavia, who seems like the classic domestic little woman modelled on Anna Alcott and Meg March, kills her sexually perverted husband by 'innocently' carrying his bondage-and-choking games just a little too far and is free to marry the Irish coachman she has always loved. The theatrical Malvinia, realizing Louisa's lifelong dream of going on the stage, becomes a celebrated and lusty actress. In a playful commentary on the lesbian subtext of Alcott's life, and on the sad disparities between the opportunities available to Alcott's dutiful heroines and those of her daring boyish heroes, the rebellious Constance Philippa Zinn actually turns into a man, makes a dashing career as a riverboat gambler and hero of the Wild West, and returns to rescue her beloved girlhood friend from a miserable marriage. Deirdre, who represents the novelist and Oates herself, is a medium haunted and tormented by voices that demand she speak for them. At the end of the novel, even the girls' mother, Prudence Zinn, sees the dawning of a new age, as she reads with shock of the feminist campaigners for dress reform, women's suffrage, and equal rights. One of them, a bold 'Miss Elaine Cottler,' has even 'stepped forward, with the support of the others, *to place herself as a candidate for the Presidency of the United States!*'

Oates also deepens and extends Alcott's critique of Emersonian and patriarchal genius, satirizing its pretensions and dangers. As in *Little Women*, and in the real Alcott family, the Zinn sisters live in a household dominated by an ineffectual but dictatorial father, a Transcendentalist sage and inventor, who eventually produces in his workshop both the electric chair and the atomic bomb. Like Hawthorne's Aylmer in 'The Birthmark', another one of Oates's key texts, the end of masculine technological genius is destruction. The man of science, consumed by envy of the reproductive powers of women and nature, tries to appropriate them, but instead of creating life, can only invent more efficient and terrific forms of death. Meanwhile, the last Zinn sister, Samantha, uses technology to make life more pleasant and easy, as she invents the disposable diaper and the washing machine.

Oates's postmodern invention offers one set of imaginative solutions to Alcott's dilemmas within the American context. In her edition of *Little Women*, Madelon Bedell speculated on whether Jo could have been 'an independent artist living an adventurous life in some sort of Bohemian quarter of Boston, supposing such a place to have existed.' But, Bedell concluded, 'that solution might be true to Jo's dreams, but not to Jo's character and certainly not her time and place. She is no George Sand; and this is America, not France.'[47]

Yet Alcott's creation also inspired women who could be independent artists. In the first volume of her autobiography, *Memoirs of a Dutiful Daughter* (1958), Simone de Beauvoir paid tribute to *Little Women*: 'I identified myself passionately with Jo, the intellectual. . . . She wrote; in order to imitate her more completely, I composed two or three short stories.'[48] As Beauvoir later explained, her identification with Jo helped her endure a lonely childhood and make decisions about her own life: 'I felt such esteem for Jo that I was able to tell myself that I too was like her, and therefore it did not matter if society was cruel, because I too would be superior and find my place.' Beauvoir learned from Jo's example, she believed,

that marriage was not necessary for me. . . . I saw that all the March girls hated housework because it kept them from what really interested them, the writing and drawing and music and so on. And I think that somehow, even when very young, I must have perceived that Jo was always making choices and sometimes they were neither well reasoned nor good. The idea of choice must have frightened me a little, but it was exhilarating as well.

It seems like a long way from Concord to St Germain-des-Près, but Alcott's American female myth shaped the lives of women of many times and places who read *Little Women*, never forgot it, and had the freedom to make different choices. Through all these Jos of the future, the independent Jo lives and writes, not as the unattainable genius, Shakespeare's American sister, but as a dearly cherished sister of us all.

4

The Awakening: Tradition and the American Female Talent

IN contrast to *Little Women*, embraced from the moment of its publication to the present by unbroken generations of women readers, Kate Chopin's *The Awakening* (1899) has been a solitary book. Generally recognized today as the first aesthetically successful novel to have been written by an American woman, it marked a significant epoch. *The Awakening* broke new thematic and stylistic ground as Chopin went boldly beyond the work of her precursors in writing about women's longing for sexual and personal emancipation. Yet the novel represents a literary beginning as abruptly cut short as the heroine's awakening consciousness. Edna Pontellier's explicit violations of the modes and codes of nineteenth-century American society shocked contemporary reviewers, who condemned the book as 'morbid,' 'essentially vulgar,' and 'gilded dirt.'[1] Banned in Chopin's home town of St Louis, and censured in the national press, *The Awakening* dropped out of sight and remained unsung by literary historians and unread by several generations of American writers.

In the early stages of her career, Chopin had tried to follow the literary advice and literary examples of others, and had learned that such dutiful efforts led only to imaginative stagnation. By the mid-1890s, when she came to write *The Awakening*, Chopin had come to believe that the true artist was one who defied tradition, who rejected both the *convenances* of respectable morality, and the conventions of literary success. When, as she was 'emerging from the vast solitude in which I had been making my own acquaintance,' she encountered a story by Maupassant called 'Solitude,' she recognized a kindred soul: 'Here was a man who had escaped from tradition and authority, who had entered into himself and looked out upon life through his own being and with his own eyes.'[2] This is very close to what happens to Edna Pontellier as she frees herself from social obligations and received opinions and begins to 'look with her own eyes; to see and to apprehend the deeper under current of life.'[3]

Chopin was also moved by Maupassant's melancholy affirmation of human separateness, when he wrote: 'Whatever we may do or attempt, despite the embrace and transports of love, the hunger of the lips, we are always alone.'[4] To a woman who had survived the illusions that friendship, romance, marriage, or even motherhood would provide lifelong companionship and identity, and who had come to recognize the existential solitude of all human beings, Maupassant's declaration became a kind of credo. Indeed, *The Awakening*, which Chopin subtitled 'A Solitary Soul,' may be read as an account of Edna's evolution from romantic fantasies of fusion with another person to self-definition and self-reliance. At the beginning of the novel, in the midst of the bustling social world of Grand Isle, caught in her domestic roles of wife and mother, Edna pictures solitude as alien, masculine, and frightening, a naked man standing beside a 'desolate rock' by the sea, in an attitude of 'hopeless resignation' (9). By the end, she has claimed a solitude that is defiantly feminine, returning to the nearly empty island off-season, to stand naked and 'absolutely alone' by the shore, and to elude 'the soul's slavery' by plunging into the sea's embrace (39). Much as she admired Maupassant, and as much as she learned from translating his work, Chopin felt no desire to imitate him. Her belief in originality and autonomy in writing is expressed by Mademoiselle Reisz, the musician in *The Awakening*, who tells Edna that the artist must possess 'the courageous soul that dares and defies' and must soar above 'the level plain of tradition and prejudice' (27).

None the less, even in its defiant solitude, *The Awakening* belongs to a historical moment in American women's writing, and Chopin could not have written without the legacy of domestic fiction to work against, and the models of the local colorists and New Women writers with which to experiment. After the Civil War, the homosocial world of women's culture began to dissolve as women demanded entrance to higher education, the professions, and the political world. The female local colorists who began to publish stories about American regional life in the 1870s and 1880s were also attracted to the male worlds of art and prestige opening up to women, and they began to assert themselves as the daughters of literary fathers as well as literary mothers. Claiming both male and female aesthetic models, they felt free to present themselves as artists and to write confidently about the art of fiction in essays like Elizabeth Stuart Phelps's 'Art for Truth's Sake.'[5] Among the differences the local colorists saw between themselves and their predecessors was the question of 'selfishness,' the ability to put literary ambitions before domestic duties. Although she had been strongly influenced in her work by Harriet Beecher Stowe's *Pearl of Orr's Island*, Sarah Orne Jewett came to believe that Stowe's work was 'incomplete' because she was unable to 'bring herself to that cold selfishness of the moment for one's work's sake.'[6]

Writers of this generation chose to put their work first. The 1870s and 1880s were what Susan B. Anthony called 'an epoch of single women,'[7] and many unmarried women writers of this generation lived alone; others were involved in 'Boston marriages,' or long-term relationships with another woman. But despite their individual lifestyles, many speculated in their writing on the conflicts between maternity and artistic creativity. Motherhood no longer seemed to be the motivating force of writing, but rather its opposite. Thus artistic fulfillment required the sacrifice of maternal drives, and maternal fulfillment meant giving up artistic ambitions.

The conflicts between love and work that Edna Pontellier faces in *The Awakening* were anticipated in such earlier novels as Phelps's *Story of Avis* (1879). A gifted painter who has studied in Florence and Paris, Avis does not intend to marry. As she tells her suitor,

My ideals of art are those with which marriage is perfectly incompatible. Success—for a woman—means absolute surrender, in whatever direction. Whether she paints a picture, or loves a man, there is no division of labor possible in her economy. To the attainment of any end worth living for, a symmetrical sacrifice of her nature is compulsory upon her.

But love persuades her to change her mind, and the novel records the inexorable destruction of her artistic genius as domestic responsibilities, maternal cares, and her husband's failures use up her energy. By the end of the novel, Avis has become resigned to the idea that her life is a sacrifice for the next generation of women. Thinking back to her mother, a talented actress who gave up her profession to marry and died young, and looking at her daughter, Wait, Avis takes heart in the hope that it may take three generations to create the woman who can unite 'her supreme capacity of love' with the 'sacred individuality of her life.'[8]

As women's culture declined after the Civil War, moreover, the local colorists mourned its demise by investing its traditional images with mythic significance. In their stories, the mother's garden has become a paradisal sanctuary; the caged bird a wild white heron, or heroine of nature; the house an emblem of the female body, with the kitchen as its womb; and the artifacts of domesticity virtually totemic objects. In Jewett's *Country of the Pointed Firs*, for example, the braided rag rug has become a kind of prayer mat of concentric circles from which the matriarchal priestess, Mrs Todd, delivers her sybilline pronouncements. The woman artist in this fiction expresses her conflicting needs most fully in her quasi-religious dedication to these artifacts of a bygone age.

The New Women writers of the 1890s no longer grieved for the female bonds and sanctuaries of the past. Products of both Darwinian skepticism and aesthetic sophistication, they had an ambivalent or even hostile relationship to women's culture, which they often saw as boring and restrictive. Their attitudes towards female sexuality were also revolutionary. A few radical feminists had always maintained that women's sexual apathy was not an innately feminine attribute but rather the result of prudery and repression; some women's rights activists too had privately confessed that, as Elizabeth Cady Stanton wrote in her diary in 1883, 'a healthy woman has as much passion as a man.'[9] Not all

New Women advocated female sexual emancipation; the most zealous advocates of free love were male novelists such as Grant Allen, whose best-seller, *The Woman Who Did* (1895), became a byword of the decade. But the heroine of New Women fiction, as Linda Dowling has explained, 'expressed her quarrel with Victorian culture chiefly through sexual means—by heightening sexual consciousness, candor, and expression.'[10] No wonder, then, that reviewers saw *The Awakening* as part of the 'overworked field of sex fiction' or noted that since 'San Francisco and Paris, and London, and New York had furnished Women Who Did, why not New Orleans?'[11]

In the form as well as the content of their work, New Women writers demanded freedom and innovation. They modified the realistic three-decker novels about courtship and marriage that had formed the bulk of mid-century 'woman's fiction' to make room for interludes of fantasy and parable, especially episodes 'in which a woman will dream of an entirely different world or will cross-dress, experimenting with the freedom available to boys and men.'[12] Instead of the crisply plotted short stories that had been the primary genre of the local colorists, writers such as Olive Schreiner, Ella D'Arcy, Sarah Grand, and 'George Egerton' (Mary Chavelita Dunne) experimented with new fictional forms that they called 'keynotes,' 'allegories,' 'fantasies,' 'monochromes,' or 'dreams.' As Egerton explained, these impressionistic narratives were efforts to explore a hitherto unrecorded female consciousness:

I realized that in literature everything had been done better by man than woman could hope to emulate. There was only one small plot left for herself to tell: the *terra incognita* of herself, as she knew herself to be, not as man liked to imagine her—in a word to give herself away, as man had given himself away in his writings.[13]

Kate Chopin's literary evolution took her progressively through the three phases of nineteenth-century American women's culture and women's writing. Born in 1850, she grew up with the great best-sellers of the American and English sentimentalists. As a girl, she had wept over the works of Warner and Stowe and had copied pious passages from the English novelist Dinah Mulock Craik's *The Woman's Kingdom* into her diary. Throughout her adolescence, Chopin had also shared an intimate friendship with Kitty Garasché, a classmate at the Academy of the Sacred Heart. Together, Chopin recalled, the girls had read fiction and poetry, gone on excursions, and 'exchanged our heart secrets.'[14] Their friendship ended in 1870 when Kate Chopin married and Kitty Garasché entered a convent. Yet when Oscar Chopin died in 1883, his young widow went to visit her old friend and was shocked by her blind isolation from the world. When Chopin began to write, she took as her models such local colorists as Sarah Orne Jewett and Mary Wilkins Freeman, who had not only mastered technique and construction but had also devoted themselves to telling the stories of female loneliness, isolation, and frustration.

Sandra Gilbert has suggested that local color was a narrative strategy that Chopin employed to solve a specific problem: how to deal with extreme psychological states without the excesses of sentimental narrative and without critical recrimination. At first, Gilbert suggests, 'local color' writing 'offered both a mode and a manner that could mediate between the literary structures she had inherited and those she had begun.' Like the anthropologists, the local colorist could observe vagaries of culture and character with 'almost scientific detachment.' Furthermore, 'by reporting odd events and customs that were part of a region's "local color" she could tell what would ordinarily be rather shocking or even melodramatic tales in an unmelodramatic way, and without fear of . . . moral outrage.'[15]

But before long, Chopin looked beyond the oddities of the local colorists to more ambitious models. Her literary tastes were anything but parochial. She read widely in a variety of genres— Darwin, Spencer, and Huxley, as well as Aristophanes, Flaubert, Whitman, Swinburne, and Ibsen. In particular, she associated her own literary and psychological awakening with Maupassant. 'Here was life, not fiction,' she wrote of his influence on her, 'for where were the plots, the old fashioned mechanism and stage trapping that in a vague unthinking way I had fancied were essential to the art of story making.'[16] In a review of a book by the local colorist Hamlin Garland, Chopin expressed her dissatisfaction with the restricted subjects of regional writing: 'Social problems, social environments, local color, and the rest of it' could not 'insure the survival of a writer who employs them.'[17] She resented being compared to George Washington Cable or Grace King.[18] Furthermore, she did not share the female local colorists' obsession with the past, their desperate nostalgia for a bygone idealized age. 'How curiously the past effaces itself for me!' she wrote in her diary in 1894. 'I cannot live through yesterday or tomorrow.'[19] Unlike Jewett, Freeman, King, or Woolson, she did not favor the old woman as narrator.

Despite her identification with the New Women, however, Chopin was not an activist. She never joined the women's suffrage movement or belonged to a female literary community. Indeed, her celebrated St Louis literary salon attracted mostly male journalists, editors, and writers. Chopin resigned after only two years from a St Louis women's literary and charitable society. When her children identified her close friends to be interviewed by her first biographer, Daniel Rankin, there were no women on the list.[20]

Thus Chopin certainly did not wish to write a didactic feminist novel. In reviews published in the 1890s, she indicated her impatience with novelists such as Zola and Hardy, who tried to instruct their readers. She distrusted the rhetoric of such feminist best-sellers as Sarah Grand's *Heavenly Twins* (1893). The eleventh commandment, she noted, is 'Thou shalt not preach.'[21] Instead she would try to record, in her own way and in her own voice, the *terra incognita* of a woman's 'inward life' in all its 'vague tangled, chaotic' tumult.

Much of the shock effect of *The Awakening* to the readers of 1899 came from Chopin's rejection of the conventions of women's writing. Despite her name, which echoes two famous heroines of the domestic novel (Edna Earl in Augusta Evans' *St Elmo* and Edna Kenderdine in Dinah Craik's *Woman's Kingdom*), Edna Pontellier appears to reject the domestic empire of the mother and the sororal world of women's culture. Seemingly beyond the bonds of womanhood, she has neither mother nor daughter, and even refuses to go to her sister's wedding. For a generation which had grown up reading about Meg's wedding in *Little Women*, this was shocking indeed.

Moreover, whereas the sentimental heroine nurtures others, and the abstemious local color heroine subsists upon meager vegetarian diets, Kate Chopin's heroine is a robust woman who does not deny her appetites. Freeman's New England nun picks at her dainty lunch of lettuce leaves and currants, but Edna Pontellier eats hearty meals of paté, pompano, steak, and broiled chicken; bites off chunks of crusty bread; snacks on beer and Gruyère cheese; and sips brandy, wine, and champagne.

Formally, too, the novel has moved away from conventional techniques of realism to an impressionistic rhythm of epiphany and mood. Chopin abandoned the chapter titles she had used in her first novel, *At Fault* (1890), for thirty-nine numbered sections of uneven length, ranging from the single paragraph of section 28 to the sustained narrative of the dinner party in section 30. The sections are unified less by their style than by their focus on Edna's consciousness, and by the repetition of key motifs and images: music, the sea, shadows, swimming, eating, sleeping, gambling, the lovers, birth. Scenes of lyricism and fantasy, such as Edna's voyage to the Chenière Caminada, alternate with realistic, even satirical, scenes of Edna's marriage.

Most important, where previous works by American women largely ignored sexuality or spiritualized it through maternity, *The Awakening* is insistently sexual, explicitly involved with the body and with self-awareness through physical awareness. Although Edna's actual seduction by Arobin takes place in the narrative neverland between sections 31 and 32, Chopin brilliantly evokes sexuality through images and details. In keeping with the novel's emphasis on the self, several scenes suggest Edna's initial autoeroticism. Edna's midnight swim, which awakens the 'first-felt throbbings of desire,' takes place in an atmosphere of erotic fragrance, 'strange, rare odors . . . a tangle of the sea-smell and of weeds and damp new-ploughed earth, mingled with the heavy perfume of a field of white blossoms'(10). A similarly voluptuous scene is her nap at Chenière Caminada, when she examines her flesh as she lies in a 'strange, quaint bed with its sweet country odor of laurel'(13).

Edna reminds Dr Mandalet of 'some beautiful, sleek animal waking up in the sun'(23), and we recall that among her fantasies in listening to music is the image of a lady stroking a cat. The image both conveys Edna's sensuality and hints at the self-contained, almost masturbatory, quality of her sexuality. Her rendezvous with Robert takes place in a sunny garden where both stroke a drowsy cat's silky fur, and Arobin first seduces her by smoothing her hair with his 'soft, magnetic hand'(31).

Yet despite these departures from tradition, there are other respects in which the novel seems very much of its time. As its title suggest, *The Awakening* is a novel about a process rather than a program, about a passage rather than a destination. It is a transitional female fiction of the *fin de siècle*, a narrative of and about the passage from the homosocial women's culture and literature of the nineteenth century to the heterosexual fiction of modernism. Chopin might have taken the plot from a notebook entry Henry James made in 1892 about

the growing divorce between the American woman (with her comparative leisure, culture, grace, social instincts, artistic ambition) and the male American immersed in the ferocity of business, with no time for any but the most sordid interests, purely commercial, professional democratic and political. This divorce is rapidly becoming a gulf.[22]

The Gulf where the opening chapters of *The Awakening* are set certainly suggests the 'growing divorce' between Edna's interests and desires and Leonce's obsessions with the stock market, property, and his brokerage business.

Yet in turning away from her marriage, Edna initially looks back to women's culture rather than forward to another man. As Sandra Gilbert has pointed out, Grand Isle is an oasis of women's culture, or a 'female colony':

Madame Lebrun's pension on Grand Isle is very much a woman's land not only because it is owned and run by a single woman and dominated by 'mother-women' but also because (as in so many summer colonies today) its principal inhabitants are actually women and children whose husbands and fathers visit only on weekends . . . [and it is situated] like so many places that are significant for women, outside patriarchal cultures, beyond the limits and limitations of the city where men make history, on a shore that marks the margin where nature intersects with culture.[23]

Edna's awakening, moreover, begins not with a man, but with Adele Ratignolle, the empress of the 'mother-women' of Grand Isle. A 'self-contained' (7) woman, Edna has never had any close relationships with members of her own sex. Thus it is Adele who belatedly initiates Edna into the world of female love and ritual on the first step of her sensual voyage of self-discovery. Edna's first attraction to Adele is erotic: 'the excessive physical charm of the Creole had first attracted her, for Edna had a sensuous susceptibility to beauty' (7). At the beach, in the hot sun, she responds to Adele's caresses, the first she has ever known from another woman, as Adele clasps her hand 'firmly and warmly' and strokes it fondly. The touch provokes Edna to an unaccustomed candor; leaning her head on Adele's shoulder and confiding some of her secrets, she begins to feel 'intoxicated' (7). The bond between them goes beyond sympathy, as Chopin notes, to 'what we might well call love' (7).

In some respects, the motherless Edna also seeks a mother surrogate in Adele and looks to her for nurturance. Adele provides maternal encouragement for Edna's painting and tells her that her 'talent is immense' (18). Characteristically, Adele has rationalized her own 'art' as a maternal project: 'she was keeping up her music on account of the children . . . a means of brightening the home and making it attractive' (9). Edna's responses to Adele's music have been similarly tame and sentimental. Her revealing fantasies as she listens to Adele play her easy pieces suggest the restriction and decorum of the female world: 'a dainty young woman . . . taking mincing dancing steps, as she came down a long avenue between tall hedges'; 'children at play' (9). Women's art, as Adele presents it, is social, pleasant, and undemanding. It does not conflict with her duties as a wife and mother, and can even be seen to enhance them. Edna understands this well; as she retorts when her husband recommends Adele as a model of an artist, 'She isn't a musician and I'm not a painter!' (19).

Yet the relationship with the conventional Adele educates the immature Edna to respond for the first time both to a different kind of sexuality and to the unconventional and difficult art of Mademoiselle Reisz. In responding to Adele's interest, Edna begins to think about her own past and to analyze her own personality. In textual terms, it is through this relationship that she becomes 'Edna' in the narrative rather than 'Mrs. Pontellier.'

We see the next stage of Edna's awakening in her relationship with Mademoiselle Reisz, who initiates her into the world of art. Significantly, this passage also takes place through a female rather than a male mentor, and, as with Adele, there is something more intense than friendship between the two women. Whereas Adele's fondness for Edna, however, is depicted as maternal and womanly, Mademoiselle Reisz's attraction to Edna suggests something more perverse. The pianist is obsessed with Edna's beauty, raves over her figure in a bathing suit, greets her as 'ma belle' and 'ma reine,' holds her hand, and describes herself as 'a foolish old woman whom you have captivated' (21). If Adele is a surrogate for Edna's dead mother and the intimate friend she never had as a girl, Mademoiselle Reisz, whose music reduces Edna to passionate sobs, seems to be a surrogate lover. And whereas Adele is a 'faultless madonna' who speaks for the values and laws of the Creole community, Mademoiselle Reisz is a renegade, self-assertive and outspoken. She has no patience with petty social rules and violates the most basic expectations of femininity. To a rake like Arobin, she is so unattractive, unpleasant, and unwomanly as to seem 'partially demented' (27). Even Edna occasionally perceives Mademoiselle Reisz's awkwardness as a kind of deformity, and is sometimes offended by the old woman's candor and is not sure whether she likes her.

Yet despite her eccentricities, Mademoiselle Reisz seems 'to reach Edna's spirit and set it free' (26). Her voice in the novel seems to speak for the author's view of art and for the artist. It is surely no accident, for example, that it is Chopin's music that Mademoiselle Reisz performs. At the *pension* on Grand Isle, the pianist first plays a Chopin prelude, to which Edna responds with surprising turbulence: 'the very passions themselves were aroused within her soul, swaying it, lashing it, as the waves daily beat upon her splendid body. She trembled, she was choking, and the tears blinded her' (9). 'Chopin' becomes the code word for a world of repressed passion between Edna and Robert that Mademoiselle Reisz controls. Later the pianist plays a Chopin impromptu for Edna that Robert has admired; this time the music is 'strange and fantastic—turbulent, plaintive and soft with entreaty' (21). These references to 'Chopin' in the text are on one level allusions to an intimate, romantic, and poignant musical *œuvre* that reinforces the novel's sensual atmosphere. But on another level, they function as what Nancy K. Miller has called the 'internal female signature' in women's writing, here a self-referential pun that alludes to Kate Chopin's ambitions as an artist and to the emotions she wished her book to arouse in its readers.[24]

Chopin's career represented one important aesthetic model for his literary namesake. As a girl, Kate Chopin had been a talented musician, and her first published story, 'Wiser Than a God,' was about a woman concert pianist who refused to marry. Moreover, Chopin's music both stylistically and thematically influences the language and form of *The Awakening*. The structure of the impromptu, in which there is an opening presentation of a theme, a contrasting middle section, and a modified return to the melodic and rhythmic materials of the opening section, parallels the narrative form of *The Awakening*. The composer's techniques of unifying his work through the repetition of musical phrases, his experiments with harmony and dissonance, his use of folk motifs, his effects of frustration and delayed resolution can also be compared to Kate Chopin's repetition of sentences, her juxtaposition of realism and impressionism, her incorporation of local color elements, and her rejection of conventional closure. Like that of the composer's impromptu, Chopin's style seems spontaneous and improvised, but it is in fact carefully designed and executed.[25]

Madame Ratignolle and Mademoiselle Reisz not only represent important alternative roles and influences for Edna in the world of the novel, but as the proto-heroines of sentimental and local color fiction, they also suggest different plots and conclusions. Adele's story suggests that Edna will give up her rebellion, return to her marriage, have another baby, and by degrees learn to appreciate, love, and even desire her husband. Such was the plot of many late-nineteenth-century novels about erring young women married to older men, such as Susan Warner's *Diana* (1880) and Louisa May Alcott's *Moods* (1881). Mademoiselle Reisz's story suggests that Edna will lose her beauty, her youth, her husband, and children—everything, in short, but her art and her pride—and become a kind of New Orleans nun.

Chopin wished to reject both of these endings and to escape from the literary traditions they represented; but her own literary solitude, her resistance to allying herself with a specific ideological or aesthetic position, made it impossible for her to work out something different and new. Edna remains very much entangled in her own emotions and moods, rather than moving beyond them to real self-understanding and to an awareness of her relationship to her society. She alternates between two moods of 'intoxication' and 'languor,' expansive states of activity, optimism, and power and passive states of contemplation, despondency, and sexual thralldom. Edna feels intoxicated when she is assertive and in control. She first experiences such exultant feelings when she confides her history to Adele Ratignolle and again when she learns how to swim: 'intoxicated with her newly conquered power,' she swims out too far. She is excited when she gambles successfully for high stakes at the race track, and finally she feels 'an intoxication of expectancy' about awakening Robert with a seductive kiss and playing the dominant role with him. But these emotional peaks are countered by equally intense moods of depression, reverie, or stupor. At the worst, these are states of 'indescribable oppression,' 'vague anguish,' or 'hopeless ennui.' At best, they are moments of passive sensuality in which Edna feels drugged; Arobin's lips and hands, for example, act 'like a narcotic upon her' (25).

Edna welcomes both kinds of feelings because they are intense, and thus preserve her from the tedium of ordinary existence. They are in fact adolescent emotions, suitable to a heroine who is belatedly awakening; but Edna does not go beyond them to an adulthood that offers new experiences or responsibilities. In her relationships with men, she both longs for complete and romantic fusion with a fantasy lover and is unprepared to share her life with another person.

Chopin's account of the Pontellier marriage, for example, shows Edna's tacit collusion in a sexual bargain that allows her to keep to herself. Although she thinks of her marriage to a paternalistic man twelve years her senior as 'purely an accident,' the text makes it clear that Edna has married Leonce primarily to secure a fatherly protector who will not make too many domestic, emotional, or sexual demands on her. She is 'fond of her husband,' with 'no trace of passion or excessive or fictitious warmth' (7). They do not have an interest in each other's activities or thoughts, and have agreed to a complete separation of their social spheres; Leonce is fully absorbed by the business, social, and sexual activities of the male sphere, the city, Caronde-let Street, Klein's Hotel at Grand Isle, where he gambles, and especially the New Orleans world of the clubs and the red-light district. Even Adele Ratignolle warns Edna of the risks of Mr Pontellier's club life and of the 'diversion' he finds there. 'It's a pity Mr. Pontellier doesn't stay home more in the evenings,' she tells Edna. 'I think you would be more—well, if you don't mind my saying it—more united, if he did.' 'Oh! dear no!' Edna responds, 'with a blank look in her eyes. "What should I do if he stayed home? We wouldn't have anything to say to each other"' (23). Edna gets this blank look in her eyes—eyes that are orig-inally described as 'quick and bright'—whenever she is con-fronted with something she does not want to see. When she joins the Ratignolles at home together, Edna does not envy them, although, as the author remarks, 'if ever the fusion of two human beings into one has been accomplished on this sphere it was surely in their union' (18). Instead, she is moved by pity for Adele's 'colorless existence which never uplifted its possessor beyond the region of blind contentment' (18).

None the less, Edna does not easily relinquish her fantasy of rhapsodic oneness with a perfect lover. She imagines that such a union will bring permanent ecstasy; it will lead, not simply to 'domestic harmony' like that of the Ratignolles, but to 'life's delirium' (18). In her story of the woman who paddles away with her lover in a pirogue and is never heard of again, Edna elaborates on her vision as she describes the lovers, 'close together, rapt in oblivious forgetfulness, drifting into the unknown' (23). Although her affair with Arobin shocks her into an awareness of her own sexual passions, it leaves her illusions about love intact. Desire, she understands, can exist independently of love. But love retains its magical aura; indeed, her sexual awakening with Arobin generates an even 'fiercer, more overpowering love' for Robert (28). And when Robert comes back, Edna has persuaded herself that the force of their love will overwhelm all obstacles; 'We shall be everything to each other. Nothing else in the world is of any consequence' (36). Her intention seems to be that they will go off together into the unknown, like the lovers in her story. But Robert cannot accept such a role, and when he leaves her, Edna finally realizes 'that the day would come when he, too, and the thought of him, would melt out of her existence, leaving her alone' (39).

The other side of Edna's terror of solitude, however, is the bondage of race as well as gender that keeps her in a prison of the self. She goes blank too whenever she might be expected to notice the double standard of ladylike privilege and oppression of black women in Southern society. Floating along in her 'mazes of inward contemplation,' Edna barely notices the silent quadroon nurse who takes care of her children, the little black girl who works the treadles of Madame Lebrun's sewing machine, the laundress who keeps her in frilly white, or the maid who picks up her broken glass. She never makes connections between her lot and theirs.

The scene in which Edna witnesses Adele in childbirth (37) is the first time in the novel that she identifies with another woman's pain, and draws some halting conclusions about the female and the human condition, rather than simply about her own ennui. Edna's births have taken place in unconsciousness; when she goes to Adele's childbed, 'her own like experiences seemed far away, unreal, and only half remembered. She recalled faintly an ecstasy of pain, the heavy odor of chloroform, a stupor which had deadened sensation' (37). The stupor that deadens sensation is an apt metaphor for the real and imaginary narcotics supplied by fantasy, money, and patriarchy, which have protected Edna from pain for most of her life, but which have also kept her from becoming an adult.

But in thinking of nature's trap for women, Edna never moves from her own questioning to the larger social statement that is feminism. Her ineffectuality is partly a product of her time; as a heroine in transition between the homosocial and the heterosexual worlds, Edna has lost some of the sense of connectedness to other women that might help her plan her future. Though she has sojourned in the 'female colony' of Grand Isle, it is far from being a feminist utopia, a real community of women, in terms of sisterhood. The novel suggests, in fact, something of the historical loss for women of transferring the sense of self to relationships with men.

Edna's solitude is one of the reasons that her emancipation does not take her very far. Despite her efforts to escape the rituals of femininity, Edna seems fated to reenact them, even though, as Chopin recounts these scenes, she satirizes and revises their conventions. Ironically, considering her determination to discard the trappings of her role as a society matron—her wedding ring, her 'reception day,' her 'charming home'—the high point of Edna's awakening is the dinner party she gives for her twenty-ninth birthday. Edna's birthday party begins like a kind of drawing-room comedy. We are told the guest list, the seating plan, the menu, and the table setting; some of the guests are boring, and some do not like each other; Madame Ratignolle does not show up at the last minute, and Mademoiselle Reisz makes disagreeable remarks in French.

Yet as it proceeds to its bacchanalian climax, the dinner party also has a symbolic intensity and resonance that makes it, as Sandra Gilbert argues, Edna's 'most authentic act of self-definition.'[26] Not only is the twenty-ninth birthday a feminine threshold, the passage from youth to middle age, but Edna is literally on the threshold of a new life in her little house. The dinner, as Arobin remarks, is a *coup d'état*, an overthrow of her marriage, all the more an act of aggression because Leonce will pay the bills. Moreover, she has created an atmosphere of splendor and luxury that seems to exceed the requirements of the occasion. The table is set with gold satin, Sèvres china, crystal, silver, and gold; there is 'champagne to swim in' (29), and Edna is magnificently dressed in a satin and lace gown, with a cluster of diamonds (a gift from Leonce) in her hair. Presiding at the head of the table, she seems powerful and autonomous: 'There was something in her attitude which suggested the regal woman, the one who rules, who looks on, who stands alone' (30). Edna's moment of mastery thus takes place in the context of a familiar ceremony of women's culture. Indeed, dinner parties are virtual set pieces of feminist aesthetics, suggesting that the hostess is a kind of artist in her own sphere, someone whose creativity is channeled into the production of social and domestic harmony. Like Virginia Woolf's Mrs Ramsay in *To the Lighthouse*, Edna exhausts herself in creating a sense of fellowship at her table, although in the midst of her guests she still experiences an 'acute longing' for 'the unattainable' (30).

But there is a gap between the intensity of Edna's desire, a desire that by now has gone beyond sexual fulfillment to take in a much vaster range of metaphysical longings, and the means that she has to express herself. Edna may look like a queen, but she is still a housewife. The political and aesthetic weapons she has in her *coup d'état* are only forks and knives, glasses and dresses.

Can Edna, and Kate Chopin, then, escape from confining traditions only in death? Some critics have seen Edna's much-debated suicide as a heroic embrace of independence and a symbolic resurrection into myth, a feminist counterpart of Melville's Bulkington: 'Take heart, take heart, O Edna, up from the spray of thy ocean-perishing, up, straight up, leaps thy apotheosis!' But the ending too seems to return her to the nineteenth-century female literary tradition, even though Chopin redefines it for her own purpose. Readers of the 1890s were well accustomed to drowning as the fictional punishment for female transgression against morality, and most contemporary critics of *The Awakening* thus automatically interpreted Edna's suicide as the wages of sin.

Drowning itself brings to mind metaphorical analogies between femininity and liquidity. As the female body is prone to wetness, blood, milk, tears, and amniotic fluid, so in drowning the woman is immersed in the feminine organic element. Drowning thus becomes the traditionally feminine literary death.[27] And Edna's last thoughts further recycle significant images of the feminine from her past. As exhaustion overpowers her, 'Edna heard her father's voice and her sister Margaret's. She heard the barking of an old dog that was chained to the sycamore tree. The spurs of the cavalry officer clanged as he walked across the porch. There was the hum of bees, and the musky odor of pinks filled the air' (39). Edna's memories are those of awakening from the freedom of childhood to the limitations conferred by female sexuality.

The image of the bees and the flowers not only recalls early descriptions of Edna's sexuality as a 'sensitive blossom,' but also places *The Awakening* firmly within the textual traditions of American women's writing, where it is a standard trope for the unequal sexual relations between women and men. Margaret Fuller, for example, writes in her journal: 'Woman is the flower, man the bee. She sighs out of melodious fragrance, and invites the winged laborer. He drains her cup, and carries off the honey. She dies on the stalk; he returns to the hive, well fed, and praised as an active member of the community.'[28] In post-Civil War fiction, the image is a reminder of an elemental power that women's culture must confront. *The Awakening* seems particularly to echo the last lines of Mary Wilkins Freeman's 'New England Nun,' in which the heroine, having broken her long-standing engagement, is free to continue her solitary life, and closes her door on 'the sounds of the busy harvest of men and birds and bees; there were halloos, metallic clatterings, sweet calls, long hummings.'[29] These are the images of a nature that, Edna has learned, decoys women into slavery; yet even in drowning, she cannot escape from their seductiveness, for to ignore their claim is also to cut oneself off from culture, from the 'humming' life of creation and achievement.

We can re-create the literary tradition in which Kate Chopin wrote *The Awakening*, but of course, we can never know how the tradition might have changed if her novel had not had to wait half a century to find its audience. Few of Chopin's literary contemporaries came into contact with the book. Chopin's biographer, Per Seyersted, notes that her work

was apparently unknown to Dreiser, even though he began writing *Sister Carrie* just when *The Awakening* was being loudly condemned. Also Ellen Glasgow, who was at this time beginning to describe unsatisfactory marriages, seems to have been unaware of the author's existence. Indeed, we can safely say that though she was so much of an innovator in American literature, she was virtually unknown by those who were now to shape it and that she had no influence on them.[30]

Not until 1928, with the publication of Nella Larsen's *Quicksand*, did black women writers attempt to deal with the sexual ideology and repression facing a woman seeking independence. Ironically, even Willa Cather, the one woman writer of the *fin de siècle* who reviewed *The Awakening*, not only failed to recognize its importance but also dismissed its theme as 'trite.'[31]

Edna's triumphant embrace of solitude had unexpected and unhappy consequences for Kate Chopin. A writer needs to cultivate solitude and independence, but literature depends on shared forms and representations of experience. Literary genres, like biological species, evolve because of significant innovations by individuals that survive through imitation and revision. Thus it can be a very severe set-back to a developing genre when a revolutionary work is taken out of circulation. Experimentation is retarded and repressed. The interruption of this process is most destructive for the literature of a minority group, since they are so often taxed with lacking originality and aesthetic boldness. Yet radical departures from literary convention are especially likely to be censured and suppressed within a minority tradition because they violate social as well as aesthetic expectations and stereotypes.

In many respects, *The Awakening* seems to comment on its own history as a novel, and to predict its own critical fate. The parallels between the experiences of Edna Pontellier, as she breaks away from the conventional feminine roles of wife and mother, and those of Kate Chopin, as she broke away from the conventions of literary domesticity, suggest that Edna's story may also be read as a parable of Chopin's literary awakening. Both the author and the heroine oscillate between two worlds, caught between contradictory definitions of femininity and creativity, and seeking whether to synthesize them or to go beyond them to an emancipated womanhood and an emancipated fiction. Edna's 'unfocused yearning' for an autonomous life is akin to Chopin's yearning to write works that go beyond female plots and feminine endings.

Edna Pontellier was no Margaret Fuller, nor was meant to be; Chopin's view of her is ironic, and her death is not held up to us as the tragic loss of a great spirit. But the death of *The Awakening* was a tragic loss for Chopin's artistry. There are signs that it would have been a pivotal work in her career. While it was in press, she wrote one of her finest and most daring stories, 'The Storm,' which surpasses the novel in terms of its expressive freedom.[32] But her career was halted by the scandal, which may have also hastened her early death. At the turn of the century, Chopin, like Edith Wharton and Willa Cather, speaks for a painful transitional age in American women's writing.

Yet we owe the rediscovery of Chopin's work not to American women writers but to male literary critics from France and

Norway as well as from the United States. Chopin's editor Per Seyersted was the one who brought her work to the attention of a new feminist generation, while her French translator Cyrille Arnavon championed her as a stylist. And while the novel has now firmly entered the academic canon, it has yet to enter women's writing as a touchstone. In fact, the most significant contemporary rewriting of *The Awakening* is not by a woman novelist. It is rather Robert Stone's *Children of Light* (1986). Stone is on the surface a most unlikely writer to be influenced by Chopin. His literary reputation has been made as a post-Vietnam reporter of a violent, drugged-out America in the dying throes of its imperialist adventures. He won the National Book Award for *Dog Soldiers*, a novel of surrealistic doom which displayed his stunning gifts for dialog and his sense of apocalyptic fatality. These elements also appear in *Children of Light*, which reimagines Chopin's novel through the eyes of a Hollywood screenwriter who has been asked to write the script for a movie of *The Awakening*. The modern Edna is the movie star Lu Anne Verger, an actress who is alcoholic and schizophrenic, and who has lost custody of her child through a messy divorce. Through the role of Edna, Lu Anne hopes to redeem herself in a superb performance that will reveal her acting gifts, and give her life meaning. But it is too late; the years of pretense and narcissism have left her locked in her own hallucinations, unable to accept either friendship with other women or love from men. Like Edna, Lu Anne 'finds out who she is and it's too much and she dies.'[33]

Stone makes Lu Anne's suicide a symbol of the corruption of art and fantasy in *fin de siècle* America. But his dialog with Chopin is an important sign that contemporary American male writers are no longer living in a different country from women and never reading their work. While *Little Women* has remained a female myth, *The Awakening* has also become part of the texture of a masculine and mainstream art. That process must be troubling to some feminists, for when American women's writing passes into the mainstream, it ceases to be solitary, 'American,' or 'feminine.' But such rereadings, rewriting, and reinhabiting of women's texts are the only way that *The Awakening*, like other lost masterpieces by American women, is finally restored to us and takes its rightful place in our literary heritage.

The Death of the Lady (Novelist): Wharton's *House of Mirth*

> The lady is almost the only picturesque survival in a social order which tends less and less to tolerate the exceptional. Her history is distinct from that of woman though sometimes advancing by means of it, as a railway may help itself from one point to another by leasing an independent line. At all striking periods of social development her status has its significance. In the age-long war between men and women, she is a hostage in the enemy's camp. Her fortunes do not rise and fall with those of women but with those of men.
>
> Emily James Putnam, *The Lady* (1910)
>
> Perfection is terrible, it cannot have children.
>
> Sylvia Plath, 'The Munich Mannequins'

A t the beginning of Edith Wharton's first great novel, *The House of Mirth* (1905), the heroine, Lily Bart, is twenty-nine, the dazzlingly well-preserved veteran of eleven years in the New York marriage market. By the end of the novel, she is past thirty and dead of an overdose of chloral. Like Edna Pontellier, who celebrates her twenty-ninth birthday by taking a lover, Lily Bart belongs to a genre we might call 'the novel of the woman of thirty,' a genre that emerged appropriately enough in American women's literature at the turn of the century. These novels pose

the problem of female maturation in narrative terms: What can happen to the heroine as she grows up? What plots, transformations, and endings are imaginable for her? Is she capable of change at all? As the nineteenth-century feminist activist and novelist Elizabeth Oakes Smith noted in her diary, 'How few women have any history after the age of thirty!'[1]

Telling the history of women past thirty was part of the challenge Wharton faced as a writer looking to the twentieth century. The threshold of thirty established for women by nineteenth-century conventions of 'girlhood' and marriageability continued in the twentieth century as a psychological observation about the formation of feminine identity. While Wharton's ideas about personality were shaped by Darwinian rather than by Freudian determinants, she shared Freud's pessimism about the difficulties of change for women. In his essay 'Femininity,' for example, Freud lamented the way that women's psyches and personalities became fixed by the time they were thirty. While a thirty-year-old man 'strikes us as a youthful, somewhat unformed individual, whom we expect to make powerful use of the possibilities for development opened up to him by analysis,' Freud wrote, a woman of thirty 'often frightens us by her psychical rigidity and unchangeability. Her libido has taken up fixed positions and seems incapable of exchanging them for others.'[2] From Wharton's perspective Lily Bart is locked into fixed positions that are social and economic as well as products of the libido. Her inability to exchange these positions for others constitutes an impasse in the age as well as the individual.

Wharton situates Lily Bart's crisis of adulthood in the contexts of a larger historical shift. We meet her first in Grand Central Station, 'in the act of transition between one and another of the country houses that disputed her presence at the close of the Newport season,'[3] and indeed *The House of Mirth* is a pivotal text in the historical transition from one house of American women's fiction to another, from the homosocial women's culture and literature of the nineteenth century to the heterosexual fiction of modernism. Like Edna Pontellier, Lily is stranded between two worlds of female experience: the intense female friendships and mother–daughter bonds characteristic of nineteenth-century American women's culture, and the dissolution of these single-sex relationships in the interests of more intimate friendships between women and men that was part of the gender crisis of the turn of the century.

The writers and feminist thinkers of Wharton's transitional generation, Elizabeth Ammons has noted, wrote 'about troubled and troubling young women who were not always loved by their American readers.' This literature, Ammons points out, 'consistently focused on two issues: marriage and work.'[4] Seeing marriage as a form of work, a woman's job, it also raises the question of work and especially of creativity. The fiction of this transitional phase in women's history and women's writing is characterized by unhappy endings, as novelists struggled with the problem of going beyond the allowable limits and breaking through the available histories and stories for women.

Unlike some other heroines of the fiction of this transitional phase, Lily Bart is neither the educated, socially conscious, rebellious New Woman, nor the androgynous artist who finds meaning for her life in solitude and creativity, nor the old woman fiercely clinging to the past whom we so often see as the heroine of the post-Civil War local colorists.[5] Her skills and morality are those of the Perfect Lady. In every crisis she rises magnificently to the occasion, as we see when Bertha insults her, her aunt disinherits her, Rosedale rejects her. Lawrence Selden, the would-be New Man to whom she turns for friendship and faith, criticizes Lily for being ' "perfect" to everyone'; but he demands an even further moral perfection that she can finally only satisfy by dying. Lily's uniqueness, the emphasis Wharton gives to her lonely pursuit of ladylike manners in the midst of vulgarity, boorishness, and malice, makes us feel that she is somehow the *last* lady in New York, what Louis Auchincloss calls the 'lone and solitary' survivor of a bygone age.[6]

I would argue, however, that Wharton refuses to sentimentalize Lily's class position but rather, through associating it with her own limitations as the Perfect Lady Novelist, makes us aware of the cramped possibilities of the lady whose creative roles are defined and controlled by men. Lily's plight has a parallel in Wharton's career as the elegant scribe of upper-class New York society, the novelist of manners and decor. Cynthia Griffin Wolff calls *The House of Mirth* Wharton's 'first Künstlerroman,' and in important ways, I would agree, Wharton's *House of Mirth* is also a fictional house of birth for the woman artist. Wolff points out that *The House of Mirth* is both a critique of the artistic representation of women—the transformation of women into beautiful objects of male aesthetic appreciation—and a satiric analysis of the artistic traditions that 'had evolved no conventions designed to render a woman as the maker of beauty, no language of feminine growth and mastery.' In her powerful analysis of Lily Bart's disintegration, Wharton 'could turn her fury upon a world which had enjoined women to spend their artistic inclinations entirely upon a display of self. Not the woman as productive artist, but the woman as self-creating artistic object—that is the significance of the brilliant and complex characterization of Lily Bart.'[7] In deciding that a Lily cannot survive, that the upper-class lady must die to make way for the modern woman who will work, love, and give birth, Wharton was also signaling her own rebirth as the artist who would describe the sensual worlds of *The Reef*, *Summer*, and *The Age of Innocence* and who would create the language of feminine growth and mastery in her own work.

We are repeatedly reminded of the absence of this language in the world of *The House of Mirth* by Lily's ladylike self-silencing, her inability to rise above the 'word-play and evasion' (p. 494) that restrict her conversations with Selden and to tell her own story. Lily's inability to speak for herself is a muteness that Wharton associated with her own social background, a decorum of self-restraint she had to overcome in order to become a novelist. In one sense, Lily's search for a suitable husband is an effort to be 'spoken for,' to be suitably articulated and defined in the social arena. Instead, she has the opposite fate: she is 'spoken of' by men, and as Lily herself observes, 'The truth about any girl is that once she's talked about, she's done for, and the more she explains her case the worse it looks' (364). To become the object of male discourse is almost as bad as to become the victim of male lust; 'It was horrible of a young girl to let herself be talked about,' the significantly named Mrs Peniston reflects in agitation. 'However unfounded the charges against her, she must be to blame for their having been made' (p. 205).

Whenever Lily defies routine, the male scandalmongers are there to recycle her for their own profit. After the *tableaux vivants*, her performance and her relationship with Gus Trenor are so racily described in *Town Talk* that Jack Stepney is perturbed, although the elderly rake Ned Van Alstyne, 'stroking his mustache to hide the smile behind it,' comments that he had 'heard the stories before' (p. 254). When Bertha Dorset announces that Lily is not returning to the yacht, the scene is witnessed by Dabham, the society columnist of 'Riviera Notes,' whose 'little eyes,' Selden fears, 'were like tentacles thrown out to catch the floating intimations with which . . . the air at moments seemed thick' (p. 347). These men can rewrite the story of Lily's life, as they can also enjoy the spectacle of her beauty and suffering.

Although Lily has a 'passionate desire' to tell the truth about herself to Selden, she can only hint, can only speak in parables he is totally unable to comprehend. Even the body language of her tears, her emaciation, and her renunciatory gestures are lost on him. On her deathbed, as she is drifting into unconsciousness, Lily is still struggling with the effort to speak: 'She said to herself that there was something she must tell Selden, some word she had found that should make life clear between them. She tried to repeat the word, which lingered vague and luminous on the far edge of thought. . . . If she could only remember it and say it to him, she felt that everything would be well' (p. 522). Yet she dies with this word of self-definition on her lips, not the bride of a loving communication, but rather the still unravished bride of quietness. After her death, Selden kneels and bends over her dead body on the bed, like Dracula or little Dabham, 'draining their last moment to its lees' (as he has earlier led Gerty on, 'draining her inmost thoughts'), 'and in the silence there passed between them the word which made all clear' (p. 533). This word, Susan Gubar argues,

is Lily's dead body; for she is now converted completely into a script for his edification, a text not unlike the letters and checks she has left behind to vindicate her life. . . . Lily's history, then, illustrates the terrors not of the word made flesh, but of the flesh made word. In this respect, she illuminates the problems Wharton must have faced in her own efforts to create rather than be created.[8]

Among the issues the novel raises is the question of writing itself, both in terms of female creativity and in terms of a relationship to literary traditions. *The House of Mirth* revises both male and female precursors, as Wharton explores not only the changing worlds of women, but also the transformation and equally limiting worlds of men. In a number of striking respects, *The House of Mirth* goes back to adapt the characteristic plot of mid-nineteenth-century 'woman's fiction' and to render it ironic by situating it in the post-matriarchal city of sexual commerce. This plot, as Nina Baym has established, concerned 'a young girl who is deprived of the supports she had rightly or wrongly depended on to sustain her throughout life and is faced with the necessity of winning her own way in the world.' Despite hardships and trials, the heroine overcomes all obstacles through her 'intelligence, will, resourcefulness, and courage.' Although she marries, as an indication that her progress toward female maturity has been completed, marriage is not really the goal of this heroine's ordeal, and men are less important to her emotional life than women.[9]

Lily Bart's story alludes to but subverts these sentimental conventions of nineteenth-century women's literature, conventions that dozens of female best-sellers from *The Wide, Wide World* to *Little Women* had made familiar. Lily has certainly been deprived of the financial and emotional supports she has been raised to expect and has been even more seriously deprived of the environment for the skills in which she has been trained. First of all, Wharton puts the question of youth itself into question. At twenty-nine, Lily sees eligible 'girlhood' slipping into spinsterdom and faces the impending destruction of her beauty by the physical encroachments of adulthood—not simply the aging process, but also anxiety, sexuality, and serious work. Secondly, in contrast to the emotionally intense relationships between mothers, daughters, sisters, and friends in most nineteenth-century women's writing, women's relationships in *The House of Mirth* are distant, formal, competitive, even hostile. Selden deplores 'the cruelty of women to their kind' (p. 352). Lily feels no loving ties to the women around her; in her moment of crisis 'she had no heart to lean on' (p. 240). Her mother is dead and unmourned; 'Her relation with her aunt was as superficial as that of chance lodgers who pass on the stairs' (p. 240). Her treatment of her cousin Grace Stepney is insensitive and distant, and Grace is bitterly jealous of her success. Lily sees and treats other women as her allies, rivals, or inferiors in the social competition; she is no different from the 'best friends' she describes to Selden as those women who 'use me or abuse me; but . . . don't care a straw what happens to me' (p. 13).

Whereas childbirth and maternity are the emotional and spiritual centers of the nineteenth-century female world, and still an issue in *The Awakening*, in *The House of Mirth* they have been banished to the margins. Childbirth seems to be one of the dingier attributes of the working class; the Perfect Lady cannot mar her body or betray her sexuality in giving birth. There are scarcely any children occupying the Fifth Avenue mansions and country cottages of Lily's friends. (Judy and Gus Trenor have two teenage daughters, briefly glimpsed, but not in their mother's company. Judy refers to them only once as having to be sent out of the room because of a guest's spicy stories.)

And whereas the heroine of women's fiction triumphs in every crisis, confounds her enemies and wins over curmudgeons and reforms rakes, Lily is continually defeated. The aunt who should come to her rescue disinherits her; Bertha Dorset, the woman friend who should shelter her, throws her out in order to protect her own reputation; the man who should have faith in her cannot trust her long enough to overcome his own emotional fastidiousness. With stark fatalism rather than with the optimism of woman's fiction Wharton takes Lily from the heights to her death. As Edmund Wilson first noted in his 1937 essay 'Justice to Edith Wharton,' Wharton 'was much haunted by the myth of the Eumenides; and she had developed her own deadly version of the working of the Aeschylean necessity. . . . She was as pessimistic as Hardy or Maupassant.'[10] Indeed, Lily's relentless fall suggests the motto of Hardy's *Tess of the D'Urbervilles*: 'The Woman Pays.' Despite being poor, in debt, disinherited, an outsider in a world of financiers and market manipulators, speculators and collectors, Lily is the one who must pay again and again for each moment of inattention, self-indulgence, or rebellion. 'Why must a girl pay so dearly for her least escape from routine?' she thinks after her ill-timed meeting with Rosedale outside Selden's apartment. But while Tess pays with her life for a real fall, Lily pays only for the appearance of one, for her inability to explain or defend herself.

In other respects, many details of the novel allude to an American female literary tradition. As Cynthia Griffin Wolff has shown, the name 'Lily' referred to a central motif of art nouveau: the representation of female purity as lilies adapted from Japanese art themes, 'Easter lilies, tiger lilies, water lilies, liquescent calla lilies, fluttering clusters of lily-of-the-valley.'[11] It was also a name with a special history in nineteenth-century American women's writing. Amelia Bloomer's temperance and women's rights journal of the 1850s was called *The Lily*, to represent, as the first issue announced, 'sweetness and purity.'[12] In women's local-color fiction, 'Lily' was a recurring name for sexually attractive and adventurous younger women, as opposed to women of the older generation more bound to sisterly and communal relation-ships. In Mary Wilkins Freeman's most famous story, 'New England Nun,' Lily Dyer is the blooming girl to whom the cloistered Louisa Ellis thankfully yields her red-faced suitor. In Freeman's later 'Old Woman Magoun,' Lily represents the femi-nine spirit of the new century, a sexuality terrifying to the old women who guard the female sanctuaries of the past. In this stark and terrifying story, Old Woman Magoun has managed to keep her pretty fourteen-year-old granddaughter, Lily, a child within a strictly female community; but when it becomes clear that she will lose the orphaned girl both to adolescence and to the predatory sexuality of the male world, the grandmother poisons her.[13]

Furthermore, Wharton's pairing of Lily Bart with her nemesis, Bertha Dorset, echoes the pairing of Berthas and Lilys in an earlier feminist text: Elizabeth Oakes Smith's *Bertha and Lily* (1854). Oakes Smith's novel describes the relationship of a mother (Bertha) and her illegitimate daughter (Lily). While the erring Bertha's life has been painful and limited, Lily's future is presented as radiantly hopeful: 'She will be an artist, an orator, a ruler . . . just as her faculties impel.' Lily seems to represent the possibilities of the creative buried self Oakes Smith felt in her own stifled career.[14]

Constance Cary Harrison's *Anglomaniacs* (1890), a successful novel of the *fin de siècle* set in the same upper-class New York milieu as *The House of Mirth*, also has a heroine named Lily, a young heiress who is pressured to marry a titled Englishman she does not love in order to satisfy her mother's social ambitions. Like Lily Bart, Lily Floyd-Curtis has the graceful figure of a 'wood-nymph,' socializes with a sensitive bachelor friend who lives 'in the Benedick with his violincello,' and attends a charity ball where the dinner table is set to represent a Veronese painting and she herself is dressed as a Venetian princess.[15]

Wharton is ironically aware of the way that Lily Bart becomes the object of male myths and fantasies, like that of the wood nymph, that must be revised from the woman's perspective. Selden insists on seeing her as a 'captured dryad subdued to the conventions of the drawing-room,' yet the image of the dryad is as much one of these drawing-room conventions as that of the woman of fashion. Indeed, Lily, as Wharton tells us, 'had no real intimacy with nature, but she had a passion for the appropriate' (pp. 19, 101). For her role in the *tableaux vivants*, Lily chooses to represent the figure of Sir Joshua Reynolds's *Mrs. Lloyd* (Figure 1), in a draped gown that revealed 'long dryad-like curves that swept upwards from her poised foot to her lifted arm' (p. 217). Selden is enraptured by her performance, finding the authentic Lily in the scene; but it is rather the carefully constructed Lily of his desire that he sees. The 'streak of sylvan freedom' he perceives in her is rather what he would make of her, and we are reminded that Ezra Pound at this same period was imposing the title 'Dryad' on the equally plastic H.D.[16]

The myth of Tarpeia was another case of differing male and female interpretations. Simon Rosedale tells it in garbled form to Lily when he comes to propose to her: 'There was a girl in some history book who wanted gold shields or something, and the fellows threw 'em at her, and she was crushed under 'em; they killed her' (p. 284). Tarpeia, the Roman who betrayed her city to the Sabines by opening the Capitoline citadel in exchange for gold bracelets and was crushed by the shields of the invading Sabine army, was also the subject of Louise Guiney's well-known poem of the 1890s that dramatized the paradox of a woman's being condemned by her society for the mercenary and narcissistic values it has encouraged.[17]

Wharton's major revision of a male text, as those critics not

Fig. 1. Sir Joshua Reynolds, portrait of *Mrs. Lloyd*

obsessed with her alleged apprenticeship to Henry James have noted, was with relation to Oscar Wilde's *Picture of Dorian Gray* (1890). Lily's picture is in one sense her mirror, but it is more fully her realization of the ways in which her society has deformed her. In contrast to Dorian Gray's portrait, Lily's monster in the mirror is not one whose perfect complexion has been marred by lines of worry, shame, or guilt, but rather a woman with a 'hard, brilliant' surface (p. 191). In the aftershock of her encounter with Gus Trenor in his empty house, Lily recognizes 'two selves in her, the one she had always known, and a new abhorrent being to which it found itself chained' (p. 238). As she tells Gerty, this self seems like a 'disfigurement,' a 'hideous change' that has come to her while she slept; a moral ugliness that she cannot bear to contemplate (p. 265).

Some feminist critics have argued that this 'stranger' in Lily, this second and abhorrent self, is the female personality produced by a patriarchal society and a capitalist economy. As Elizabeth Ammons notes, 'the system is designed to keep women in divisive and relentless competition' for the money and favor controlled by men. 'Forbidden to aggress on each other directly, or aggress on men at all, women prey on each other—stealing reputations, opportunities, male admirers—all to parlay or retain status and financial security in a world arranged by men to keep women suppliant and therefore subordinate.' Women employ, exploit, and cheat each other as cold-bloodedly as their Wall Street husbands carry out deals, but 'by nature' women 'feel no necessity to harm each other.'[14]

Yet the nature of both men and women is in question in the novel rather than given. It is often overlooked that Wharton develops a full cast of male characters in *The House of Mirth*, whose dilemmas parallel those of the women. As historians now recognize, the period 1880–1920 redefined gender identity for American men as well as for American women. Among the characteristics of progressivism and of the masculinity crisis was the increased specialization of men as workers marginal to the family and culture: 'According to the capitalistic ethos, men were expected to promote industry and commerce, which they did in abundance, often spending long hours at the office, the plant, or in the fields and forests. With their energies spent, they came home too weary and worn to devote much time and interest to family or friends.'[19]

Wharton's critique of the marriage system is not limited to the economic dependency of women but also extends to consider the loneliness, dehumanization, and anxiety of men. Lily's father, a shadowy figure in the prehistory of the novel, establishes the theme of the marginal man. This 'neutral-tinted father, who filled an intermediate space between the butler and the man who came to wind the clocks,' is a dim and pathetic fixture of Lily's scant childhood memories (p. 45). 'Effaced and silent,' patient and stooping, he is an exhausted witness to the stresses his society places on men. Even on vacation at Newport or Southampton, 'it seemed to tire him to rest, and he would sit for hours staring at the sea-line from a quiet corner of the verandah, while the clatter of his wife's existence went on unheeded a few feet off' (pp. 45–6). Mr Bart does not so much die as get discarded; to his wife, once he had lost his fortune 'he had become extinct,' and she sits at his deathbed 'with the provisional air of a traveller who waits for a belated train to start' (p. 51). Unable to love her father, to feel more for him than a frightened pity or to mourn him, Lily none the less comes to identify with him in her own trial, recalling his sleepless nights in the midst of her own and feeling suddenly 'how he must have suffered, lying alone with his thoughts' (p. 266).

The story of Mr Bart, who in his enigmatic solitude and marginality here strongly resembles Mr Bartleby, lingers in our consciousness as we read *The House of Mirth*, coloring our impression of even the crudest male characters. If Gus Trenor is beefy and stupid, he is none the less repeatedly used by the women in the book, and there is some justice in the words, if not the tone, of his complaint to Lily: 'I didn't begin this business— kept out of the way, and left the track clear for the other chaps, till you rummaged me out and set to work to make an ass of me— and an easy job you had of it, too' (p. 234). To Lily, we have seen earlier, Trenor is merely 'a coarse dull man . . . a mere supernumerary in the costly show for which his money paid; surely, to a clever girl, it would be easy to hold him by his vanity, and so keep the obligation on his side' (p. 137). Lily repays her financial debt to Trenor, but never her human one.

If women in this system harm each other, they also do an extraordinary amount of harm to men. It's hard not to feel a sympathy for shy Percy Gryce when Lily sets out to appeal to his vanity and thus to make an ass of *him*: 'She resolved so to identify herself with her husband's vanity that to gratify her wishes would be to him the most exquisite form of self-indulgence' (p. 78). Despite the loss to Lily, we must feel that Gryce is better off with even the 'youngest, dumpiest, dullest' of the Van Osburgh daughters (p. 146).

Edmund Wilson described the typical masculine figure in Edith Wharton's fiction between 1905 and 1920 as 'a man set apart from his neighbours by education, intellect, and feeling, but lacking the force or the courage either to impose himself or to get away.'[20] Selden is obviously such a figure, a man who seems initially to be much freer than Lily but who is revealed to be even more inflexible. His failed effort to define himself as the New Man parallels Lily's futile effort to become a New Woman; 'In a different way,' as Wharton points out, 'he was, as much as Lily, the victim of his environment' (p. 245). Selden's limitations are perhaps those of the New Man in every period of gender crisis. Cautious about making a commitment, successful and energetic in his law practice, fond of travel, taking enormous pleasure in his Manhattan apartment with its 'pleasantly faded Turkey rug,' its carefully chosen collectibles, and its opportunities for intimate entertaining. Selden lacks only jogging shoes and a copy of *The Color Purple* on his coffee-table to fit into the culture of the 1980s.

Real change, Wharton shows us in the novel, must come from outside the dominant class-structures. Thus the figure of Simon Rosedale, the Jewish financier making it big on Wall Street, takes on increasing importance as the novel develops. He plays one of the main roles in the triangle with Lily and Selden, and while Selden asserts too late that he has faith in Lily, Rosedale demonstrates his faith by coming to see her in her dingy exile and by offering her money to start again. Rosedale's style is certainly not that of the Perfect Gentleman, and even to the last Lily's ladyhood cannot quite accept him: 'Little by little, circumstances were breaking down her dislike for Rosedale. The dislike, indeed, still subsisted; but it was penetrated here and there by the perception of mitigating qualities in him: of a certain gross kindliness, a

rather helpless fidelity of sentiment, which seemed to be struggling through the surface of his material ambitions' (p. 485). In
order to break out of the social cage, Lily must make compromises with elegance, compromises that ultimately are beyond her
scope. But Rosedale, the only man in the novel who likes children
(we see him through Lily's eyes 'kneeling domestically on the
drawing room hearth' with Carry Fisher's little girl (p. 401)),
offers the hope of continuity, rootedness, and relatedness that
Lily finally comes to see as the central meaning of life.

Lily's changing perceptions of Rosedale are a parallel to the
most radical theme in the novel: her growing awareness and
finally her merger with a community of working women. With
each step downward, each removal to a smaller room, Lily's life
becomes more enmeshed with this community, and she sees it in
more positive terms. We see her first as an exceptional figure,
silhouetted against a backdrop of anonymous female drones in
Grand Central Station, 'sallow-faced girls in preposterous hats
and flat-chested women struggling with paper bundles and palm-
leaf fans' (p. 5). For the observant Selden, the contrast to 'the
herd' only brings out Lily's high gloss: 'The dinginess, the
crudity of this average section of womanhood made him feel how
specialized she was' (p. 6).

The crudest of these women is the charwoman, Mrs Haffen,
whose appearance frames the first part of the novel as that of the
typist Nettie Struther frames the end. Leaving Selden's apartment, Lily encounters this woman scrubbing the stairs, stout,
with 'clenched red fists . . . a broad, sallow face, slightly pitted
with smallpox, and the straw-coloured hair through which her
scalp shone unpleasantly' (p. 20). In her hardness, ugliness,
poverty, and age, Mrs Haffen is the monstrous specter of everything Lily most dreads, the very heart of dinginess. Trying to
make money out of Bertha Dorset's love letters, she also em-
bodies the moral corruption Lily has come to fear in herself, the
willingness to sacrifice all sense of value to the need to survive.

Lily's gradual and painful realization that her status as a lady
does not exempt her from the sufferings of womanhood is
conveyed through her perceptions of her own body as its exquisite ornamentality begins to decline. Her luxuriant hair begins
to thin, as Carry Fisher notices (p. 404); her radiant complexion

too will become 'dull and colourless' in the millinery workshop (p. 455). In the beginning, she is one of the lilies of the field, who neither toils nor spins, nor, certainly, scrubs; her hands are not the 'clenched red fists' of anger, labor, rebellion, but art objects 'polished as a bit of old ivory' (p. 10). Yet in her confrontation with Gus Trenor, Lily is suddenly aware that these lovely hands are also 'helpless' and 'useless' (p. 237). Lily has had fantasies of her hands as creative and artistic, dreaming of a fashionable shop in which 'subordinate fingers, blunt, grey, needle-pricked fingers' would do all the hard work, while her delicate fingers added the distinctive finishing touch (pp. 456–7). In reality, she learns, her 'untutored fingers' are blundering and clumsy; like the hands of the working women, her hands too have 'been formed from childhood for their special work,' the work of decoration and display, and they can never compete in the workaday world (p. 477). When Selden sees her for the last time in his apartment, noting 'how thin her hands looked' against the fire, it is as if they are fading and disappearing, vestigial appendages useless to her solitary existence (p. 501).

At the center of Lily's awakening to her kinship with other women is Gerty Farish's Working Girls' Club. Gerty works with a charitable association trying 'to provide comfortable lodgings, with a reading-room and other modest distractions, where young women of the class employed in down-town offices might find a home when out of work, or in need of a rest' (p. 179).[21] Visiting this club as Lady Bountiful, Lily none the less makes the first imaginative identification between herself and the working girls, 'young girls, like herself, some perhaps pretty, some not without a trace of her finer sensibilities. She pictured herself leading such a life as theirs—a life in which achievement seemed as squalid as failure—and the vision made her shudder sympathetically' (p. 179).

Yet when she 'joins the working classes,' Lily also sees 'the fragmentary and distorted image of the world she had lived in, reflected in the mirror of the working-girls' minds' (p. 461). They idealize the society women whose hats they trim. Lily Bart herself has become a kind of romantic heroine for Nettie Struther, the working girl she meets in Bryant Park on her return from Selden's apartment. Nettie has followed Lily's social career in the newspapers, reading about her dresses, thinking of her as 'being so high up, where everything was just grand' (p. 505). She has named her baby daughter 'Marry Ant'nette' because an actress playing the queen reminded her of Lily. Their encounter is the strongest moment of female kinship in the novel, as Lily also sees herself mirrored in Nettie and her baby, and recognizes that Nettie's achievement is far beyond any she has previously conceived for herself.

Nettie is a typist who has had an unhappy affair with a man from a higher social class, a man who promised to marry her but deserted her. Although Nettie felt that her life was over, she was given the chance to begin again by a man who had known her from childhood, knew that she had been seduced, and loved her enough to marry her anyway. There is even an ambiguity about the paternity of the child; Nettie may have been pregnant when George married her. This testament of male faith and female courage stands in sharp contrast to Selden's caution and Lily's despair.

The scene between the two women is unique in *The House of Mirth* for its intimacy and openness (Lily too tells Nettie that she is unhappy and in trouble), for its setting in the warm kitchen (the ritual center of much nineteenth-century women's fiction), for the presence of the baby, and for its acknowledgment of physical needs. In holding Nettie's baby, the untouchable Lily gives in at last to her longing for touch. Holding the baby, she is also being held, expressing her own hunger for physical bonding: 'As she continued to hold it the weight increased, sinking deeper, and penetrating her with a strange sense of weakness, as though the child entered into her and became a part of herself' (p. 510).

Some feminist critics, however, have tended to see the images of the mother and child in this scene, and in Lily's deathbed hallucination of holding the infant, as sentimental and regressive. Patricia M. Spacks, for example, criticizes Lily's 'escapist fantasy of motherhood.'[22] Cynthia Griffin Wolff maintains that the scene with Nettie 'gives poignant evidence of Lily's inability to conceive of herself in any other way than as the object of aesthetic attention,' that she is once again self-consciously arranging herself in a *tableau vivant* for Nettie's admiration. Wolff also argues that in her death Lily is relinquishing her 'difficult pretenses to adulthood.' Thus in Wolff's view the extraordinary passage in which Lily, as she is succumbing to the drug, feels 'Nettie Struther's child . . . lying on her arm . . . felt the pressure of its little head against her shoulder' is a sign of Lily's own retreat into the safety of infantilization.[23]

It seems to me, however, that this hallucination speaks rather for Lily's awakened sense of loving solidarity and community, for the vision she has had of Nettie's life as repressing 'the central truth of existence' (p. 517). That Nettie should be the last person to see Lily alive and that Gerty should be the first to discover her death suggests that Lily's death is an acknowledgment of their greater strength. Doing justice to Lily Bart requires that we see how far she has come even in her death. Unlike the infantilized Edna Pontellier, who never awakens to the dimensions of her social world, who never sees how the labor of the mulatto and black women around her makes her narcissistic existence possible, Lily is a genuinely awakened woman, who fully recognizes her own position in the community of women workers. Whereas Edna's awakening is early, easy, incomplete, and brings a warm liquid sense of satisfaction, Lily's enlightenment is gradual and agonizing: 'It was as though a great blaze of electric light had been turned on in her head. . . . She had not imagined that such a multiplication of wakefulness was possible; her whole past was re-enacting itself at a hundred different points of consciousness' (p. 520). Although her awakening proves unendurable, she really tries to overcome rejection, failure, and the knowledge of her own shortcomings. *The House of Mirth* ends not only with a death, but with the vision of a new world of female solidarity, a world in which women like Gerty Farish and Nettie Struther will struggle hopefully and courageously. Lily dies—the lady dies— so that these women may live and grow. As Elizabeth Ammons observes, 'In the arms of the ornamental, leisure-class Lily lies the working-class infant female, whose vitality succors the dying woman. In that union of the leisure and working classes lies a new hope—the New Woman that Wharton would bring to mature life in her next novel.'[24]

For Edith Wharton as novelist, then, *The House of Mirth* also marked a transition to a new kind of fiction. Like Lily Bart, Wharton had retreated from touch, from community, from awakenings to her own sexuality and anger. While the standard pattern for nineteenth-century American women writers was a strong allegiance to the maternal line and the female community, Wharton belonged to the more troubled and more gifted counter-tradition of women writers who were torn between the literary world of their fathers and the wordless sensual world of their mothers. Like Margaret Fuller, Edith Wharton felt that 'the kingdom of her father's library' was the intellectual center of her development. But unlike Fuller, she did not have the childhood alternative of her mother's garden—a space of sensuality, warmth, and openness. Instead Lucretia Wharton was a chilly woman who censored her daughter's reading, denied her writing paper (as a child Wharton was 'driven to begging for the wrappings of the parcels delivered at the house'), withheld physical affection, and met her literary efforts with 'icy disapproval.'[25]

None the less in her literary memoir, *A Backward Glance*, Wharton called her writing a 'secret garden,' echoing the title of Frances Hodgson Burnett's popular novel for girls.[26] The connection with maternal space (in Burnett's novel it is the dead mother's garden, lost and overgrown) may have come from her sense of writing as a forbidden joy. From childhood Wharton was possessed with what she called the 'ecstasy' of 'making up,' almost a form of illicit sexual indulgence: 'The call came regularly and imperiously and . . . I would struggle against it conscientiously.'[27]

The House of Mirth marks the point at which Wharton found herself able to give in to her creative desire, to assert her power as a woman artist, and to merge the male and female sides of her lineage into a mature fiction that could deal seriously with the sexual relationships of men and women in a modern society. Writing *The House of Mirth* had important professional, literary, and psychological consequences for Wharton's career, and it is clear that she herself thought of it as a turning point in her life as a writer. In her autobiography, Wharton described the process of writing *The House of Mirth* as a serial for *Scribner's Magazine* as one that taught her the work of writing, that transformed her 'from a drifting amateur into a professional.' Because she had agreed to complete the book within five months, Wharton was forced to exchange the leisurely rhythms of the lady novelist's routine, with its manifold 'distractions of a busy and hospitable life, full of friends and travel, reading and gardening' for the 'discipline of the daily task.' The necessity for 'systematic daily effort' also redefined and excused the pleasures of 'making up' as part of her process of gaining 'mastery over my tools.'[28]

Under the pressures of the deadline, Wharton also made tough choices about her narrative, choices that reflected her own transition to a more serious artistic professionalism, craftsmanship, and control. In choosing to have Lily die, Wharton was judging and rejecting the infantile aspects of her own self, the part that lacked confidence as a working writer, that longed for the escapism of the lady's world and feared the sexual consequences of creating rather than becoming art. Secondly, Wharton mastered her emotional conflicts as material for art, learning through the process that anger and other strong emotions, including sexual desire, could be safely expressed.[29] The death of the lady is thus also the death of the lady novelist, the dutiful daughter who struggles to subdue her most powerful imaginative impulses. If Lily Bart, unable to change, gives way to the presence of a new generation of women, Edith Wharton survives the crisis of maturation at the turn of the century and becomes one of our American precursors of a literary history of female mastery and growth.

6

The Other Lost Generation

'I NEVER was a member of a "lost generation,"' the poet Louise Bogan wrote to her friend Morton Zabel in the 1930s, trying to account for the problems she was facing in her career.[1] Bogan meant that she had not belonged to the famous group of literary pilgrims who fled the United States in disillusionment after World War I, to cultivate their Muse in London or Montparnasse. Yet in another, and more important sense, Bogan and her female contemporaries *were* members of a generation lost to literary history and to each other. For—despite the presence of Edith Wharton, Gertrude Stein, Katherine Anne Porter, and other women—the post-war literary movement that we have come to call the Lost Generation was in fact a community of men. In the 1920s, according to the critic John Aldridge, 'the young men came to Paris. With their wives and children, cats and typewriters, they settled in flats and studios along the Left Bank and in the Latin Quarter.'[2] Functional and anonymous as typewriters to male literary historians, the wives of the expatriates were none the less often ambitious writers themselves. Their marginalization, moreover, paralleled the dilemma of other American women writers who stayed at home. While the 'lost generation' of Ernest Hemingway and F. Scott Fitzgerald became literary legend, another generation of American women writers suffered a period of conflict, repression, and decline.

For the literary women who came of age in the 1920s, the post-war hostility to women's aspirations, the shift from the feminist to the flapper as the womanly ideal, and especially the reaction against the feminine voice in American literature in the colleges and the professional associations made this decade extraordinarily and perhaps uniquely difficult. American society's expectations of modern womanhood were strikingly at odds with its image of artistic achievement. Women writers who had established their careers in the earlier part of the century found themselves out of touch with the new ideals; as Willa Cather would later remember, 'the world broke in two in 1922 or thereabouts;' and for many women of her older generation it was impossible to cross the divide.

In order to understand the problems of American women writers in the 1920s and 1930s, we must also look at what was happening to American women generally during this period. First we need to look at the feminist crash of the 1920s—the unexpected disintegration of the women's movement after the passage of the Nineteenth Amendment. The 1920s were feminism's awkward age. The political coalitions of the suffrage campaign had dissolved into bitter and warring factions. While the suffragists had prophesied that an enfranchised female electorate would bring sweeping social reform to the United States, they were grievously disappointed when women did not press *en masse* for an end to war, prostitution, and poverty. To many feminists, moreover, Democratic and Republican party politics seemed crude, boorish, and mundane after the heightened utopian rhetoric and ennobling sense of sisterly mission conferred by suffrage activism. By the mid-1920s, it was widely acknowledged that the women's vote had failed to materialize. Women did not seem able to deliver a united vote that would give them power at the polls; instead they voted like their fathers and husbands, or simply stayed at home. Even one of the new female politicians, Democratic committeewoman Emily Newell Blair, acknowledged that the ballot had not brought women either power or political solidarity: 'I know of no woman today who has any influence or political power because she is a woman. I know of no woman who has a following of other women. I know of no politician who is afraid of the woman vote on any question under the sun.'[4]

As articles began to appear in the popular press on the 'failure' of women's suffrage, there were also signs of failure and disillusion on the personal level. The feminism of an earlier generation had been forged in the intense personal relationships of women's culture. Many female intellectuals and activists of the pre-war generation—women like Jane Addams or Sarah Orne Jewett—had been raised to believe that women were the purer sex, blessed with little sexual appetite. The novelist Mary Austin recalled in 1927 that in her youth 'nobody, positively *nobody*, had yet suggested that women are passionately endowed even as men are.'[5] Many ambitious women had forgone marriage and satisfied their emotional needs in intimate friendships with other women, or in communal female living in women's colleges or settlement houses. What they sacrificed in sexual passion they made up for in independence and the freedom to devote all their creative energies to their work.

But 'modern' women read Freud and struggled to liberate themselves from outmoded sexual inhibitions. The heroine of the Jazz Age became the flapper, with her bobbed hair, short skirts, bathtub gin, and easy kisses. The feminism of the suffragettes seemed irrelevant or dated to the young women of the 1920s, who had been exposed to the messages of psychoanalysis, advertising, and Hollywood. The women's colleges that had been the avant-garde for the previous generation felt the shock wave of major changes in the 1920s. No longer intellectual sanctuaries where bright girls were initiated into intense female communities, they became sites of struggle over regulations and restrictions about heterosexual mixing. Even Bryn Mawr, the last holdout, offered tea dances by 1929 and allowed Princeton students to play the men's parts in student plays. The rituals and traditions that had united women students as a group withered away as students demanded more personal freedom and interaction with men. Ambitious women of the 1920s expected that they could have careers of their own, without surrendering the traditional feminine experiences of romance, marriage, and motherhood. 'By the time I grew up,' Lillian Hellman recalled, 'the fight for the emancipation of women, their rights under the law, in the office, in bed, was stale stuff. My generation didn't think much about the place or the problems of women.'[6]

But these fantasies of lives that successfully balanced love and work were premature in a society where the husband's role was unexamined and unaltered, where wives were still expected to serve their men and their families, where in fact women's reproductive, marital, legal, and vocational rights were few. Encountering the real tensions between their writing and their personal lives led to disillusionment for women of Hellman's generation. Older feminists too felt bitter and betrayed. The younger generation did not seem to recognize their sacrifice or wish to emulate it. For a pioneer of women's higher education like Wellesley's Vida Scudder, the 1920s were 'the bleakest years of her life.'[7]

While this shift in female attitudes towards personal achievement caused anxiety and conflict for women planning literary careers in the 1920s and 1930s, hostility towards female authorship and feminine values in academia and the literary establishment further stigmatized women's writing. A country taking new pride in its cultural heritage after the war saw only weakness and sentimentality in the contribution women had made to our national literature. In the years following the war, women writers were gradually eliminated from the canon of American literature as it was anthologized, criticized, and taught.

We can see the signs of this devaluation of women's writing as public honors for a few celebrated token figures were accompanied by mockery of women readers and writers in private literary correspondence and exclusion of women's literature from serious critical consideration. Although Willa Cather received an honorary degree from Princeton in 1931—the first woman to be so honored—her critical reputation, like that of her contemporary Edith Wharton, diminished. Both women were scorned by critics of the 1930s as decorous relics of a bygone age. While at the beginning of his career Fitzgerald acknowledged the influence of such important novelists as Cather and Wharton, he also complained that the American novel was being emasculated by female conventionality and propriety. Yet there was little tolerance for female unconventionality, originality, and impropriety from the very men who lamented the dictatorship of feminine prudery. Hemingway, for example, learned what he needed from Gertrude Stein, but could not imagine her being part of his literary circle. 'There is not much future in men being friends with great women,' he wrote in his memoir of Paris, *A Moveable Feast* (published posthumously in 1964), 'and there is usually even less future with truly ambitious women writers.'

Perhaps the worst casualties of the inter-war period were the women poets. The image of the woman poet, or 'poetess,' as she might still be called, was much more stereotyped and limiting than that of the novelist. The popular image of the American 'female lyrist' was that of a 'sweet singer' with three names, a pretty, youthful creature who wrote about love and renunciation, in a song as spontaneous, untaught, and artless as the lark's. After the war, however, American women poets needed to search for precursors who could define the shape of a serious woman poet's career as she matured and grew in artistry, range, and technique. Some, like Sara Teasdale, Edna St Vincent Millay, and H. D. (Hilda Doolittle), looked to Sappho, the Greek lyricist whose work existed only in fragments; and indeed reinvented her to provide a poetic matrilineage for themselves. Many turned to the English poets Elizabeth Barrett Browning and Christina Rossetti. Others welcomed the rediscovery of a uniquely American female poetic voice, heralding the critical revival of Emily Dickinson in the late 1920s. Amy Lowell championed Dickinson's poetic genius and praised her unorthodox meters and rhymes during a period when mainstream critics regarded her work as eccentric, and her place in American literary history as inconspicuous. Genevieve Taggard's biography of Dickinson in 1931 was one of the first written outside of the poet's family circle, and Taggard was editing a collection of Dickinson's poems and letters when she died.

Yet none of these precursors seemed wholly satisfying either in their personal lives or in their poetic careers. Amy Lowell's poem 'The Sisters' (1925) summarized her generation's sense of marginality and eccentricity:

> Taking us by and large, we're a queer lot
> We women who write poetry. And when you think
> How few of us there've been, it's queerer still.

Reviewing the work of her 'older sisters' in poetry—Sappho ('a leaping fire'), Barrett Browning ('squeezed in stiff conventions'),

and Dickinson ('she hung her womanhood upon a bough')—
Lowell regretfully concludes that none offers her a model for the
kind of poetry she wants to write:

> Goodbye, my sisters, all of you are great,
> And all of you are marvellously strange,
> And none of you has any word for me.
> I cannot write like you.

American women poets like Lowell were particularly troubled
by the advent of a modernist poetic aesthetic. Before the war,
there had been a place for the female poet in American culture,
albeit a limited and sentimental one. But T. S. Eliot and Ezra
Pound, among others, proclaimed the need for a severe poetry
that transcended personal experience and emotion—precisely the
modes in which women lyric poets had been encouraged to
specialize. Serious, or 'major,' poetry, Eliot, Pound, and their
disciples argued, was intellectual, impersonal, experimental, and
concrete. Furthermore, they believed, women were by nature
emotional creatures who could inspire major poems but lacked
the genius to produce them. As John Crowe Ransom declared in
an essay entitled 'The Poet as Woman' (1936), 'A woman lives for
love. . . . safer as a biological organism, she remains fixed in her
famous attitudes, and is indifferent to intellectuality.' Even lauda-
tory reviews of particular women poets frequently included
derisory generalizations about the deficiencies of women's poetry
as a genre; Theodore Roethke, for example, provided a lengthy
catalogue of 'charges most frequently levelled against poetry by
women': 'lack of range—in subject matter and emotional tone—
and lack of a sense of humor . . . the embroidering of trivial
themes; a concern with the mere surfaces of life . . . lyric or
religious posturing . . . lamenting the lot of the woman; cater-
wauling, writing the same poem about fifty times, and so
on.'[8]

Even when women produced feminine versions of modernism, reimagining myths, for example, from female perspectives
(such as Bogan's 'Cassandra' and 'Medusa', Millay's 'An Ancient
Gesture,' describing Penelope, and H. D.'s 'Eurydice'), as James
Joyce and T. S. Eliot had modernized the myths of Ulysses and
the Grail, their experiments were ignored or misunderstood. As

they attempted to forge a new tradition for themselves against this patronizing aesthetic, American women poets struggled with the conflict between their ambitions to create and their internalized obligations to behave as beautiful and selfless Muses for men. This conflict can be seen as the common thread in a number of otherwise disparate poetic careers.

Sara Teasdale was one of the most famous female poets of her era. Yet she had been raised to believe in the romantic feminine myth of love as woman's whole experience, and she could never allow herself to acknowledge a primary commitment to art. 'Art can never mean to a woman what it means to a man,' she reassured an admirer. 'Love means that.' Believing that 'a woman ought not to write . . . it is indelicate and unbecoming,' Teasdale sought to curb her poetic ambitions, as she also repressed her sexual energies. Her early poems were wistful love lyrics that corresponded to her sense of feminine delicacy and decorum. When Teasdale married in 1914, her businessman-husband boasted that 'she has put the duties of her womanhood (mother-hood and wifehood) above *any* art and would I believe rather be the fond mother of a child than the author of the most glorious poem in the language.' A rejected suitor, the Populist poet Vachel Lindsay, foresaw a new role for Teasdale in which her 'woman heart' would express itself in verse that was both maternal and modest in scope: 'You ought to make yourself the little mother of the whole United States,' he enthusiastically suggested.

Yet marriage did not bring the ecstasies that she had antici-pated, or the motherly role men envisioned for her. Only a few years later, Teasdale had an abortion, unable to imagine mater-nity and poetic creativity as other than antagonistic roles. In the 1920s she retreated into isolation and psychosomatic illness, as her poetry took up themes of frustration and suffering. As a young woman, Teasdale had believed that the woman who wished to be a poet should 'imitate the female birds, who are silent—or, if she sings, no one ought to hear her music until she is dead.' In 1933, convinced that her lyrics had become unfashion-able, but unable to develop a new and strong poetic voice, she took her own life.[9]

Another strategy for American women poets of the period seeking to reconcile femininity and creativity was the celebration of the miniature and the decorative, in exquisitely crafted sonnets and lyrics. Elinor Wylie, for example, specialized in images of whiteness, crystal, ice, glass, porcelain, and jewels. Unlike that of Teasdale, Wylie's life had been full of scandal, including adultery, divorce, and the desertion of her son. The precision of her poetic forms and the chilliness of her imagery helped Wylie defend herself against charges of overwrought feminine emotionalism and sexual promiscuity. Her most famous poems, such as 'Velvet Shoes,' about walking in the snow, and a series of sonnets about winter landscapes, established her persona as a daughter of the Puritans devoted to austerity, silence, and self-denial. In such books as *Nets to Catch the Wind* (1921) and in her essay 'Jewelled Bindings' (1923), Wylie presented her view of the lyric poem as a 'small jeweled receptacle' in two or three well-polished stanzas. The image associated the female lyric with the female body itself, especially since Wylie was celebrated for her silver gowns, dresses like a kind of metallic armor, in which her slender body reminded Van Wyck Brooks of 'some creature living in an iridescent shell.'[10]

The themes of reticence, confinement, and silence so prominent in the work and personae of Teasdale and Wylie can be seen as the dominant ones of the modernist women poets; and we can understand them as in part a response to anxieties about female creativity. In the Imagism of 'H. D.' and the elipses of Marianne Moore, subjective elements were made ambiguous or obscure. Moore's difficult and allusive poems withheld any hint of a self behind the text; the critic Hugh Kenner's remark that Moore was a 'poet of erasures' for whom deletion 'was a kind of creative act' suggests that the aesthetic of reticence demanded vigilant self-control.[11] Léonie Adams and Louise Bogan also chose a severely impersonal poetry, dissociating themselves from what they saw as the sentimental excess of much women's writing. Bogan was outspoken about her contempt for a female tradition in poetry, although she did not recognize the self-hatred behind her stance. Rejecting a proposal to edit an anthology of women's verse in 1935, she wrote that 'the thought of corresponding with a lot of female songbirds made me acutely ill. It is hard enough to bear with my own lyric side.'[12]

Yet these cautious choices also seemed to restrict the poets to minor status. Writing about Marianne Moore in the *Literary History of the United States* (1948), for example, a critic remarked that 'she is feminine in a very rewarding sense, in that she makes no effort to be major.' While Moore's self-effacement might seem rewarding in contrast to the bawling ambition of her male contemporaries, this is a revealing statement about the way in which femininity and minority status were linked in the critical mind. For many women poets of the period, feeling '*very* minor,' as Bogan noted, was a painful reminder of their dilemma. At the same time that Bogan pursued her austere credo of withdrawing 'her own personality from her productions,' she envied male poets their scope, ambition, variety, and freedom to express personality.

Often Bogan's sense of creative inhibition was expressed in physical images of size and weight. In a review of Edna St Vincent Millay's poetry, Bogan noted that 'women who have produced an impressively bulky body of work are few.' Just as she lamented the absence of a female precursor with a substantial body of work, Bogan longed to write 'fat words in fat poems,' like her friend Theodore Roethke, instead of the spare, chiseled, even anorexic verses she could allow herself.[13]

At the beginning of her career, Edna St Vincent Millay showed promise of becoming the most daring and successful presence in her generation of women poets. After her widely publicized youthful debut in 1912, when her poem 'Renascence' won a prize sponsored by a poetry society, Millay became as notorious for her love affairs as for her art. Her first book, *A Few Figs from Thistles* (1920), established her as a bold voice for the New Woman. Such flippant lines as these from 'First Fig'—'My candle burns at both ends; | It will not last the night; But ah, my foes, and oh, my friends— | It gives a lovely light!'—suggested that Millay would insist upon the kind of sexual freedom and emotional independence that had always been the prerogative of men. Raised by a strong mother in a family of loving and talented sisters, and a student at Vassar during the height of the suffrage movement, Millay became a passionate lifelong feminist. Unlike some of her contemporaries, she took pride in the achievements of other women. 'Isn't it wonderful how the lady poets are coming along?' she wrote in delight after reading Louise

Bogan.[14] Millay dedicated her powerful sonnet-sequence *Fatal Interview* to the memory of Elinor Wylie, and even in unsuccessful poems like 'Menses' she made a daring attempt to explore taboo female sexual experience and bring it into the realm of acceptable poetic subjects.

Yet Millay, too, suffered from the period's critical resistance to the first-person lyric as a serious art form. Working with such traditional poetic genres as the ballad, lyric, and sonnet, she was patronized by critics favoring formal and linguistic experimentation. In the 1930s, as she sought to incorporate her political interests into her writing, she disappointed an audience that expected her to remain a romantic laureate. Like Teasdale, she suffered a series of breakdowns as her popularity waned.

Millay was not the only woman poet of this generation who found it increasingly difficult to create as she grew older. Many seemed to run out of suitably 'impersonal' subjects, and were finally silenced by years of self-censorship. Léonie Adams, having published two widely praised volumes of 'metaphysical' poetry in the 1920s, virtually stopped writing by 1933. Louise Bogan simply could not imagine a woman poet who survived as an artist when youth, beauty, and romance were past: 'Has there ever *been* an old lady poet?' she sadly inquired.[15] Between 1941 and 1968, Bogan wrote only ten poems and was frequently hospitalized for depression.

One way to resist the label of 'minor woman lyricist' was to write poems reflecting the political struggles of the Great Depression. Genevieve Taggard began her career with *For Eager Lovers* (1922), a book of poems about love, courtship, and pregnancy that reminded reviewers of Teasdale and Millay. Yet Taggard, a socialist and radical who had written for *The Masses* and who was active in left-wing organizations and writers' groups, became impatient with this limited cultural role. 'I have refused to write out of a decorative impulse,' she explained, 'because I conceive it to be the dead end of much feminine talent.' Neither could she accept the impersonal mask of the modernist aesthetic. Acknowledging the importance of Eliot as a poet, she none the less sharply criticized his elitist politics, his anti-Semitism, and his contempt for women.[16] Believing that the most personal lyric could reveal the feelings of a whole community, Taggard used the form to write about the experience of the working class, in collections that critics promptly denounced as mere propaganda.

Ironically, women poets like Taggard and Millay who turned to politics in the 1930s as a way of establishing their strength and universality found themselves condemned by yet another set of double sexual and literary standards. As the historian Elinor Langer has noted, 'the radical movement of the 1930s was a male preserve.'[17] Like other left-wing groups, the Communist Party of America welcomed women into its ranks but elevated few to leadership and presented few as candidates for public office. Leftist groups saw feminist issues as not only potentially divisive but also as less important than the struggle of the working class. Women's roles and needs were subordinated to those of workers, and women organizers were expected to sacrifice personal ambitions, family, and children for the good of the party. Political work—picketing, demonstrating, writing, and distributing party leaflets and tracts—demanded enormous commitments of women's time and energy.

Moreover, as the historians Alice Kessler-Harris and Paul Lauter have pointed out, 'The cultural apparatus of the Left in the thirties was, if anything, more firmly masculist than its political institutions.'[18] Women were only token members of left-wing cultural and literary organizations such as the John Reed Clubs, and they were also underrepresented on the editorial boards and pages of radical journals: six women were listed among fifty-five editors and writers on the masthead of *The New Masses*. At the *Partisan Review*, also, male editors expected women to be frivolous, less than intellectually and politically serious. Mary McCarthy recalled that when she started writing for the *Partisan Review* she was given the job of drama critic because 'I was a sort of gay, good-time girl from their point of view. . . . They thought the theater was of absolutely no consequence.'[19]

Finally, the literary and aesthetic values of the Left favored male writers, male protagonists, and masculine themes. In 'Go Left, Young Writers,' an editorial for *The New Masses* in 1929, Michael Gold described the advent of a new kind of American writer, 'a wild youth of about twenty-two, the son of working-class parents, who himself works in the lumber camps, coal mines, and steel mills, harvest fields and mountain camps of America.' The vogue of this tough-guy artist implicitly cast doubt on the more private or domestic subject matter of women's fiction, even though for men, too, the lumberjack role was often a pose. In addition, the insistence that left-wing art should focus on economic oppression and the workplace created special problems for women. Only 25 percent of all women, and less than 15 percent of married women, worked outside the home during the 1930s; and few of these worked in the coal mines or steel mills. Once more women's special experiences were devalued or ignored.

What were the effects of political involvement for women writing during the 1930s? Despite their difficulties, some women felt nourished and inspired by the urgency of the issues before them and by the excitement of sharing revolutionary goals with male and female comrades. They found encouragement, communion, and fellowship in left-wing organizations. For the novelist Meridel Le Sueur, for example, the 1930s were a period of satisfying literary productivity and of 'nourishing' associations with political men and working women. From her point of view, the decade was 'a good time to be a woman writer, or any kind of writer.'[20] Like other politically active women in the decade, such as Josephine Herbst, Martha Gellhorn, Tillie Olsen, and Mary Heaton Vorse, Le Sueur developed new forms of reportage, combining journalism with a committed personal voice that made the work a precursor of the 'nonfiction novel' of the 1970s. Her best-known essays are outspoken, colloquial, graphic vignettes of female experience during the Depression. 'Women Are Hungry' (1934) describes the special anguish of women on the breadlines:

The women looking for jobs or bumming on the road, or that you see waiting for a hand-out from the charities, are already mental cases as well as physical ones. A man can always get drunk or talk to other men, no matter how broken he is in body and spirit; but a woman, ten to one, will starve alone in a hall bedroom until she is thrown out, and then she will sleep alone in some alley until she is picked up.

Yet there were other women on the Left trying to write about gender as well as class, who were isolated from each other, and who had no support either from women's groups or Communist Party networks. Furthermore, as Le Sueur admitted, the party demanded a particular style of writing from its members and had little tolerance for other literary forms. Most Marxist literary critics were hostile to the formal and linguistic experiments of modernist writers such as James Joyce, D. H. Lawrence, and Virginia Woolf; they dismissed such aesthetic preoccupations with language as bourgeois or decadent. Instead they advocated 'proletarian realism,' the theory that literature should describe and celebrate the lives, struggles, and triumphs of working-class people under capitalism. Literary innovation was to take the form of recording the language and dialect of the working class, or the 'folk,' extending reportage and documentary into a narrative form.

But even Le Sueur had been profoundly influenced by Lawrence, whose writing about sexuality helped her overcome the puritanism of her Midwest upbringing and gave her a model for some of her lyrical short stories of the 1920s about female sexuality and pregnancy. Such subjects, however, were taboo among left-wing critics in the 1930s, as were the styles and subjectivities of women's writing. When left-wing women writers moved away from the permitted subjects to discuss private female experiences, their work was harshly condemned by radical male critics. Whittaker Chambers rebuked Le Sueur for the 'defeatist attitude' of her essays about women, and other reviewers disparaged her fictional efforts to describe women's feelings and their sexuality. Le Sueur struggled during the decade to purge her fiction of what she called its 'narcissistic' elements; but later she ruefully recalled that the Communist Party tried 'to beat the lyrical and emotional out of women.'[21]

We can see the effects of this pressure on the development of her writing during the period. In her early work, Le Sueur had been drawn to explorations of women's awakening sexual consciousness in the tradition of Kate Chopin's *The Awakening* and Edith Wharton's *Summer*, and to almost mythic projections of the cycle of separation from the mother, reproduction, and death. 'Persephone' is a haunting allegory about a young girl's abduction from her mother, a Demeter-figure identified with nature and fertility. In subsequent stories such as 'Wind' and 'Annunciation,' Le Sueur described female rites of passage, including sexual initiation and pregnancy. Yet her major fictional work of the 1930s, a novella called *The Girl* (1936), which describes a community of women from different backgrounds who help each other to survive the Depression, was rejected by her publisher and remained unpublished until 1971.

Tillie Olsen has written in her book *Silences* (1978) about the periods of creative paralysis that beset writers and especially women writers, listing among the causes the moments when 'political involvement takes priority.' Olsen's own experiences in the 1930s are a case in point. Coming from a socialist immigrant background in Nebraska, Olsen grew up aware of the suffering of women and the poor, and familiar with both a radical and a feminist literary tradition. She had read the work of Rebecca Harding Davis, Willa Cather, Olive Schreiner, and Agnes Smedley, as well as that of John Dos Passos and Langston Hughes. When she joined the Young Communist League as a talented young writer in 1931, Olsen was assigned to a series of political tasks in the Midwest, including organizing women in factories and writing skits and plays for the Communist Party. During these years, too, she was working at a series of low-paid jobs and taking care of two daughters. For Olsen, 'it was not a time that my writing self could be first.'[22] Her writing self, indeed, had to be postponed until many years later, and in some sense it has never been fully recovered; a prizewinning book of short stories, *Tell Me a Riddle* (1961), and an unfinished novel, *Yonnondio* (1974), are fragments of a career that was damaged by long deferral.

Yonnondio, like *The Girl*, was begun in the 1930s and only published forty years later. Like Le Sueur's book, it is about the struggle for survival: a family moving from mining to tenant farming and finally to the slaughterhouses and packing plants of Omaha. Yet the novel has a strong subjective and experimental quality. It is the story of the daughter, Mazie, an autobiographical heroine who, in Olsen's original plan, was to have become a writer, and her mother Anna. But Olsen was never able to finish the book. In the tradition of feminist writers like Olive Schreiner, she wanted a place for the lyric, the personal, the mythic, and the fantastic. But her immersion in the aesthetic of proletarian realism made it difficult for her to develop the psychological elements of her story—the wrenchingly intense mother–daughter bond, the conflicts of sexual desire and feminine respectability, and the power struggles of marriage. These had to be suppressed in favor of a more impersonal account of the struggle between workers and bosses. Olsen was silenced by her internal conflicts as well as by the external pressures of family and work.

Josephine Herbst was another significant novelist on the Left whose work was both nourished and distorted by the formulas of the 1930s. While Herbst was never an active feminist, her life and career were shaped by her profound feelings about other women. Her mother's stories first stimulated her imagination and made her want to become a writer; in the early 1920s her favorite sister's death after an abortion was a never-to-be-forgotten blow. Although Herbst was married to the left-wing writer John Herrmann, she also had two profound love affairs with women. Deep friendships with other women writers, especially Katherine Anne Porter and Genevieve Taggard, gave her a stronger base in a female literary community than Olsen or Le Sueur had enjoyed. Herbst's political radicalism was also an important part of her life, although at many times she recognized that she was being marginalized or used as a token woman.

For Herbst's fictional development, however, the times were mixed. In 1920 she had an affair with Maxwell Anderson, then a married young reporter; when she became pregnant, he insisted on an abortion. The bitter novel she finished in 1922, 'Unmarried,' was never published. In a trilogy of novels based on her family's history in America, Herbst later tried to avoid the 'constricted "I"' deplored by Marxist critics and to submerge autobiography in an epic story of American society. But the documentary devices and the mixture of social consciousness and personal narrative that worked for male writers like Dos Passos struck readers as less significant when the central protagonists were women. Herbst's reputation declined, and although she worked for many years on a memoir of her life in the 1920s and 1930s, when she died it was found unfinished.[23]

Another neglected writer of the 1930s was Tess Slesinger. The daughter of a cultured and prosperous Jewish family, Slesinger studied writing at Swarthmore and Columbia. In 1928 she married Herbert Solow, assistant editor of the *Menorah Journal*, and through him met many of the young left-wing New York intellectuals of the period. The couple were divorced in 1932, and Slesinger drew on this experience for her only novel, *The Unpossessed* (1934). Like Le Sueur and Olsen, Slesinger was drawn to the literary experiments of the modernist writers, and her novel was strongly influenced in its style and narrative technique by Katherine Mansfield and Virginia Woolf; its stream-of-consciousness technique is especially akin to Woolf's *Mrs. Dalloway* (1925). Slesinger uses two heroines to represent the modern woman of the 1930s: Margaret Flinders, the working woman married to a Marxist intellectual, and Elizabeth Leonard, a boyish art student, who has bohemian love affairs and reads *Ulysses*. Through her account of the founding of a left-wing journal, Slesinger satirizes the sexism of the literary Left. One intellectual leader proclaims that 'the point about a woman . . . is her womb'; and the women heroines wonder how to reconcile their desires for marriage and motherhood with their intelligence and their political ideals. In the bitter concluding section, 'Missis Flinders,' Margaret is made to have an abortion by her husband Miles, who fears that becoming parents would make them soft and bourgeois. The death of their child is clearly a signal of the death of their marriage, and perhaps also of their political movement. Slesinger ends with a despairing image of Margaret's barrenness and emotional sexlessness: 'She had stripped and revealed herself not as a woman at all, but as a creature who would not be a woman and could not be a man.' Published independently of the book, 'Missis Flinders' was one of the first stories about abortion to appear in an American magazine.

But Slesinger's insistence that personal relationships as well as political ones needed to be revolutionized was lost on her male contemporaries. While the mainstream press generally praised her book, the work offended male radical critics, such as Philip Rahv, who complained in the *Partisan Review* that it lacked 'a disciplined orientation for radicalized intellectuals;' Joseph Freeman in the *Daily Worker* called it 'bourgeois and reactionary.' In the late 1930s, Slesinger went to Hollywood as a film writer and became active in the Screen Writers' Guild. Her last, unfinished novel, left in fragments when she died of cancer in 1944, was a study of Hollywood written from the perspective of the film industry's workers, rather than its tycoons or stars.[24]

The frustration, fragmentation, and silencing that plagued women poets and novelists generally during the 1920s and 1930s were especially acute for black women writers, who struggled not only with personal conflicts but also with racism and with pressures to conform to the aesthetic ideals of the Harlem Renaissance. As in the Left, the cultural theory and practice of the Harlem Renaissance was strongly male-dominated. Influential critics of the period, such as Alain Locke in *The New Negro* (1925), argued that the black writer should strive for positive expressions of black culture and for racial uplift, as well as for pure art. In the 1930s, when some leading black intellectuals such as Richard Wright joined the Communist Party, they argued that the black artist had a primary responsibility to portray racial oppression and struggle. Women were expected to provide loving maternal nurturance for the new movement and its artists, not to lead it. The novelist Dorothy West recalled how in 1926 she joined a literary group in Harlem, but because she was 'young and a girl . . . they never asked me to say anything.' The highly educated and sophisticated women writers who participated in the movement often felt estranged from the working-class black community whose experiences they were expected to represent. Insulted by racist stereotypes of the black woman as erotic and primitive, they also felt hampered by family and religious pressures to deny their sexuality.

One of the most gifted women of the group the Harlem Renaissance called the 'ultrarespectables' was the novelist Jessie Redmon Fauset. Educated at Cornell, where she was elected to Phi Beta Kappa, Fauset went on to graduate study at the University of Pennsylvania and the Sorbonne. From 1919 to 1926 she was the literary editor of the NAACP journal *The Crisis*. Fauset's male contemporaries admired her intelligence and culture, especially in her conventionally feminine role as the mentor or 'midwife' for young black writers. Langston Hughes recalled her parties for the black intelligentsia in which conversations about literature sometimes took place in French. Claude McKay praised her for being 'as prim and dainty as a primrose.' But her refined hyperfemininity affronted those fighting oppression or defending the folk sources of black consciousness. Fauset's novels were as deeply concerned with problems of female sexual identity as with racial conflict; they show how race and gender together create permutations of power and powerlessness. Yet her romantic plots were mocked as 'sophomoric, trivial and dull,' or as 'vapidly genteel, lace-curtain romances.' Even McKay called her novels 'fastidious and precious,' and to critics of the Harlem Renaissance, Fauset is sometimes described as the 'Rear Guard.'

Fauset's own relationship to her literary community, however, was more critical and innovative than these condescending terms would suggest. On the one hand, she deplored the cult of primitivism and the limits that white publishers set on the portrayal of blacks in fiction. Most publishers, she wrote in protest, 'persist in finding only certain types of Negroes interesting and if an author presents a variant they fear that the public either won't believe in it or won't stand for it.' Indeed, Fauset's first novel, *There Is Confusion* (1924), was rejected by publishers because it contained 'no description of Harlem dives, no race riot, no picturesque abject poverty.' 'White readers just don't expect Negroes to be like this,' her publishers complained.[25]

On the other hand, Fauset's portraits of black middle-class women, struggling with sexual politics as well as with racial tensions, challenged the stereotypes of black male readers. Fauset's most important novel, *Plum Bun* (1929), uses a contrast between two sisters, the light-skinned Angela and the dark Virginia, to dramatize the temptations of 'passing' for her gifted black women. For Fauset, the theme of 'passing' has a double meaning; it refers both to the racial conflicts of the mulatto who can enter the white world and to the divided sensibility of the woman artist who must conceal or sacrifice her vision in response to social definitions of femininity. As one character in the novel remarks, 'God doesn't like women.' Each sister represents an aspect of Fauset's own identity. Through the vivid Jinny, a teacher in Harlem, she describes the intellectual world of the Harlem Renaissance and its male idols, like the spellbinding theorist Van Meier. Through the gifted artist Angela, who studies in New York and Paris, Fauset shows the steady subversion of female talent by myths of romance and domesticity. Whether she is courted by the cynical white playboy Roger or the idealistic black painter Anthony, Angela fears that she will risk losing love and security if she appears strong or insists on putting her art first; to be beloved and feminine she must be 'dependent, fragile . . . to the point of ineptitude.' In marrying Anthony, she determines to make his happiness her career: 'At the cost of every ambition which she had ever known she would make him happy. After the manner of most men his work would probably be the greatest thing in the world to him. And he should be the greatest thing in the world to her.'

Similar themes of female sexuality and frustrated ambition are explored in the remarkable novels of Nella Larsen. The daughter of a Danish mother and a West Indian father, Larsen studied at Fisk University and the University of Copenhagen, and trained as a nurse in New York. Later she became a librarian. Her literary career was brief and intense. On the basis of her two novels, *Quicksand* (1928) and *Passing* (1929), she was offered a Guggenheim Fellowship for creative writing in 1930—the first black woman to be so honored. But Larsen never finished another book. After her return from Europe, as she dissolved her marriage to a prominent black physicist, her career ended in silence and obscurity.

We may look for the clues to Larsen's unhappy career in the tensions of her two novels about cultivated women of mixed parentage trying to find a place for themselves in the Harlem art world, in white society, or in the black rural South. In *Quicksand*, the mulatto heroine Helga Crane is intellectual and cosmopolitan, but she feels alienated and alone wherever she goes. At the black Southern college where she teaches English, she is repelled by the caution of her black colleagues and by their self-denying emphasis on racial uplift. In Harlem, she is both intrigued by the glamor and imagination of black society and irritated by its obsession with race. Yet when she goes to live with relatives in Denmark, Helga misses the company of other blacks, experiencing a belated sense of racial identity she had not even known she possessed. Resisting marriage, moreover, she is tormented by the intensity of sexual desires that are unacceptable in all her social worlds. Larsen imagines a grim resolution to

Helga's dilemma; wandering into a black revivalist prayer meeting in New York, she finds a release for her stifled emotions in the Bacchic frenzy of worship and song. 'In the confusion of seductive repentance,' she marries the evangelical preacher and goes to live with him in Alabama, a marriage that sentences her to permanent imprisonment in childbearing and poverty. Although she is gifted with intelligence and beauty, Helga seems doomed by both her sexuality and her race.

The most important and productive woman writer of the Harlem Renaissance, Zora Neale Hurston, experienced similar conflicts in her life, but managed to transcend them in her work. Raised in the all-black community of Eatonville, Florida, where her father was the mayor, Hurston grew up with the direct experience of rural Southern society that writers like Fauset and Larsen from the urban Northeast had missed. In 1925, however, having begun to establish a reputation in Harlem as one of the most talented and irreverent young writers, Hurston won a scholarship to Barnard College, where she was the only black student. Trained as an anthropologist by Franz Boas, and subsidized by a wealthy white patron of black writers whom she called 'Godmother,' Hurston returned to the South with the eyes of an observer, and with the methods of a social scientist rather than an artist. The tall tales of her childhood had been redefined as 'folklore,' and her task was to collect and analyze them. Yet Hurston kept her aesthetic identity intact; she survived both the pressure of the academic community to distance herself from black culture and the pressure of the white literary community to romanticize it. The books she wrote in the 1930s—most notably *Mules and Men* (1935), *Their Eyes Were Watching God* (1937), and *Moses: Man of the Mountain* (1939)—are memorable for what Hurston called 'a Negro way of saying,' a subtle, pungent, and original style that draws force from the black vernacular but is carefully crafted and influenced by literary models as well. However, Hurston's determination to write from inside black culture and to withstand fashionable issues of racial tension or oppression ('I do not belong to the sobbing school of Negrohood,' she wrote in 'How It Feels to Be Colored Me') antagonized her male contemporaries. Richard Wright, Sterling A. Brown, and Ralph Ellison accused her of pandering to a white audience and attacked her use of dialect humor as 'minstrel technique.' Like Fauset and Larsen, Hurston had to make her way as an independent and strong female artist in the face of male opposition.

Hurston's finest book, *Their Eyes Were Watching God*, blends several traditions of American writing. In technique, it is a modernist novel that incorporates surreal elements into its realism, and that alternates between the sophisticated verbal range of an omniscient narrator and a more intimate folk idiom that represents the consciousness of the heroine, Janey. Hurston's use of dialect, folklore, and a mulatto heroine roots her in the Afro-American literary tradition as well. But the novel is primarily the story of a woman's evolution from loneliness to independence. In what it includes and what it leaves out, it demonstrates Hurston's commitment to traditions of female narrative. Unlike her predecessors in the 1920s, Hurston was not afraid to make female sexuality a central theme in her fiction. Janey's growth to personal maturity is reflected by the sexual as well as emotional terms of her three marriages, which represent three stages of her inner development. Married at sixteen to an older man for whom she feels no desire and who would turn her into a 'mule' (one who carries a burden passed by white men to black men to black women), she bolts. Her second marriage, to the domineering and possessive Joe Starks, becomes a power struggle that ends with her silencing and subordination. After Joe's death, Janey chooses Tea Cake, a younger man, who insists that she 'partakes wid everything,' that she share both his work and his play. Tender and affectionate, Tea Cake teaches her to fish and to shoot; he cooks for her and encourages her to tell stories with the men. Yet at the end of the novel, after Tea Cake has been bitten by a rabid dog, Janey is forced to shoot him.

Why does Hurston arrange her plot so that her heroine is forced to destroy a loving and egalitarian hero, if not because her heroine's survival meant more to her than romantic love? Having learned how to speak and to work, Janey must end on her own, free to make her own way in the world. Hurston's strong resistance to saddling her heroine with domestic burdens, however idealized, is made clear by the fact that despite three marriages, in two of which sex plays an important role, Janey has no children; in fact, the novel seems deliberately constructed to make us look away from this striking omission, to make us ignore such a lapse in its realism. In *Quicksand*, Helga Crane ends up pregnant and immobilized with her fifth child; in *Their Eyes Were Watching God*, Janey remains unencumbered and so is free to realize her dreams.

The 1930s did not end happily for American women writers. Within the academic institutions of American literature, women were increasingly marginalized. In 1935, the first edition of a standard college textbook, *Major American Writers*, included no women at all. Even the great best-sellers of the decade, such as Pearl Buck's *The Good Earth* (1931) and Margaret Mitchell's *Gone with the Wind* (1936), were taken as confirmations of women's talent for a popular literature that could never compete with male art. During the last years of her life, Zora Neale Hurston moved from job to job, forgotten and neglected. When she died in 1960, she was living in a welfare home, working as a maid. Her grave was unmarked.

Yet despite all the difficulties and defeats, American women writers in the 1920s and 1930s produced an important body of work that has finally become influential, as we begin to incorporate it into a three-dimensional understanding of American literary history. Although the feminist movement waned during these decades, many strong women writers resisted the pressures to abandon their own visions and voices. In every genre— poetry, the short story, the novel—women writers between the wars advanced the honest exploration of female experiences and female lives. Moreover, many revised the aesthetic techniques and narrative strategies of their male contemporaries, in order to record uniquely female perspectives. As the feminist critics Sandra Gilbert and Susan Gubar have noted, the sonnet sequences of Wylie and Millay expressed female sexual desires within a genre traditionally devoted to the expression of male desire.[26] The more experimental poets of the period—Gertrude Stein, H.D., Marianne Moore—contested the linguistic, syntactical, and thematic conventions of what Stein called 'patriarchal poetry.' Women novelists on the Left infused the stiff formulas of proletarian realism with psychological nuance and lyric force. And the women writers of the Harlem Renaissance insisted on telling their own stories despite neglect, condescension, or critical abuse.

Ultimately, the value of the literature of the past has to be measured in terms of its continued impact on readers, writers, and critics. No book is ever lost as long as there are new generations of readers to enjoy it, new generations of writers to be stimulated by it, new generations of critics to reveal its fuller meanings. By this standard, women writers between the wars have already established their place in our literary tradition. Ignored or misunderstood in their own day, they often died in disappointment. Several of their most ambitious books were left incomplete. But their achievement has survived, making them significant precursors of the world in which we live as well as the one in which we read and write. Like the contemporary renaissance in American women's poetry and fiction, the development of a female tradition of political writing has been founded upon the work of women writers of the 1920s and 1930s. Perhaps the fate of Zora Neale Hurston, in many ways the most painfully 'lost' member of a lost generation, can serve as an example for all. When Hurston died, her books were out of print; histories of Afro-American writing ignored or disparaged her work; aspiring young writers studied American literature without even encountering her name. But today she is recognized not only as a gifted black woman writer but also as what the novelist Alice Walker, who made a pilgrimage in the 1970s to put a headstone on Hurston's grave, called 'a genius of the South.' For Walker and for many of the leading women writers, black and white, of the 1980s, *Their Eyes Were Watching God* has become one of the most important books in a literary tradition that continues to inspire them and to enable their work. As we continue to enlarge that tradition, the lost generation of American women's writing may offer further surprises and riches. We must not let it become lost again.

7

American Female Gothic

O NE of the earliest critical manifestations of the change in consciousness that came out of the women's liberation movement of the late 1960s was the theorization of the Female Gothic as a genre that expressed women's dark protests, fantasies, and fear. The first great feminist theorist of the genre was Ellen Moers, a brilliant and pioneering critic who died of breast cancer in 1971 at the age of fifty. Her book, *Literary Women: The Great Writers* (1975), was a highly personal, loosely organized study of women writers across national lines. The chapters on the Female Gothic were particularly striking. Moers distinguished between two types of female Gothic novel: Ann Radcliffe's origination in *The Mysteries of Udolpho* of a mode in which 'the central figure is a young woman who is simultaneously persecuted victim and courageous heroine,' and Mary Shelley's turn of the genre in *Frankenstein*, a story with a heroine but very powerfully a 'birth myth,' a tale of hideous progeny both literary and physiological. As Moers maintained, *Frankenstein* is 'A *woman's* mythmaking on the subject of . . . what follows birth: the trauma of the after-birth,' fear and guilt, anxiety and depression.[1] No woman who has ever read the book will forget Moers's description of the newborn infant, taken directly from Dr Spock:

This chapter is dedicated to the memory of Joan Liddoff.

A baby at birth is usually disappointing-looking to a parent who hasn't seen one before. His skin is coated with wax . . . his face tends to be puffy and lumpy, and there may be black and blue marks . . . the head is misshapen . . . The baby's body is covered all over with fuzzy hair . . . and some babies have black hair on the scalp which may come far down on the forehead.

Moers extended her theory of Female Gothic to self-hatred and self-disgust directed towards the female body, sexuality, and reproduction. The Gothic, in her view, had to do with women's anxieties about birth and creativity, including the anxiety of giving birth to stories in a process that society could deem un-natural. Her ideas were crucial to the work of such feminist critics as Sandra Gilbert and Susan Gubar, and to others who looked at Mary Shelley as the paradigm of the Gothic woman writer.

In the late 1970s Moers's work was rethought and revised by a number of psychoanalytically oriented feminist critics influenced by object-relations theory and especially the work of Nancy Chodorow. They viewed the Female Gothic as a confrontation not just with maternity, but with the reproduction of mothering, and 'the problematics of femininity which the heroine must con-front.'[2] In the Female Gothic, Claire Kahane asserts, 'the heroine is imprisoned not in a house but in the female body, which is itself the maternal legacy. The problematics of femininity is thus reduced to the problematics of the female body, perceived as antagonistic to the sense of self, as therefore freakish.'[3] The Gothic castle is, above all, the house of the dead mother. The heroine *thinks* that she is trapped in the haunted castle by a sinister and seductive older man; but she is really on a quest to find the mother, who holds the secrets of feminine existence:

Within an imprisoning structure, a protagonist, typically a young woman whose mother has died, is compelled to seek out the center of a mystery, while vague and usually sexual threats to her person from some powerful male figure hover on the periphery of her consciousness. Following clues that pull her onward and inward—bloodstains, myste-rious sounds—she penetrates the obscure recesses of a vast labyrinthean space and discovers a secret room sealed off by its association with death. In this dark, secret center of the Gothic structure, the boundaries of life and death seem confused. Who died? Has there been a murder? Or merely a disappearance?[4]

In the mid-1980s another group of feminist critics influenced by poststructuralism and Lacanian psychoanalysis saw the Female Gothic as a mode of writing corresponding to the feminine, the romantic, the transgressive, and the revolutionary. For them, its key texts were novels like Charlotte Brontë's *Villette*, in which the Gothic erupted despite Brontë's stated desire to express herself in the bourgeois and patriarchal language of reason. Reading the Female Gothic through Freud's *Studies on Hysteria*, 'Dora,' and 'Das Unheimliche,' as well as through Lacan and Kristeva, critics equated the Gothic with the feminine unconscious, and with the effort to bring the body, the semiotic, the imaginary, or the pre-Oedipal [M]Other Tongue into language.

Several of these critics systematized their readings of Female Gothic under the rubric of hysteria. In the preface to her book *The Coherence of Gothic Conventions*, Eve Sedgwick calls 'the heroine of the Gothic a classic hysteric, its hero a classic paranoid.'[5] The hysterical heroine graphically expresses through her body what cannot be spoken about the self or come into existence as narrative. Similarly, when Mary Jacobus asks, 'what is the literary status of that version of the uncanny known to feminist critics as "female Gothic,"' she replies that the heroine is a hysteric and the Female Gothic text is a hysterical narrative.[5]

But 'hysterical readings' that dehistoricize the Female Gothic make it a timeless universal mode, one that threatens to reinstate the familiar duality linking women with irrationality, the body, and marginality, while men retain reason, the mind, and authority. As Terry Eagleton remarks, 'if women speak the discourse of the body, the unconscious, the dark underside of formal speech—in a word, the Gothic—they merely confirm their aberrant status.'[6] And if 'Gothic' becomes the word that totalizes and encapsulates these positions, it loses its capacity to mediate between the uncanny and the unjust. Like other genres, the Female Gothic takes on different shapes and meanings within different historical and national contexts. Borrowing many of its conventions from the English and European traditions, it has become one of the most versatile and powerful genres of American women's writing, with elements that have changed in relation to changes in women's roles and American culture.

We could trace a long history of American Female Gothic. The popularity of the Gothic genre in American fiction began within a decade of Ann Radcliffe and Monk Lewis, and flourished in the first years of the Republic, despite the difficulty of finding appropriate equivalents of the 'haunted castle, the ruined abbey, the dungeons of the Inquisition' in rural Connecticut and Long Island.[7] In the introduction to her book *Woman's Record* (1852), Sarah J. Hale explained the influences which had led her to become 'the Chronicler of my own sex.' 'The first regular novel I read,' she recalled,

was 'The Mysteries of Udolpho,' when I was quite a child. I name it on account of the influence it exercised over my mind. I had remarked that of all the books I saw, few were written by Americans and none by *women*. Here was a work, the most fascinating I had ever read, always excepting 'The Pilgrim's Progress,' written by a woman! How happy it made me! The wish to promote the reputation of my own sex, and do something for my own country, were among the earliest mental emotions I can recollect.

For many nineteenth-century American women readers and writers, the Gothic suggested independence, adventure, narrative boldness, and self-reliance. It allowed writers otherwise subject to the narrative restrictions of gentility and patriotism to find covert outlets for their sexuality and to imagine exotic or European settings for transgressive plots.

Yet for much of this century, when American critics theorized about the American Gothic, lurid women writers were not on their list. Most interpretations of the Gothic saw it as a myth of male power, arousing terror through incestuous or Oedipal plots, whether 'a helpless daughter confronting the erotic power of a father or brother'; or 'the son's rebellious confrontation with paternal authority.'[8] When Leslie Fiedler, for instance, argued in *Love and Death in the American Novel* (1960) that the Gothic was the 'form that has been most fruitful in the hands of our best writers,' he was not thinking of Louisa May Alcott, Harriet Spofford, or Flannery O'Connor, but rather of Poe, Brockden Brown, Melville, Twain, Hemingway, and Faulkner. The essence of American literature, Fiedler asserted, was 'non-realistic, even anti-realistic; long before *symbolisme* had been invented in France and exported to America, there was a full-fledged native tradition of symbolism.' But American women's writing did not share this symbolist essence. In fact, American Gothic could not be written *by* women because it was a protest *against* women, a flight from the domestic and the feminine. Women stood for the dreary or repellent 'physical data of the actual world' or 'the maternal blackness, imagined by the gothic writer as a prison' below the 'crumbling shell of paternal authority.' In order to 'avoid the facts of wooing, marriage, and childbearing,' then, American writers created a 'nonrealistic and negative, sadistic and melodramatic' Gothic fiction, a literature of 'darkness and the grotesque in a land of light and affirmation.'[9] Women could only be totemic figures along the masculine Gothic trail, seductive Dark Ladies or lachrymose Little Evas.

A story that challenged this narrative of American Gothic was Charlotte Perkins Gilman's *The Yellow Wallpaper*. First published in the *New England Magazine* in 1892, the story had dropped out of the American literary canon. It was rediscovered and reprinted in 1972 by the Feminist Press, with an introduction by Elaine Hedges which used the language of Kate Millett's recently published feminist best-seller to call it a narrative of 'sexual politics' in which a woman rebels against patriarchal power. Throughout the decade, as Jean Kennard has explained, feminist critics produced numerous readings of the story which depended on new conventions and interpretations of such terms as patriarchy, madness, and quest.[10] Now considered 'one of the most famous feminist literary works,'[11] it is also an American classic. (The author is certainly not well known in England, where a recent review called her 'Charlotte Perkins Gilmore').[12] Yet paradoxically, when 'The Yellow Wallpaper' was adapted for Masterpiece Theater, a program that specializes in bringing television versions of the English classics to American audiences, it was set in Victorian England. The story may have been too Gothic to seem American.

Told in a series of brief paragraphs of one or two sentences, 'The Yellow Wallpaper' is a first-person narrative of a woman who has been taken by her physician husband to a secluded house in the country—'a colonial mansion, a hereditary estate'—in order to cure a nervous illness, 'a slight hysterical tendency,' she has developed after the birth of a son. The house is 'quite alone, standing well back from the road, quite three miles from the village.' On the extensive grounds, there are 'hedges and walls and gates that lock,' and at the top of the house, a large room with barred windows, rings on the walls, an iron bed nailed down to the floor with a canvas mattress, and a gate barring the stairs. The floor is 'gouged and splintered,' the bedstead 'gnawed,' and the yellow wallpaper ripped.

The narrator wants to write, and indeed confides her story in secrecy to the 'dead paper' of a journal which becomes the text. Her husband and his sister think it is the writing that has made her sick. But gradually the enforced passivity and confinement breaks down her mind; she begins to have crying spells, fatigue, and hallucinations in which the 'florid arabesque' of the wallpaper becomes a living paper, 'budding and sprouting in endless convolutions.' Ultimately she sees a woman creeping behind the pattern of the paper, who becomes many women trapped and trying to climb through. At the story's end, the narrator is completely mad. When her husband breaks into the room where she has locked herself, she has ripped off all the paper and is creeping around the floor. 'I've got out at last in spite of you,' she tells him, and when he faints in shock, she creeps over his body.

Gilman gives the account of the breakdown and treatment that motivated her to write the story in her autobiography and also in an essay called 'Why I Wrote "The Yellow Wallpaper."' In 1887, after the birth of her daughter, Gilman became severely depressed. Her husband at first tried to cheer her up by hiring a maid and by reading her Margaret Fuller's *Woman in the Nineteenth Century*; when neither remedy worked, he sent her to Philadelphia for six weeks to take Dr Weir Mitchell's rest cure. A prominent and successful nerve specialist, Mitchell had developed a therapy for intellectual women, Edith Wharton among them, that involved complete bed rest, no visitors, no intellectual activity of any sort, including reading, and a rich diet intended to produce a weight gain of fifty to seventy pounds, a kind of pseudo-pregnancy in which the symbolism of biological creativity displaced artistic and intellectual creativity. The body imagery of the rest cure also implied the inverse relation of female body and female mind; women who wished to produce a large body of work had to starve themselves physically, and women who nurtured or indulged their appetites would pay with artistic sterility.[13]

Ordered never to 'touch pen, brush, or pencil as long as you live,' Gilman came close to insanity. She recovered only when she left her husband and child for a short trip, an experience that made her decide on a therapeutic divorce; 'it seemed plain that if I went crazy it would do my husband no good and be a deadly injury to my child.'[14] Casting Weir Mitchell's advice to the winds, she began to write again. Later she remarried, and had a remarkable career as a feminist journalist and activist.

Like Fuller's work, Gilman's Gothic had its roots in the father's library. Gilman's father, a distinguished librarian, had abandoned the family when she was a year old. In her memory, the father's library stood not only for patriarchal knowledge and language, but also the absence of love and support. As she wrote in her autobiography, 'The word Father, in the sense of love, care, one to go to in trouble, means nothing to me, save indeed in advice about books and the care of them—which seems more the librarian than the father.'[15] After her breakdown, tellingly, she found herself unable to tolerate the paraphernalia and spaces associated with her father; she could not 'read a heavy book,' or 'look down an index,' and 'a library, which was once to me as a confectioner's shop to a child, became an appalling weariness just to look at.'[16] The father's library could indeed become the locus for both hysteria and rage. Gilman's contemporary Alice James described her fantasies of violence as she 'used to sit immovable reading in the library with waves of violent inclination suddenly invading my muscles, taking some one of their myriad forms such as throwing myself out of the window, or knocking off the head of the benignant pater as he sat with his silver locks, writing at his table.'[17]

Gilman's heroine too has violent fantasies against men, but expresses her rage against herself and against her child in the form of self-destructive illness, suicidal feelings, and infanticidal impulses. The realistic subtext of the story is that the heroine's husband and sister-in-law are afraid that she may injure her baby or herself during a postpartum psychosis. For this reason, they are indeed keeping her under tacit surveillance. The heroine wonders why the house has gone so long unrented, and why they got it so cheaply; but it seems clear that it is an abandoned private mental hospital. The barred windows are not to protect children, but to prevent inmates from jumping out. The walls and the bed have been gouged and gnawed by other prisoners. The women she sees creeping in the hedges are perhaps the ghosts of former patients. Some of these ghosts are literary; 'as readers versed in female gothic,' Mary Jacobus points out, 'we know that Bertha Mason haunts this text.'[18]

But more than women's reading haunts *The Yellow Wallpaper*. Psychosis, involving hallucinations and delusions, can develop from postpartum depressions marked by crying spells, confusion, sleeplessness, and anxiety. Victorian doctors already knew what recent studies have documented: that 'it's during a psychotic depression that mothers are at a great risk of killing their babies.'[19] We learn about the heroine's violent feelings through the fantasies she projects on the patterned yellow wallpaper in the room. Although she claims to love her child and simply be tired of caring for him, ('Such a dear baby! And yet I *cannot* be with him, it makes me so nervous') her perceptions of the wallpaper reveal images of strangling: 'There is a recurrent spot where the pattern lolls like a broken neck and two bulbous eyes stare at you upside down.' Berman suggests that 'the new mother's description of the wallpaper evokes an image of an insatiable child who seems to be crawling everywhere, even into the nursery which remains her only sanctuary.'[20] The guilt engendered by these involuntary images, while never conscious, forms her system of defenses. She congratulates herself on the baby's 'fortunate escape' from having to 'occupy this nursery with the horrid wallpaper'; and puts herself in the child's place: 'I can stand it so much easier than a baby, you see.'

Because the specter of infanticide is too appalling to be faced, the heroine transforms her violent wishes against the child to self-destructive ones. Soon there is a woman crawling behind the wallpaper,

and she is all the time trying to climb through. But nobody could climb through that pattern—it strangles so; I think that is why it has so many heads. They get through, and then the pattern strangles them off and turns them upside down, and makes their eyes white! If those heads were covered or taken off it would not be half so bad.

Childbirth becomes at once the tortuous emergence of the self, and a fantasy of engulfment by many-headed offspring, hungry and crying.

By the end of the story—the heroine's last, logically impossible journal entry, when she is completely mad—her self-punishing suicidal urges have come to the surface. She thinks about burning down the house, 'to reach the smell' of the yellow wallpaper that torments her. She has found a rope, useful only for hanging herself, and she admits 'I am getting angry enough to do something desperate. To jump out of the window would be admirable exercise, but the bars are too strong even to try.' Instead she turns herself into the infant, creeping around the room, even over the body of her husband who has fainted at the sight of what she has become.

Such a 'thematic' feminist reading of *The Yellow Wallpaper* cannot, as Mary Jacobus would argue, 'account for the . . . uncanny elements present in the text.'[21] But the scenario of confinement and madness in Gilman's Gothic corresponds to the scripts of repression and incarceration typical of late nineteenth-century psychiatric practice, and of late nineteenth-century American Female Gothic plots.

In *Literary Women*, Ellen Moers suggested that the keynote of the modern, post-war American Female Gothic was its obsession with freaks. She pointed to Southern Gothic writers such as Flannery O'Connor, Katherine Anne Porter, and Carson McCullers, whose adolescent heroines see the discomforting changes in their bodies mirrored in grotesques and freaks. In O'Connor's story 'A Temple of the Holy Ghost,' a hermaphrodite in a blue dress tells the twelve-year-old heroine, 'God made me this way and if you laugh he may strike you the same way.' In McCullers's *Member of the Wedding*, the adolescent Frankie visits a circus where she stands horrified before the booth of the Half-Man, Half-Woman: 'She was afraid of all the Freaks, for it seemed to her that they had looked at her in a secret way and tried to connect their eyes with hers, as though to say: we know you.' Katherine Anne Porter's Miranda also goes to the circus where a dwarf with 'not-human golden eyes' grimaces at her 'imitating her own face.'

Looking at freaks in the 1940s and 1950s signified a woman artist's determination to confront the forbidden without flinching, to activate a powerful female gaze. Freaks and feminists were weirdly bonded. Moers was particularly struck by Diane Arbus's photographs of urban outcasts—drag queens, circus people, lunatics, nudists, and giants. Starting out in 1950 as a fashion photographer for *Glamour* magazine, the well-bred Arbus initially seemed like the ideal American girl. 'Diane fitted perfectly into the white-glove syndrome,' a colleague remembered. 'I was astonished when she surfaced with all those freak pictures.'[22] From the photographers Lisette Model and Weegee, and the filmmaker Emile de Antonio, Arbus learned to photograph the forbidden: 'the androgynous, the crippled, the deformed, the dead, the dying.' As Model recalled, 'she never looked away, which took courage and independence.'[23] With her cameras as a shield, Arbus entered an underworld, an urban space usually off-limits to women.[24] Her gothic quest included following her subjects home; as she told a reporter for *Newsweek*, 'I love to go to people's houses—exploring—doing daring things I've not done before—things I'd fantasized about as a child. I love going into people's houses—that's part of the thrill of seduction for woman—to see how he lives.'[25] In her celebrated photograph of triplets, Arbus represented her own three faces in the American culture of the 1950s: 'Triplets remind me of myself when I was an adolescent,' she said. 'Lined up in three images: daughter, sister, bad girl, with secret lusting fantasies, each one with a tiny difference.'[26]

These images were central to the plots of American Female Gothic of the 1950s, in which such writers as Jean Stafford and Shirley Jackson were obsessed by the good girl/bad girl split. Arbus, Plath, and Marilyn Monroe, who appeared to Plath in a dream to give her 'an expert manicure' (perhaps to cure her of a man), and to promise her 'a new, flowering life,' were all Gothic heroines of a decade in which female artistic ambition as well as sexuality were deviant.[27] 'Write laundry lists,' not poems, Adlai Stevenson had exhorted Sylvia Plath's graduation class of Smith in 1953, as if in reference to the Gothic debunking of *Northanger Abbey*.[28]

Women artists of the period attempted to resolve their sense of freakishness by rejecting and exorcising the Mother. In her journals in the late 1950s, Plath also jotted down numerous descriptions of plots for Female Gothic stories, 'an analysis of the Dark Mother, the Mummy, Mother of Shadows. An analysis of the Electra complex.' *The Bell Jar* (1962) is set in several of the Women's Houses of the 1950s, suffocating equivalents of the Gothic castle. Far from being idyllic female communities of sisterly support, these are cloying sickly spaces where women betray each other, as the female body betrays: the Amazon Hotel, for 'girls . . . with wealthy parents who wanted to be sure their daughters would be living where men couldn't get at them and deceive them'; *Ladies Day* magazine where Esther Greenwood gets food poisoning; the suburban houses where she shares a bedroom with her mother and thinks about strangling her; the women's dormitory at the mental hospital that reminds her of college.

Pregnant women especially seem like freaks to Esther, whether the Catholic Dodo Conway with her six babies, and 'grotesque protruding stomach,' or the anaesthetized woman whose delivery her boyfriend takes her to watch, with 'an enormous spider-fat stomach and two little ugly spindly legs.' Plath 'equated maternal love with self-denial, self-sacrifice, and ultimately self-destruction; and it is no coincidence that [her] writings are filled with matricidal and infanticidal imagery.'[29] Fear of childbirth and its restrictions is a powerful weapon against female sexuality. 'A man doesn't have a worry in the world,' Esther tells her psychiatrist, 'while I've got a baby hanging over my head like a big stick to keep me in line.' Part of the fear is the appropriation of childbirth by a dehumanizing male medicine. The woman in the delivery room is 'on a drug that would make her forget she's had any pain . . . she was in a kind of twilight sleep.' Esther thinks 'it sounded just like the sort of drug a man would invent.' The drug is in fact nembutal, used by obstetricians in twilight sleep anaesthesia. While the movement made the concept of painless childbirth more acceptable, 'by encouraging women to go to sleep during their deliveries, the twilight sleep movement helped to distance women from their bodies.'[30] As Adrienne Rich notes, 'no more devastating image could be invented for the bondage of woman: sheeted, supine, drugged, her wrists strapped down and her legs in stirrups, at the very moment when she is bringing new life into the world.'[31] Plath equates twilight sleep with electroshock treatment, also a kind of birth process engineered by men.

The Bell Jar offers us several possible endings to Esther Green-wood's gothic quest. One is sexual freedom through birth control. When Esther gets her first diaphragm, it is like a ticket on the Underground Railroad: 'I climbed up on the examination table, thinking "I am climbing to freedom."' Another is killing off the lesbian self Plath associated with the 'career woman' in the suicide of Esther's double Joan Gilling. It's at Joan's funeral that Esther wonders 'what I thought I was burying' and hears the 'old brag' of her heart: 'I am I am I am.' A third is the rhetorical murder of the Mother. 'I hate her,' she tells the psychiatrist, who smiles 'as if something had pleased her very, very much.' And guided 'as by a magical thread' she steps into the hospital boardroom to pass her final examination in sanity.

Hating one's mother was the enlightenment of the pre-feminist 1950s and 1960s. But matrophobia is really only a metaphor for self-hatred. Since the daughter shares the maternal body, the dead mother continues to haunt her. In Adrienne Rich's important book *Of Woman Born: Motherhood as Experience and Institution* (1976), matrophobia is interpreted as 'a womanly splitting of the self, in the desire to become individuated and free. The mother stands for the victim in ourselves, the unfree woman, the martyr.' Rich insisted that the split be healed in a genuine reunion not only with the maternal principle, but with the real mother. No feminist, she argued, can be truly at peace with herself until she has made her peace with her own mother and sisters.

Rich's volumes of poems and essays called upon the feminist 'will to change,' upon women's decisions to use their anger, sexuality, and energy to confront confining institutions and to assert control of their lives. But these feminist fantasies of the liberated will characteristic of the late 1960s came up against an external limit, as did the utopian fantasies of other revolutionary movements in politics and civil rights. Despite the expansion of vocational and political opportunities during the 1970s, women also became more imprisoned and paralyzed by the fear of male violence. Susan Brownmiller's *Against Our Will: Men, Women, and Rape* (1975) was a pivotal book of the decade, one which made a strong case for the politicization of rape as a feminist issue. As Brownmiller observed, 'The ultimate effect of rape upon the woman's mental and emotional health has been accomplished *even without the act.* For to accept a special burden of self-protection is to reinforce the concept that women must live and move about in fear and can never expect to achieve the personal freedom, independence, and self-assurance of men.'

While contemporary American Female Gothic has increasingly dealt with rape, assault, and murder, it has received far less attention from feminist critics than the narratives of maternity, madness, or the grotesque. An early and influential example of this genre was Joyce Carol Oates's short story 'Where Are You Going, Where Have You Been' (1966). Dedicated to Bob Dylan, the story begins realistically. Fifteen-year-old Connie has a mind 'all filled with trashy daydreams.' She lies to her parents and spends her evenings flirting with boys and being picked up at the mall or the drive-in restaurant. The title thus suggests the parent's questions to the rebellious teenager. But Connie is threatened and finally abducted by a mysterious man posing as a teenager in a gold convertible who calls himself Arnold Friend. He looks like James Dean or Marlon Brando, with 'shaggy black hair that looked crazy as a wig,' sunglasses that are 'metallic and mirrored everything in miniature,' and 'tight faded blue jeans stuffed into black scuffed boots.' A. Friend speaks to Connie with shocking directness:

I'm your lover, honey. You don't know what that is yet but you will . . . But look: it's real nice and you couldn't ask for nobody better than me or more polite. I'm always nice at first, the first time. I'll hold you so tight you won't think you have to try to get away or pretend anything because you'll know you can't.

When he takes her away from her house in his gold car, it is clear that she is going to her death. By the story's chilling end, they have become mythic figures in a Female Gothic landscape of the True West:

My sweet little blue-eyed girl, he said in a half-sung sigh that had nothing to do with her brown eyes, but was taken up just the same by the vast sunlit reaches of the land behind him and on all sides of him—so much land that Connie had never seen before and did not recognize except to know she was going to it.

Some have attributed such plots to the overheated and morbid imaginings of the author. In an essay called 'Why Is Your Writing

So Violent?' Joyce Carol Oates muses on the reason she is so often asked why she doesn't leave 'war, rape, murder and the more colorful minor crimes' to men, and focus her writing on '"domestic" and "subjective" material, in the manner . . . of Jane Austen or Virginia Woolf. The implication is that if Jane Austen and Virginia Woolf had lived in Detroit they might have been successful at "transcending" their environment and writing novels in which not a hint of "violence" could be detected.'[32] Oates has explained however that the story came to her 'more or less in a piece' after hearing Bob Dylan's song 'It's All Over Now, Baby Blue,' and then reading about a killer in the Southwest and thinking about 'the old legends and folk songs of Death and the Maiden.'[33] According to Oates, Arnold Friend is 'a fantastic figure: he is Death, he is the elf-knight of the ballads, he is the Imagination, he is a Dream, he is a Lover, a Demon, *and all that*.'[34]

The plot is based on a real incident. In 1966 twenty-three-year-old Charles Howard Schmid of Tucson, Arizona was charged with the murder of three teenage girls and became the subject of a feature story in *Life* called 'The Pied Piper of Tucson.'[35] The article told how Schmid, or Smitty, as he was called, had sought to 'create an exalted, heroic image of himself.' To the bored teenagers in his crowd, he was a 'folk hero . . . more dramatic, more theatrical, more *interesting* than anyone else in their lives.' With a face that was his own aesthetic creation, the hair dyed black, heavy make-up, and a beauty mark on one cheek, Smitty cruised Tucson in a gold convertible, looking in all the teen hangouts for pretty girls. Bragging about his sexual exploits, claiming to have made vast amounts of money selling drugs, Charles Schmid had assembled himself so consciously from movies and popular culture that its hard to say that he, rather than Arnold Friend, is not the fictional character. Oates does not see the Gothic as a revelation of female hysteria, but rather as the indictment of an American social disorder, the romanticization of the violent psychopath and serial killer.

Yet there is also a muted maternal subtext in the story. Connie lives restlessly inside 'her daddy's house,' the house of domesticity, of the housewife married to her four walls. Connie's mother haunts the little house, always picking on her pretty daughter, who wishes they both were dead. What Connie's mother calls her 'trashy daydreams' are inarticulate longings for something different, something more than having to be 'sweet and pretty and give in.' At the mall and the roadhouse, she becomes another person, someone who experiences sexual pleasures that are tender, 'the way it was in movies and promised in songs.' To experience sexual desire, for the American maiden of 1966, is to risk pregnancy, maternity, the destruction of one's identity. It means becoming the mother and therefore dead. But twenty years later, in the film version of the story, *Smooth Talk* (1986), Connie goes off with her demon lover and comes home again, gentler, cured of her restlessness and rage. For the American maiden of the 1980s, sexual initiation is not fatal, but the beginning of understanding and maternal kinship.

The Shadow Knows (1974) by Diane Johnson is both an artful and terrifying study of female vulnerability, and a novel about race, sexuality, and fear in 1970s America. Johnson has been called a member of the 'California Gothic' School of fiction;[36] her fiction is an extended exploration of American irrationality, danger, and the bizarre. *The Shadow Knows* is narrated by 'N. Hexam,' a thirty-four-year-old divorced mother of four, who lives in a housing project in Sacramento, California. With her lives Ev, a black woman who cares for the children while N. goes to graduate school in structural linguistics. Pregnant by her married lover, N. has had an IUD put in to produce an abortion. As she receives obscene phone calls, has her door vandalized, and her tires slashed, N. believes that someone is trying to kill her, and she may be right. Anyone could do it: her ex-husband, her best friend, her lover, his wife, the crazy former maid Osella. While meditating on her enemies, N. reflects on male hatred of women: 'husbands killing wives—that's an especially recurrent sort of murder . . . I don't understand the sources of male vanity and rage that turn them into killers. Who suckles them on these bitter poisons of expectation? Women, I know.'

Carrying the burden of guilt for her sexuality, her infidelity, her intelligence, her love and resentment for her children, N. feels that perhaps she deserves to be punished. 'If someone is trying to kill you, do you perhaps deserve it?' Her efforts at abortion also torment her: 'I have reason to believe myself a murderess.' She sees the mess smeared on her front door by unknown vandals as 'fetal membranes and blood from inside me,' the 'murdered new life.'

The urban context of crime and racial tension adds to the atmosphere of the novel. According to Johnson, *The Shadow Knows* was 'about race relations, the evil in human nature, and social fear.'[37] Furthermore, 'it was meant to be about persons on the fringe; they happen to be women, and what happens to them is meant to be particular to America in the seventies.'[38] The maid, Ev, who lacks N.'s white-skin privilege, is a daily wrenching reminder to her of the desperation of women's lives at the edges of the American dream. Ev's lovers 'slash and beat . . . and steal from her.' She values herself so little that she often burns and cuts herself, and is deeply scarred, like Queequeg or 'the vandalized statue of a great Nubian queen.' Ev's death—of acute pancreatitis? of murder?—surprises no one, not even her grieving parents. She has long been a victim.

At the gothic center of the book is the relationship between N. and Osella, the enormously fat, crazy, black ex-nursemaid. Osella makes threatening phone calls to N., accusing her of witchcraft and promiscuity. Is she the mysterious vandal? Suspecting Osella of the crime, N. goes to see her perform at the Club Zanzibar, where she works as a stripper:

She seemed to have been oiled, for she shone so; one saw nothing but the gleaming immense breasts lying across her huge belly, breasts astoundingly full and firm like zeppelins overhead. She wore little trunks of purple satin and nothing else but a gold armlet around the expanse of her upper arm—a brilliant stroke, a rather Egyptian, goddess-like adornment calling to mind one of those frightening and horrifying fertility goddesses with swollen bodies and timeless eyes and the same engulfing infinitely absorbing quality Osella radiated now.

Osella is N.'s double and shadow; Kali, the dark jungle queen, the mother-man-eater. While N. is a thin little woman, Osella is immense, 'a sort of super-female.' Her huge body exudes heat; like other fat ladies and freaks in American Female Gothic, she represents the terrifying essense of female appetite and desire.[39]

Is N. a reliable narrator? Is anyone trying to kill her or is she simply paranoid, racist, neurotic? The threats may only be the projections of her own violence and rage. N. describes the 'ordinary misery of mothers of small children'; the loneliness and desperation; 'you must carry them. Their little arms are tightly around your throat, their sticky little fingers are on your glasses.' She has fantasized killing her husband on a fishing trip: 'It simply occurred to her to push him in the river.' Johnson's title alludes to the popular American radio show of the 1940s called *The Shadow Knows*, about the detective Lamont Cranston, whose eerie laugh accompanied the famous opening question; 'Who knows what evil lurks in the hearts of men?' Read with the conventions of the detective story it parodies, the novel suggests the Agatha Christie device of the first-person killer.

Yet Johnson has told an interviewer that she meant N. to be a 'reliable narrator and the events more or less real, and the fear certainly real.'[40] While N. is not murdered, Ev apparently is; and at the end of the novel N. is raped by a mysterious assailant, an event Johnson presents as a fate better than death, almost a relief. The rape is N.'s punishment for breaking the rules, for protesting and making trouble, for going to graduate school instead of working for the telephone company. Johnson has commented that 'the rape scene was meant to be a final symbol of ambiguity and everybody's complicity in evil. I wrote that last scene lightly, before my consciousness was raised about the political implications of rape.'[41] Reviewing Brownmiller's book for the *New York Review of Books*, Johnson realized that 'from a woman's earliest days she is attended by injunctions about strangers, and warnings about dark streets, locks, escorts and provocative behavior. She internalizes the lessons contained therein, that to break certain rules is to invite or deserve rape.'[42] In an interview shortly afterwards, she admitted that a woman who was raped would feel 'angry, resentful, vengeful, guilty—a whole bunch of things which N. in *The Shadow Knows* doesn't feel. And maybe now that I've read Susan Brownmiller, I would not have had the book end that way.'[43]

Some of this raised consciousness about women's internalization of the responsibility for male violence came out in 1980 when Johnson wrote the screenplay for Stanley Kubrick's film version of *The Shining*, an American Male Gothic novel by Stephen King, which portrays a woman who fears that her husband may be trying to kill her from the point of view of the husband. Jack

Torrance, the blocked writer who is the protagonist of *The Shining*, has been beaten by his father as a child, and remembers seeing his mother beaten as well. In a pattern psychologists have established as valid, he projects his rage onto his wife and child: 'You have to kill her, Jacky, and him too. Because a real artist must suffer. Because each man kills the thing he loves. Because they'll always be conspiring against you, trying to hold you back and drag you down.'

The collaboration of Johnson and Kubrick on the script for *The Shining* is a fascinating instance of the re-gendering of Gothic plots. Johnson and Kubrick wrote together during an eleven-week period in London. What initially struck Johnson about King's book was 'the horror, of course—the whole atmosphere of growing fear within the domestic circle was the core.' In the adaptation, Kubrick wrote Jack's lines, while Johnson wrote those of the wife Wendy. But most of Wendy's lines ended up on the cutting-room floor. Johnson comments, 'I was interested to see that finally the Wendy that came out on the screen was much quieter than the Wendy I had written, who was more like a female character in my novels, I suppose, in that she had a lot to say.'[44] Nevertheless, aficionados of the slasher film were disappointed in *The Shining*. They thought it had too much psychological nuance and feminist perspective, and too little blood. Stephen King himself did not like the film. 'Neither Stanley Kubrick nor his screenwriter Diane Johnson had any knowledge of the genre,' he complained. 'It was like they had never seen a horror movie before.'[45]

Changing expectations of what horror means in the horror movie will not happen overnight, and the gender gap in American Gothic remains enormous. Yet ironically, if the contemporary Female Gothic has come increasingly to be perceived as an American mode it is because its concerns are now consistent with a larger change in American fiction towards 'violence-centered plots' and a Gothic revival representing 'alternative strategies for depicting an ever more terrifying reality.'[46] If *American Psycho* is the masculine Gothic of the 1990s, Female Gothic looks more and more like a realist mode.

8

Common Threads

Susan glaspell's story 'A Jury of Her Peers' (1917) has a Gothic plot in which the woman takes a desperate revenge. Adapted from her play *Trifles*, the story begins with two women accompanying their husbands to a cold farmhouse where the local miser, John Wright, has been strangled in his sleep, and his wife Minnie jailed for the crime. Mrs Peters is the wife of the sheriff; Mrs Hale is the wife of his deputy; and thus both, as the sheriff jokes, are 'married to the law.' But this is a perplexing case. There seems to be no evidence of a motive for the crime; the men futilely search the house and barn for clues, while the women clean up the strangely disordered kitchen. Gradually, however, the women begin to notice domestic details eloquent of Minnie Foster Wright's troubled mind and of her oppression in a cruel and childless marriage. The most telling clues are the blocks of her unfinished quilt, left in the sewing basket. The 'crazy sewing' of a Log Cabin block pieced all askew alerts them to the anger and anguish of a woman who cannot control her feelings enough to create an orderly art. As Mrs Peters and Mrs Hale discover the other missing evidence—the body of a pet canary whose neck had been twisted by the husband—they recognize their own bonds within a cultural system meaningless to men,

This chapter is dedicated to the memory of Gail Kraidman, Administrative Assistant of the NEH Summer Seminar on 'Women's Writing and Women's Culture' at Rutgers University in 1984, gifted scholar of American women's writing and lover of quilts.

and their own responsibility for the isolation and loneliness of a former friend, long abandoned, who has been driven mad. In a moment of silent conspiracy, they resew the pieces and destroy the damning evidence, under the very eyes of their uncomprehending husbands who make fun of their feminine obsession with trifles. 'Have you decided whether she was going to quilt it or knot it?' Mr Hale mockingly asks his wife. 'WE think she was going to—knot it,' Mrs Hale replies. The patchwork would have been knotted, as Minnie Wright has knotted the rope around her husband's neck. But also in declaring 'knot it' at the end of the story, the women signal their infidelity to patriarchal law and serve as a jury of Minnie Foster's peers to acquit her of murder.[1]

The conceptual patterns Glaspell represents seem like they might offer a way to address the common threads of American women's culture and writing, and the significance of patchwork as its symbol. Both theme and form in women's writing, piecing and patchwork have also become metaphors for a Female Aesthetic, for sisterhood, and for a politics of feminist survival. In the past two decades especially, they have been celebrated as essentially feminine art forms, modes of expression that emerge naturally from womanly impulses of nurturance and thrift, and that constitute a women's language unintelligible to male audiences or readers.[2] Indeed, for feminist critics of American literature, 'A Jury of Her Peers' has been taken since the mid-1970s as a metaphor for feminist reading itself. As Annette Kolodny observes,

Glaspell's narrative not only invites a semiotic analysis, but, indeed, performs that analysis for us. If the absent Minnie Foster is the 'transmitter' or 'sender' in this schema, then only the women are competent 'receivers' or 'readers' of her message, since they alone share not only her context (the supposed insignificance of kitchen things), but, as a result, the conceptual patterns which make up her world.[3]

Yet to emphasize quilting as the aesthetic domain of women is to lose sight of the way it has been constructed over time in the contexts of changing ideological definitions of femininity as well as strongly gendered separations of the spheres of craft and art. To perpetuate the idea that women have a *natural* inclination for quilting as an expressive mode can serve as an explanation for their absence from the masterpieces of art history, suggesting that 'women are to patchwork as men are to painting.'[4] Furthermore, as the quilt-maker Radka Donnell argues,

there is more to the problem than the art/craft controversy. . . . More than anything, it is sexism, not just elitism, that has kept quilts from a share of space on museum walls. Quilts, after all, have been and are still made almost exclusively by women in a culture where the work, concerns, and accomplishments of women are inexorably dismissed as meaningless and unimportant.[5]

Feminizing the quilt, as the feminist art historian Lisa Tickner has explained, 'keeps women's work marginal and identifies it with the characteristics of a reproductive and domestic femininity, which are understood not to be the characteristics of great art.'[6]

Because of the devaluation, even stigma, of the domestic, the feminine and craft within the value systems of cultural history, the incorporation of quilt methods and metaphors in American women's writing has always been risky. Quilts, like those who write about them, are thought to be trifling; they have been seen as occupying a female sphere outside of high culture. Indeed, as Roszika Parker and Griselda Pollock point out in their book *Old Mistresses*, 'any association with the traditions and practices of needlework and domestic art can be dangerous for an artist, especially when that artist is a woman.'[7]

But the history of piecing and writing in the United States, and the literary or rhetorical history of the quilt metaphor, shows that conventions and styles that were originally associated with a women's culture have been gradually transformed in new configurations and adapted in the service of new ideological ends. Like other American cultural practices and symbols, quilting has also undergone a series of gender transformations, appropriations, and commodifications within the larger culture. While quilting does have crucial meaning for American women's texts, it can't be taken as a transhistorical and essential form of female expression, but rather as a gendered practice that changed from one generation to the next, and that has now become the symbol of American identity at the *fin de siècle*.

To see how the metaphor of quilting has evolved, we might begin by seeing how the history of the quilt identified it with women's culture, and why piecing offered a particularly moving symbolism of the American democratic ideal. While the practice of piecing and quilting was brought to America from its very different sources in England and Africa, it early became a distinctive feature of American society. Quilting was a practical and economic necessity in a country where ready-made bedding could not be easily obtained before the 1890s, and where in the cold New England or prairie winter each family member might need five thick quilts. All American girls were taught to piece and to quilt, and autobiographies of this period 'frequently begin with a childhood memory of learning patchwork' and doing a daily 'stint.'[8] Moreover, early art, writing, and mathematical exercises taught to little girls emphasized geometric principles of structure and organization, and such lessons were applied practically to the design of quilts. An American girl was encouraged to finish her first small quilt in time for a fifth birthday, and by the time she was engaged, she aspired to have a dozen quilts in her dower chest; the thirteenth quilt of the trousseau was the Bridal Quilt, made of the most expensive materials the family could afford, and stuffed, backed, and quilted by the bride's female relatives and by the most expert needlewomen of her community at a special quilting bee.

Furthermore, the social institutions of quilting helped forge bonds between women. At the quilting bee women celebrated a birth or an engagement; they shared rituals of grief as well when they pieced funeral quilts to line a baby's coffin or to commemorate a friend. Quilting bees were also places where women came together to exchange information, learn new skills, and discuss political issues; it was at a church quilting bee in Cleveland, for example, that Susan B. Anthony gave her first speech on women's suffrage. Even when they rebelled against the task of learning to quilt, American women had internalized its aesthetic concepts and designs, and saw it as a fundamental part of their tradition.[9]

Moreover, American quilt-making crossed racial, regional, and class boundaries, and its immense aesthetic vitality came from its fertilization by other design traditions. Black women in

ELLE

MARC HISPARD

SUBSCRIBE AND SAVE

☐ 1 Year (12 issues) $28.00—
Save $9.00

☐ 2 Years (24 issues) $49.00—
Save $25.00

☐ 3 Years (36 issues) $66.00—
Save $45.00

NAME _____ 4G4S

ADDRESS _____

CITY _____

STATE/ZIP _____

☐ **Payment enclosed.**   ☐ **Bill me**

BUSINESS REPLY MAIL

FIRST-CLASS MAIL   PERMIT NO. 1257   BOULDER, CO

POSTAGE WILL BE PAID BY ADDRESSEE

ELLE®

PO BOX 51266
BOULDER CO 80323-1266

the South adapted design elements from West African textiles, including strips, bright colors, large figures, multiple patterns, asymmetry, and improvisation.[10] The quilts made by slaves for their own use were different from those made according to the patterns prescribed to them as seamstresses; as Houston and Charlotte Baker point out, 'the hands that pieced the master's rigidly patterned quilts by day were often the hands that crafted a more functional design in slave cabins by night.'[11] African-American quilt-making took from its sources 'a percussive manner of handling textile color,' and an exuberant 'acceptance of accident and contingency.'[12] Native American quilt-makers incorporated traditional patterns from Navaho or Sioux rugs. The non-representational Amish and Mennonite traditions contributed strikingly modern color-field designs. In Hawaii, quilt-making in the 1820s was supervised by the Queen dowager, and only aristocratic women were allowed to participate in making quilts with strongly colored floral and flag patterns.

To the appliqué and string techniques brought from England and Africa, American women added the piecing technique which would become the dominant feature of quilting. Making a patch-work quilt involves four separate stages of artistic composition. The quilt-maker first selects her colors and fabrics, traditionally using recycled clothing or household material with emotional associations; and cuts out small, geometrically-shaped pieces. These fragments are then 'pieced' or joined together in a particular pattern to form a larger square unit called a 'patch' or 'block.' The patches are joined together into an overall pattern, usually a traditional one with a name that indicates its regional, political, or spiritual meaning. Finally, the entire fabric is stitched to a padding and heavy backing with a variety of large-scale embroidery motifs.

Piecing is thus an art of making do and eking out, an art of ingenuity, and conservation. It reflects the fragmentation of women's time, the scrappiness and uncertainty of women's creative or solitary moments. As the art critic Lucy Lippard observes, 'the mixing and matching of fragments is the product of the interrupted life. . . . What is popularly seen as "repetitive", "obsessive", and "compulsive" in women's art is in fact a necessity for those whose time comes in small squares.'[13]

But piecing also represents a triumph over time and scarcity. As a Texas quilter explains,

You're given just so much to work with in a life and you have to do the best you can with what you got. That's what piecing is. The materials is passed on to you or is all you can afford to buy . . . that's just what's given to you. Your fate. But the way you put them together is your business. You can put them in any order you like. Piecing is orderly.[14]

This metaphor is central to the historical tradition of American women's writing, and is deeply connected to the creative vision American women writers have shared. For American women, housekeeping, as Lydia Maria Child said in *The American Frugal Housewife* (1829) 'is the art of gathering up all the fragments so that nothing be lost.' Piecing these fragments together into a beautiful design, Harriet Beecher Stowe explains in her novel *The Minister's Wooing*, is an emblem of 'that household life which is to be brought to stability and beauty by reverent economy in husbanding and tact in arranging the little . . . morsels of daily existence.'

Moreover, piecing is not a repetitious recycling of design elements, but a series of aesthetic decisions that involve the transformation of conventions. Even when working with such well-known patterns as the Star, Sun, or Rose, 'the quilt artist exploited the design possibilities through her colors, contrasts, and inventive variations on the original pattern.'[15] In the African-American quilt tradition, improvisation has also led to distinctive and unique designs. As Stowe comments in *The Minister's Wooing*, quilting gave women an outlet for their originality: 'Many a maiden, as she sorted and arranged fluttering bits of green, yellow, red, and blue, felt rising in her breast a passion for somewhat vague and unknown, which came out at length in a new pattern of patchwork.' And piecing and quilting were not anonymous or collective arts. As Patricia Mainardi has pointed out, 'The women who made quilts knew and valued what they were doing: frequently quilts were signed and dated by the maker, listed in her will with specific instructions as to who should inherit them, and treated with all the care that a fine piece of art deserves.'[16]

Finally, the quilt process corresponds to the writing process, on the level of the word, the sentence, the structure of a story or novel, and the images, motifs, or symbols that unify a fictional work. Parallels between piecing and writing emerge in the earliest days of the Republic. In the 1830s and 1840s, album quilts, today the most prized and expensive examples of American quilt art, were the dominant genre of female craft. Album quilts are composed of pieced or appliquéd squares 'that are entirely different, even if their construction has been carefully planned and orchestrated by a single quilter. The effect is as if each square were a page in a remembrance book.'[17] They were made to be presented to young men on their 21st birthdays (known as Liberty quilts), or exchanged among women friends (Medley or Engagement quilts), and were signed square by square (Friendship quilts). Many, like the Betsy Lee Wright quilt made in 1851, had poems and messages written on their squares. The most elaborate album quilts were made beginning in 1846 by a small community of Methodist women in Baltimore, among whom were the master quilt-makers Acsah Goodwin Wilkins and Mary Evans, professional needlewomen who worked on commission and whose work now brings between \$70,000 and \$100,000 at auctions (Figure 2).

A number of nineteenth-century women's texts discuss the problem of reading a quilt, of deciphering the language of piecing like pages in an album. In 'The Patchwork Quilt,' an anonymous essay by a factory girl printed in *The Lowell Offering* in 1845, the author's quilt is described as 'a bound volume of hieroglyphics.' But only a certain kind of reader can decipher these female signifiers. To the 'uninterested observer,' the narrator declares, it looks like a 'miscellaneous collection of odd bits and ends,' but to me 'it is a precious reliquary of past treasure.' She locates the significance of the quilt in the individual piece, as if it were a textile scrapbook. The quilt's pieces, taken from the writer's childhood calico gowns, her dancing school dress, her fashionable young ladies' gowns, her mother's mourning dress, her brother's vest, are thus a record of the female life cycle from birth to death.[18]

During the same period the standard genre of American women's writing was the sketch or piece written for annuals,

Fig. 2. Mary Evans, Album Quilt, Baltimore

which became popular in the 1820s, and which often accepted only American materials.[19] While the sustained effort of a novel might be impossible for a woman whose day was shattered by constant interruption, the short narrative piece, quickly imagined and written, could be more easily completed. Harriet Beecher Stowe's literary career, for example, began in the 1840s with a series of pieces written for Christmas gift annuals, ladies albums, and religious periodicals. A 'piece' could be written in a day, and bring in $2.00 a page, and Stowe thought of her writing in terms of temporal blocks which could be set aside when financial pressure demanded. 'When the family accounts wouldn't add up,' Stowe recalled, 'Then I used to say to my faithful friend and factotum Anna . . . Now if you will keep the babies and attend to the things in the house for one day I'll write a piece and then we shall be out of the scrape.'[20] Working with the piece or story, Judith Fetterley has argued, freed American women from the pressures of the novel form, the one 'most highly programmed and most heavily burdened by thematic and formal conventions.' Short story forms allowed them more freedom, for 'in territory less clearly marked, the woman's story that these writers wished to tell could perhaps be better told.'[21] As the book and novel form became more important in the American market, women gathered their pieces together in books such as *Fern Leaves from Fanny's Portfolio*, a model Whitman would later borrow and masculinize in *Leaves of Grass*. At first simply gatherings of disparate pieces, these collections evolved in some cases into novels with narrative structures developed out of the piecing technique.

By the mid-nineteenth century, the most popular American pieced-quilt pattern was the Log Cabin (Figure 3). It begins with a central square, usually red to represent the hearth; and its compositional principle is the contrast between light and dark fabric. Each block is divided into two triangular sections, one section executed in light-colored fabrics, the other in dark. When the blocks are pieced together to make the quilt, dramatic visual effects and variations such as Light and Dark, Barn Raising, Courthouse Steps, and Streak of Lightning, can be created depending on the placement of the dark sections.

When she began to write *Uncle Tom's Cabin*, serialized in short

Fig. 3. Log Cabin Quilt

weekly installments, Stowe continued to think of her writing as the stitching together of scenes. Uncle Tom's log cabin, first described in the fourth chapter, is a metanarrative marker of the Log Cabin quilt, which in its symbolic deployment of boundaries, is particularly apt for Stowe's novel of the borders and conflicts between the states, the races, and the sexes. In the novel, Uncle Tom's cabin becomes the iconographic center upon which narrative blocks are built up. Each block of the novel is similarly centered on a house, and around it Stowe constructs large contrasts of black and white society. The novel does not obey the rules which dictate a unity of action leading to a denouement, but rather operates through the cumulative effect of blocks of event structured on a parallel design.

The coded formal considerations which lie behind Stowe's novels can also be seen in other women's literary genres of the American Renaissance, especially in the poetry of Emily Dickinson. Dickinson's famous use of the dash for punctuation makes her poems resemble patches, and emphasized the way she joined her poems together in stitched booklets called fascicles. Barton St Armand has suggested that while Dickinson's poetic sequences follow no traditional literary models, 'the art of quilting offers an alternative model for coherence and design.' St Armand argues that 'the discipline of the pieced quilt is as rigorous as that of the sonnet,' and that it provides us with a 'model or metaphor for Dickinson's art that is visual rather than verbal, yet that was also . . . firmly a part of her own culture.'[22] In the heyday of the female world of love and ritual, the woman's rite had serious meaning and dignity.

But by the 1860s, piecing had begun to seem old-fashioned, an overly-moralized exercise in feminine decorum. Louisa May Alcott's children's story, 'Patty's Patchwork,' which appeared as part of her series *Aunt Jo's Scrap-Bag*, shows how tendentiously the process was allegorized to teach feminine behavior. Ten-year-old Patty, visiting her Aunt Pen while her mother has a new baby, grows impatient with her patchwork, and flings the pieces into the air, declaring that 'something dreadful ought to be done to the woman who invented it.' But Aunt Pen has a different point of view. The quilt, she explains, is a 'calico diary,' a record of a female life composed of 'bright and dark bits . . . put together so that the whole is neat, pretty, and useful.' As a project, Patty sets out to make a 'moral bed-quilt' for her aunt to read and decipher, while she herself is learning to become a 'nice little comforter,' the epitome of female patience, perseverance, good nature, and industry. When the infant sister dies, Patty none the less goes on to finish the quilt, which Aunt Pen not only reads and interprets as a journal of her psychological maturity, but which she also inscribes—that is, writes upon—with verses and drawings that became a textual criticism of both the work and the life. Ironically, Aunt Pen is a figure for Alcott herself in her role as dispenser of moral pap to the young, a role she particularly loathed and deplored.[23]

By the *fin de siècle* changes in technology as well as in attitude influenced the ideology and aesthetics of the quilt. In 1870 Singer sold 127,833 sewing machines, which both transformed the time invested in quilts and could also be a 'boon, a challenge, and inspiration' to quilters: 'The machine's speed and its technical possibilities,' along with aniline dyes, the availability of commercial cotton batting, and other technological developments, acted as a stimulus to ambitious designs, especially since home-made quilts were no longer a domestic necessity.[24] Styles in quilts had changed as well. The 'calico patchwork quilt had become associated with the past and with backward rural regions,'[25] and the new trend was for the virtuoso techniques of the crazy quilt, which flourished during the 1880s and 1890s, and which reflected a more cosmopolitan awareness. The styles of crazy quilting, otherwise known as puzzle, mosaic, kaleidoscope, or Japanese patchwork, were inspired by oriental ceramics, textiles, and prints displayed at the Centennial Exposition of 1876 in Philadelphia. Embroidery, the use of silver and gold, and especially the 'jagged patterns in which irregular, triangular and circular patterns overlap' linked Eastern art with Western crazy-quilt design; the combination of many patterns was influenced by a form of Japanese textile called 'kirihame,' and alluded to the crazing in the ceramic glazes used in China and Japan.[26] Crazy quilts incorporated ribbons, commemorative images, photographs, masonic emblems and symbols of religious and sororal societies, and machine-made appliqués. Designs were embroidered on the individual pieces with silk floss, metallic thread, or ribbon; inscriptions were also handwritten, printed, or painted on the cloth.

By the 1880s quilting became identified with an older, dying generation, and especially with the temperance movement. In 1878 the Crusade quilt made by 3,000 Temperance women was shown at the national WCTU convention in Baltimore, testifying to 'women's patience in matters of detail' as well as their hatred of the Demon Rum.[27] To many New Women, such as the suffragist Abigail Duniway, bed-quilts were 'primary symbols of women's unpaid subjection.'[28] Filled with 'a profound horror of the woman's life,' the suffragist Inez Haynes Irwin vowed as a student at Radcliffe in the 1890s that she would 'never sew, embroider, crochet, knit;—especially would I never learn to cook.'[29] Parallels between piecing and women's writing were being more self-consciously, but often negatively or satirically, explored by American women writers, wishing to assert themselves as artists. The stories of the local colorists are often more explicitly about the frustrations of the woman writer struggling to create an appropriate form for her experience within a literary culture increasingly indifferent or even hostile to women's domestic lives. These are stories that represent women's culture as sour or comic, and that frequently end in its defeat.

We can see the generational contrast in two related stories about the quilting bee, Ann S. Stephens's 'The Quilting-Party,' written in the 1850s, and Mary Wilkins Freeman's 'A Quilting-Party in Our Village,' written in 1898. In Stephens's story, the 'quilting frolic' is an all-day festival of female bonding; a bevy of girls in silk dresses stitch merrily away on a rising-sun pattern, while they sing romantic ballads. At night there is a lavish feast, and the gentlemen arrive to dance in a room filled 'with a rich fruity smell left by dried apples and frost grapes.' In this story, women's culture is at its ripest and most romantic moment of plenitude, comfort, and harmony. In Freeman's story, however, the quilting bee takes place on the hottest day of a July heatwave. Wearing their oldest dresses, the quilters set grimly to their task, gossiping among themselves about the bride's age, ugliness, and stinginess. The supper is sickening in its vulgar abundance, and when the gentlemen arrive for a sweaty dance, the women nearly come to blows competing for their attention. The rising-sun pattern which they also quilt now seems like a mocking allusion to the setting sun of women's culture, and to the disappearance of its sustaining rituals.[30]

Similarly, in 'Mrs. Jones's Quilting' (1887) by Marietta Holley, the quilting bee for the minister's wedding is an occasion for ripping up other women's reputations rather than sisterly solidarity or communal piety:

> The quilt was made of different kinds of calico; all the wimmen round had pieced a block or two, and we took up a collection to get the batten and linin', and the cloth to set it together with, which was turkey red, and come to quilt it it looked well; we quilted it herrin' bone and a runnin' vine round the border. After the post-master was demoralized, the school-mistress tore to pieces, the party to Ripleys scandelized, Miss Brown's baby voted an unquestionable idiot, and the rest of the unrepresented neighborhood dealt with, Lucinder Dobbs spoke up, as sez she: 'I hope the minister will like the bed-quilt.'

When sisterhood has unravelled, it takes more than a quilt to stitch it up.

'Elizabeth Stock's One Story,' by Kate Chopin, takes up the issue of piecing and narrative design, originality, and appropriation. Elizabeth Stock is a postmistress in a secluded town who longs to be a writer, but is stymied by her inability to imagine a narrative both in conformity with a patriarchal literary tradition and in creative relation to it: 'Since I was a girl I always felt as if I would like to write stories,' but 'whenever I tried to think of one, it always turned out to be something that some one else had thought about before me.' Despairing of her efforts to imitate male traditions of plot that are 'original, entertaining, full of action, and goodness knows what all,' Elizabeth Stock turns to the female tradition which seems to offer a more authentic, but also less orderly plot: 'I . . . walked about days in a kind of a dream, twisting and twisting things in my mind just like I often saw old ladies twisting quilt patches to compose a design.' After her death of consumption at the age of thirty-eight, Elizabeth Stock's desk is found to contain 'scraps and bits of writing.' Out of this 'conglomerate mass,' the male editor, who may be either her nephew or her longtime suitor, assembles the only pages which seem to resemble a 'connected or consecutive narration.'

Finally her scraps and bits of writing, her stock of experience, will be edited, condensed, and preserved according to the consecutive and linear models of the male tradition, with all their craziness and originality lost.[31]

Following the introduction of Cubism to the United States at the New York Armory Show in 1913, the *New York Sun* published a cartoon of the crazy quilter as the 'original Cubist' (Figure 4). Dorothy Canfield Fisher's story 'The Bedquilt,' published in 1915, describes the design and creation of a magnificent quilt, a great work of art, by an elderly spinster. At the age of sixty-eight, Aunt Mehetabel suddenly conceives a great artistic project: a spectacular quilt, pieced according to a dramatically difficult and original design. As Fisher writes,

She never knew how her great idea came to her. Sometimes she thought she must have dreamed it, sometimes she even wondered reverently, in the phraseology of her weekly prayer-meeting, if it had been 'sent' to her. She never admitted to herself that she could have thought of it without other help. It was too great, too ambitious, too lofty a project for her humble mind to have conceived. . . . By some heaven-sent inspiration, she had invented a pattern beyond which no patchwork quilt could go.

As Aunt Mehetabel becomes absorbed in the 'orderly, complex, mosaic beauty' of her pieces, so too her family begins to give her recognition, praise, and a sewing table of her own. The story of Aunt Mehetabel's prize-winning quilt is obviously applicable to Fisher's own literary fantasies. A Columbia Ph.D. who had abandoned academia to become a writer, Fisher confessed her anxieties about 'the enormous difficulties of story telling, often too great for my powers to cope with.' Her ambitions to create an extraordinary new form for the novel are figured in the image of the ultimate quilt. The literary masterpiece Fisher feared was beyond her as a woman writer is transformed into the mastery of pieces in the great quilt; and her sense of alienation from narrative convention takes shape in the form of a new and inspired pattern, whose 'mosaic beauty' suggests both complex form and spiritual liberation.[32]

Yet modernism, despite its celebration of the fragment in Cubism and in such poetic epics as Eliot's *Waste Land*, disparaged and suppressed women's fragmented art. Women's poetry,

FIG. 4. "The Original Cubist," *New York Evening Sun*, 1913

Theodore Roethke observed, was largely 'the embroidery of trivial themes.' At the same time art historians, despite the impact of Cubism, belittled even the most basic elements of quilt practice as feminine, trivial, and dull. In one 1925 treatise, for example, the authors proclaimed that

the geometric style is primarily a feminine style. The geometric orna-ment seems more suited to the *domestic*, pedantically tidy, and at the same time superstitiously careful spirit of women than that of men. It is, considered purely aesthetically, a petty, lifeless, and despite all its inventiveness of colour, a strictly limited mode of art.[33]

Thus we should not be surprised that many serious women writers scorned needlework metaphors in an effort to dissociate their work from the insulting imputations of feminine triviality. Beginning her career in the mid-1920s, Genevieve Taggard disparaged much women's lyric poetry as 'literary needle-work.'[34]

Piecing and quilting underwent an aesthetic revival only after the women's movement in the late 1960s had encouraged a new interest in women's art. In 1971 the curator Jonathan Holstein broke through the barrier that had relegated quilts to the level of craft, when he organized a major exhibit on 'Abstract Designs in American Quilts' at the Whitney Museum in New York. Several American women artists such as Judy Chicago and Miriam Schapiro 'found new artistic inspiration and self-validation in women's needlework.'[35] Indeed, the pieced quilt has become one of the most central images of the new feminist art lexicon. As the art critic Lucy Lippard explains, 'Since the new wave of feminist art began around 1970, the quilt has become the prime visual metaphor for women's lives, for women's culture.'[36]

In feminist literary theories of a Female Aesthetic, piecing became the metaphor for the decentered structure of a woman's text. According to Rachel DuPlessis, a pure *écriture feminine* would be 'nonhierarchic . . . breaking hierarchical structures, making an even display of elements over the surface with no climactic place or moment, having the materials organized into many centers.' In the 'verbal quilt' of the feminist text, she argued, there is 'no subordination, no ranking.'[37] Radka Donnell-Vogt, a Bulgarian quilt-maker living in Boston who was featured in the documentary 'Quilts in Women's Lives,' wrote about piecing as a primal women's art form, related to the body, to mother–daughter bonding, to touch and texture, and to the intimacy of the bed and the home.[38] Using a vocabulary from psychoanalysis, feminism, and poststructuralism, Donnell-Vogt has been the Kristeva of quilting.[39]

Most of the women writers adopting quilt imagery in their poems and novels, however, were not quilt-makers themselves. In contemporary American women's writing, Elaine Hedges has written, the quilt often stands for an idealized past, 'a way of bridging the gulf between domestic and artistic life that until recently women writers have found such difficulty in negotiating.' Textile imagery, 'especially imagery associated with quilts, the piecing together of salvaged fragments to create a new pattern of connections, and integrated whole . . . provides the elements . . . for a new transformative vision.'[40] This imagery is nostalgic and romantic. Marge Piercy's 'Looking at Quilts' describes

> Pieced quilts, patchwork from best gowns,
> winter woolens, linens, blankets, worked jigsaw
> of the memories of braided lives, precious
> scraps: women were buried but their clothing wore on.

Joyce Carol Oates's poem 'Celestial Timepiece' sees quilts as women's maps and history, 'their lives recorded in cloth.' In Adrienne Rich's poem 'Natural Resources,' the humble 'things by women saved' become

> scraps, turned into patchwork,
> doll-gowns, clean white rags
> for stanching blood
> the bride's tea-yellow handkerchief,
> that have the power to 'reconstitute the world.'

In 'Transcendental Etude' the 'bits of yarn, calico, and velvet scraps' along with objects from the natural world, such as 'small rainbow-colored shells,' 'skeins of milkweed,' and 'the dry darkbrown lace of seaweed,' become the substance of what Rich calls 'a whole new poetry beginning here,' a poetry as much 'whole' as 'new,' that is, that makes an effort to re-member, reconstruct, and remake. The imagery of common threads in

American women's quilts offers Rich a model for her 'dream of a common language' of women.

At the same time, the 'common language' of American women's quilting was being challenged by the rediscovery of black women's quilts, which were displayed in highly successful museum exhibits in Dallas, San Francisco, New York, Mississippi, and Washington DC. Houston and Charlotte Baker have argued that the patchwork quilt is 'a trope for understanding black women's creativity in the United States.' Piecing represents 'a signal instance of a patterned wholeness in the African diaspora.'[41] As the Bakers conclude,

In order to comprehend the transient nature of all wholes, one must first become accustomed to living and working with fragments. . . . Finally it is the 'self,' or a version of humanness that one calls the Afro-American self, that must, in fact, be crafted from fragments on the basis of wisdom gained from preceding generations.[42]

The patchwork quilt appealed not only to black women artists but also to a new generation of African-American intellectuals, artists, and critics seeking powerful and moving symbols of racial identity. In the context of the Black Aesthetic movement, blues and jazz had been posited as the definitive Afro-American art forms; by the late 1970s scholars began to argue that quilts too incorporated the improvisational techniques important to African-American music. In 1979 Maude Wahlman and John Scully organized an exhibition of 'Black Quilters' which emphasized analogies between piecing and the blues. Elements of spontaneity and novelty in the work of twentieth-century black quilt-makers were cited as crucial to 'Afro-Atlantic aesthetics,' just as 'fresh' was the 'all-purpose encomium on the streets of black and Puerto Rican New York.'[43]

For Alice Walker, piecing and quilting have come to represent both the aesthetic heritage of Afro-American women, and the model for what she calls a 'womanist,' or black feminist, writing of reconciliation and connection. In her essay 'In Search of Our Mothers' Gardens,' Walker identified the quilt as a major form of creative expression for black women in the South. 'In the Smithsonian Institution in Washington, D.C.,' Walker writes, there hangs a quilt unlike another in the world. In fanciful, inspired, and yet simple and identifiable figures, it portrays the story of the Crucifixion . . . Though it follows no known pattern of quiltmaking, and though it is made of bits and pieces of worthless rags, it is obviously the work of a person of powerful imagination and deep spiritual feeling. Below this quilt I saw a note that says it was made by 'an anonymous Black woman in Alabama a hundred years ago.'

The quilt Walker is describing from memory is in fact one of two extant narrative quilts by Harriet Powers (1836–1911), born a slave in Georgia. The Powers quilt at the Smithsonian illustrates Bible stories, while the one in the Boston Museum of Fine Arts mingles Bible tales with folklore and astronomical events such as shooting stars and meteor showers.[44] For Walker, genuine imagination and feeling can be recognized without the legitimacy conferred by the labels of 'art' or the approval of museums. Paradoxically this heritage survives because it has been preserved in museums; but it can be a living art only if it is practiced.

The theme of Walker's quilt aesthetic is most explicitly presented in her early story 'Everyday Use.' Like much of her work, it uses a contrast between two sisters to get at the meaning of the concept of 'heritage': a privileged one who escapes from Southern black culture, and a suffering one who stays or is left behind. The younger daughter, Maggie, has stayed at home since she was horribly scarred in a house fire ten years before. Dee is the bright and confident sister, the one with 'faultfinding power.' Dee has learned fast how to produce herself. 'At sixteen she had a style of her own: and knew what style was.' Now having chosen the style of radical black nationalism, her name changed to 'Wangero,' and spouting Swahili, Dee returns to claim her heritage from her mother in the form of 'folk art': the worn benches made by her father, the butter churn whittled by an uncle, and especially the quilts pieced by her grandmother. 'Maggie can't appreciate these quilts,' Dee exclaims. 'She'd probably be backward enough to put them to everyday use.' Walker thus establishes a contrast between 'everyday use' and 'institutional theories of aesthetics.'[45] In a moment of epiphanic insight, the mother, who has always been intimidated by Dee's intelligence and sophistication, decides to give the quilts to Maggie. 'She can always make some more,' the mother responds. 'Maggie knows how to quilt.' Maggie cannot speak glibly about her 'heritage' or about 'priceless' artifacts, but unlike Dee, she understands the quilt as a process rather than as a commodity; she can read its meaning in a way Dee never will, because she knows the contexts of its pieces, and loves the women who have made it. The meaning of an aesthetic heritage, according to Walker's story, lies in continual renewal rather than in the rhetoric of nostalgia or appreciation. In writing *The Color Purple*, Walker herself took up quilt-making as well as using it as a central metaphor in the novel.

The issues of cultural heritage, female creativity, and order are differently explored in Bobbie Ann Mason's 'Love Life,' which appeared in the 29 October 1984 *New Yorker*, and is the title story of her recent collection. Like Walker, Mason is a Southern writer, from western Kentucky, a region in which most of her powerful and disturbing fiction is set. But for Mason, the legacies of Southern women's culture are not simply healing; they also have a darker side that speaks of secrecy and repression, of women's self-destructive commemoration of the patriarchal traditions in which their own freedoms had been thwarted, and of commodification within a sentimentalizing ideology of American womanhood.

In 'Love Life,' two unmarried women represent two generations of women's culture—Aunt Opal, the retired schoolteacher, the old woman who is the caretaker of tradition; and her niece Jenny, the New Woman of the 1980s, whose casual love affairs and backpack existence suggest the dissolution of the female world and the loss of its cultural traditions. Returning to Kentucky, Jenny pleads with Opal to see the family's celebrated but secret and hidden burial quilt. Mason here alludes to a regional quilt genre which flourished in nineteenth-century Kentucky, as a version of the funeral-quilt tradition. Funeral quilts were rituals of mourning in which family members and friends, and sometimes even the dying person, worked together in making a memorial quilt out of fragments recalling the person's life. Burial quilts, however, were more like records of mortality. The best-known surviving example is Elizabeth Roseberry Mitchell's Kentucky Coffin Quilt, done in Lewis County in 1839, and now in the collection of the Kentucky Historical Society (Figure 5).

When a member of Mitchell's family died, she would remove a labelled coffin from the border and place it within the graveyard depicted in the center of the quilt.

Aunt Opal's burial quilt is made of dark pieced blocks, each appliquéd with a named and dated tombstone. Its 'shape is irregular, a rectangle with a clumsy foot sticking out from one corner. The quilt is knotted with yarn, and the edging is open, for more blocks to be added.' According to family legend, a block is added whenever someone dies; the quilt stops when the family name stops, so 'the last old maids finish the quilt.' Who will be the last old maid? Ironically, Aunt Opal has rejected the cultural roles of the past. To her, the quilts mean only 'a lot of desperate old women ruining their eyes.' The burial quilt is a burden, 'ugly as homemade sin,' a depressing reminder of failure, loneliness, and servitude. Opal plans to take up aerobic dancing, to be modern; meanwhile she spends all her time watching MTV. 'Did Jenny come home just to hunt up that old rag?' she thinks about the burial quilt. Jenny, however, plans to learn how to quilt. She will use the burial quilt to stitch herself back into history, to create her context.

Using the familiar nineteenth-century women's narrative model of an emotional interaction between aunt and niece, Mason brings us back, through Aunt Opal's Scrap Bag, to a sense of continuity and renewal in an American female literary and cultural tradition. But the story also suggests that these traditions may be burdens rather than treasures of the past, and that there may be something morbid, self-deceptive, and even self-destructive in our feminist efforts to reclaim them. Is it time to bury the burial quilt rather than to praise it?

The stories by Walker and Mason both reflect the commodification of quilts in the 1970s, and the popularity that made them available as cultural metaphors to many different groups. In 1976 the celebration of the Bicentennial led to a regendering of the quilt aesthetic in relation to American identity. Every state commissioned a Bicentennial quilt, and many towns and communities made their own album quilts with patches by schoolchildren, senior citizens, women's groups, and ethnic groups. By 1984 a survey indicated that fourteen million Americans had made, bought, sold, or had something to do with a quilt.

Fɪɢ. 5. Elizabeth Roseberry Mitchell Graveyard Quilt, Lewis County, Kentucky, 1839

The bonding activities of quilting had great appeal to Americans wishing to come together after the traumas of Watergate and Vietnam. The 1980s, as Annette Kolodny points out, 'were to be the decade of healing and consolidation . . . three presidents in a row—Gerald Ford, Jimmy Carter, and Ronald Reagan—called upon the country to bind up its wounds, heal its divisions, and commit itself anew to shared traditions.'[46] Both communal quilts and collective literary histories seemed to represent the endurance of American traditions.

But the 1980s were also the decade which questioned the monolithic concepts of American exceptionalism. As Sacvan Bercovich notes,

now it is said, in reaction against those who speak of an American literature or a national culture, that this country is sheer heterogeneity. The ruling elite has an American ideology; the people have their own patchwork-quilt (rather than melting-pot) American multifariousness: 'America' is—many forms of ethnicity, many patterns of thought, many ways of life, many cultures, many American literatures.[47]

The melting-pot, with its associations of alchemy, industry, and assimilation, had 'shaped American discourse on immigration and ethnicity' for most of the twentieth century. Its major literary source was Israel Zangwill's 1909 melodrama *The Melting-Pot*, which proclaimed, 'America is God's crucible, the great Melting Pot where all the races of Europe are melting and reforming.' The Ford Motor Company dramatized this image too in the graduation ceremonies for their English School, in which male factory workers in their ragged native garb marched into a huge caldron on the company athletic field, merging on the other side in natty American suits waving little American flags. Sometimes plant managers stirred the giant pot with huge ladles, while the Ford band played patriotic songs.[48]

But since World War II, the image of the melting-pot had carried unpleasant associations, not only the macabre echoes of cannibalism and the crematorium, but also distasteful connotations of processed identical robots. Americans needed a new metaphor of national identity, one that acknowledged ethnic difference, heterogeneity, and multiplicity, that incorporated contemporary concerns for gender, race, and class.

Thus the patchwork quilt came to replace the melting-pot as the central metaphor of American cultural identity. In a very unusual pattern, it transcended the stigma of its sources in women's culture and has been remade as a universal sign of American identity. Like other national symbols, the quilt can be adopted and transformed by many groups. Thus, while on the one hand quilts have come to signify a kinder, gentler upper-class Republican America as they appear in fashions by Ralph Lauren, on the cover of the Horchow catalog, and on the boxes of high-fiber cereals, their potential for a more radical political symbolism has also been recognized. It was most fully expressed in Jesse Jackson's speech before the Democratic National Convention in Atlanta in July 1988, when he called for a Democratic 'quilt of unity'.

America is not a blanket woven from one thread, one color, one cloth. When I was a child growing up in Greenville, South Carolina, and grandmomma could not afford a blanket, . . . she took pieces of old cloth—patches—wool, silk, gaberdeen, crockersack—only patches, barely good enough to wipe off your shoes with. But they didn't stay that way very long. With sturdy hands and strong cord, she sewed them together into a quilt, a thing of beauty and power and culture. Now, Democrats, we must build such a quilt.

Jackson's unity quilt called for patches from farmers, workers, women, students, Blacks, Hispanics, gays and lesbians, conservatives and progressives, 'bound by a common thread' in a great multicolored quilt of the American people.[49]

In a tragic irony Jackson had not anticipated, the phrase *Common Threads* has become best known as the title of a documentary about the NAMES Project, usually called the AIDS Quilt, which has become the material embodiment of Jackson's metaphor. In 1987 the San Francisco gay activist Cleve Jones had the vision of a 'unifying quilt in memory of those who had died of AIDS.' As Jones has explained, he saw the quilt both as a memorial which demonstrated the magnitude of the epidemic, and 'a way for survivors to work through their grief in a positive, creative way. Quilts represent coziness, humanity, and warmth.'[50] The national monument to the holocaust of AIDS, then, like the Vietnam War Memorial, would not be an anonymous abstraction, but a space that would allow personal mourning and remembrance. All the names of the dead would be included, in quilt blocks made by their friends, families, and lovers. Working out of a store on Market Street in the Castro, San Francisco's gay neighborhood, NAMES Project volunteers raised money, sewed, and received quilt panels sent to them by grieving friends of those who had died. In many respects, the AIDS Quilt draws on the traditions and rituals of burial quilts developed in women's culture.

But the AIDS Quilt is also very different from those pieced by American women, and its differences suggest the transition from private to public symbols, from women's culture to American culture, from feminine imagery to masculine imagery, and from separate spheres to common threads. First of all, there is its enormous scale. Quilt panels are each three by six feet long, and thus about twenty-five times as large as a standard quilt block. By October 1987 there were 1,920 panels that had been attached with grommets to white fabric walkways. When it was first displayed on the Mall of the Capitol in Washington, the quilt, according to news releases, covered an area the size of 'two football fields' and weighed 6,890 pounds. By 1988, as the AIDS Quilt was exhibited in twenty-five major American cities, usually in parks or huge convention halls, it had to be lifted by cranes, and was transported from city to city by an air cargo company called the Flying Tigers. By fall 1989 it weighed thirteen tons, and included 11,000 panels (Figure 6). Now it is so huge that it can no longer be shown in its entirety.

Secondly, the quilt panels themselves are not pieced. They are made out of every conceivable material from baby clothes to black leather and gold lamé, and are 'laden with mementos, possessions, and final farewells'—medals, locks of hair, jock straps, toys, messages.[51] Most are cloth rectangles to which shapes have been appliquéd or glued; they are painted and written on with crayons and marking pens, often only with names of the dead, but also with phrases and slogans. In contrast to traditional burial quilts, which take several months to make, and become part of the work of grieving, the AIDS Quilt blocks are so simply designed and crudely made that they are very rapidly completed, over periods ranging from a few hours to a few weeks at most.

Fig. 6. The AIDS Quilt exhibited in Washington, across from the White House, in October 1989

Folklorists have debated whether the AIDS Quilt belongs to the authentic tradition of women's quilt-making, or whether it reflects the immensity and distance more characteristic of masculine monuments. The AIDS Quilt cannot be treasured, stroked, held, used to solace sleep. It is not an 'intimate object.'[52] Its attendant metaphors of football, sales conventions, and cargo planes evoke a normative American masculinity, perhaps in a deliberate effort to counter the stigma of homosexuality associated with AIDS. To some, the promotional rhetoric of the Project seems commercial; to others, sentimental.

Yet the AIDS Quilt has clearly added its own symbols, rituals, and images to the tradition, and must be read in its own new terms. Its pieces are a solace for grief not because they are made privately in a slow process, but because they link individual mourning to a national loss. The funerary elements seen as morbid in stories like Mason's 'Love Life' take on different meanings in the NAMES Project as making the quilt block became for some a way of preparing for death, a farewell letter and last testament. The large blocks are the size of coffins, and represent the missing graves of AIDS, like a national cemetery of those fallen in war. This symbolism is especially important for the San Franciscans who began the Project, since most of the people who have died there of AIDS

have no grave or headstones; they are cremated and their ashes are scattered over the mountains or in San Francisco Bay. Even those who are buried disappear—to the cemetery town of Colma, just to our south—because an old law forbids graveyards within the city limits. After the memorial service, the scattering of ashes, and the garage sale, there isn't much left.[53]

The scale and visibility of the quilt testifies to remembrance of lost lives too easily forgotten (Figure 7).

Moreover, the AIDS Quilt has evolved its own powerful rituals and ceremonies: the blessing and unfolding of the huge segment of the quilt by volunteers dressed in white; the reading aloud of the names in each segment by the bereaved. What is perhaps most moving and impressive about this project initiated within the gay community is its refusal to privilege the loss of any individual or group over another. Love and grief are the common

Fig. 7. Mourners at the AIDS Quilt

threads that bind mothers, fathers, wives, lovers; here hemophiliac children, gay men, straight women, the famous and the obscure, the addicted and the caretakers, are equally remembered and mourned. The British AIDS theorist Simon Watney is one of many witnesses whose initial cynicism about the quilt was overcome by its emotional power:

I was skeptical about it before I saw it. Falling back on a rationalist perspective, I thought, Oh, God, this is so sentimental. But when I finally saw it, despite the ghastly New Age music booming overhead, it was a completely overwhelming experience. To have this social map of America. To have Liberace alongside Baby Doe, to have Michel Foucault alongside five gay New York cops. In many ways it's a more accurate map of America than any other I've ever seen.[54]

What is important about the AIDS Quilt is not its 'authenticity' in folklore terms, or its fidelity to the feminine traditions of piecing. In it we see the continued vitality of the quilt metaphor, its powers of change and renewal, and its potential to unify and to heal. Like the literary traditions that have grown out of American women's culture, the quilt tradition created and nurtured by American women has never been more meaningful, even as it ceases forever to belong to us alone.

Are there still common threads that bind American women's writing, despite the changes which have opened it to the world? If American women are 'unequal sisters' divided by the multicultural force fields of racial, regional, religious, economic, and erotic difference, do we still share a conversation and a correspondence?[55]

Surely one element which unites us and which permeates our literature and our criticism is the yearning for community and continuity, for the bonds of even an unequal sisterhood. To a striking degree, American women writers have rejected the Oedipal metaphors of murderous 'originality' set out as literary paradigms in Harold Bloom's *Anxiety of Influence*; the patricidal struggle defined by Bloom and exemplified in the careers of male American writers, has no matricidal equivalent, no echo of denial, parody, exile. Instead, Alice Walker proclaims, 'each writer writes the missing parts to the other writer's story.'[56] Similarly, Joyce Carol Oates has said,

The living are no more in competition with the dead than they are with the living. . . . All of us who write work out of a conviction that we are participating in some sort of communal activity. Whether my role is writing, or reading and responding, might not be very important. . . . By honoring one another's creation, we honor something that deeply connects us all and goes beyond us.[57]

Virginia Woolf's image of a room of one's own, so enabling for women modernists in England seeking privacy and autonomy, seems somehow isolated and remote for American women writers, especially black writers, today. In the writer's need to reach her audience, the room of one's own, writes Hortense Spillers, 'explodes its four walls to embrace the classroom, the library . . . conferences, the lecture platform, the television talk show, the publishing house, the "best seller," and collections of critical essays.'[58] Moreover, as the work of Alice Walker suggests, 'Art, and the thought and sense of beauty in which it is based, is the province not only of those with a room of their own, or of those in libraries, universities, and literary Renaissances.' The power of creating also belongs to those who 'work in kitchens and factories, nurture children and adorn homes, sweep streets or harvest crops, type in offices or manage them.'[59]

To recognize that the tradition of American women's writing is exploding, multi-cultural, contradictory, and dispersed is yet not to abandon the critical effort to piece it together, not into a monument, but into a literary quilt that offers a new map of a changing America, an America whose literature and culture must be replotted and remapped. Indeed, that work of exploration and assembly must be carried on, for until feminist critics took up their cause, few American women writers, black or white, were seen as part of the national literary landscape at all. The pages of the ongoing history of women's writing to which this book is a contribution will have to give up the dream of a common language and learn to understand and respect each sister's choice; but we can still choose to read American women's stories and to ask American questions about their past and future.

NOTES

❧

CHAPTER I

1. This novel and several others are discussed in David Reynolds's original and provocative *Beneath the American Renaissance* (New York: Alfred A. Knopf, 1988), 347.

2. Bronson Alcott, *Journals* (1870), quoted in Joel Myerson, '"Our Children Are Our Best Work": Bronson and Louisa May Alcott,' in Madeleine Stern (ed.), *Critical Essays on Louisa May Alcott* (Boston: G. K. Hall, 1984), 263.

3. *The Selected Letters of William Carlos Williams*, ed. John C. Thirlwell (New York: McDowell Oblensky, Inc., 1957), 69; quoted in Albert Gelpi, *The Tenth Muse* (Cambridge, Mass.: Harvard University Press, 1975), 9.

4. Kenneth W. Warren, 'Delimiting America: The Legacy of Du Bois,' *American Literary History*, 1 (1988), 186.

5. *Afro-American Poetics: Revisions of Harlem and the Black Aesthetic* (Madison: University of Wisconsin Press, 1988), 11–12.

6. 'American Things/Literary Things: The Problem of American Literary History,' *American Literature*, 57 (1985), 471.

7. Emory Elliott, 'Introduction,' *Columbia Literary History of the United States*, ed. Emory Elliott (New York: Columbia University Press, 1988), xvii.

8. Emory Elliott, quoted in Annette Kolodny, 'The Integrity of Memory: Creating a New Literary History of the United States,' *American Literature*, 57 (May 1985), 294.

9. Alice Jardine and Anne M. Menke, 'Exploding the Issue: "French" "Women" "Writers" and "the Canon"? Fourteen Interviews,' *Yale French Studies*, No. 75 (1988), 229–58. Ironically, Jardine and Menke were so shocked by the French women writers' attitudes that they had to admit to themselves that they were more 'American' than they had realized. Furthermore, despite their protestations to the contrary, the French women writers revealed more concern with these issues than they wished to admit.

10. 'Feminist Literary Criticism in America and England,' in Moira Monteith (ed.), *Women's Writing* (Brighton, Sussex: Harvester, 1986), 90.

11. 'Introducing Feminism,' *Paragraph*, 8 (Oct. 1986), 100–1.
12. *Kanthapura* (New York: New Directions, 1938), vii.
13. For an account of the language issues in post-colonial literature, see Bill Ashcroft, Gareth Griffiths, and Helen Tiffin, *The Empire Writes Back* (London: Routledge, 1989), 38–77.
14. See 'Criticism in the Jungle,' in *Black Literature and Literary Theory*, ed. Henry Louis Gates, Jr. (New York: Methuen, 1984), 4; Rámon Saldívar, 'Ideologies of Self: Chicano Autobiography,' *Diacritics*, 15 (Fall 1985), 25–34; and Naomi Schor, *Men in Feminism*, ed. Paul Smith and Alice Jardine (New York: Methuen, 1988), 110.
15. Kimberley W. Benston, 'I yam what I am: The topos of (un)naming in Afro-American Literature,' in Gates (ed.), *Black Literature and Literary Theory*, 153.
16. 'Unhiding the Hidden: Recent Canadian Fiction,' *Journal of Canadian Fiction*, 3 (1974), 43.
17. On the veil in women's writing, see Sandra M. Gilbert and Susan Gubar, *The Madwoman in the Attic* (New Haven, Conn.: Yale University Press, 1979), 468–77; on the veil in Afro-American literature, see Houston A. Baker, Jr., *Modernism and the Harlem Renaissance* (Chicago: University of Chicago Press, 1987), 51–2, 57. On the black 'redeemer-poet,' see Henry Louis Gates, Jr., *The Signifying Monkey: A Theory of Afro-American Literary Criticism* (New York: Oxford University Press, 1988), 174–5.
18. 'The Third Space,' in Jonathan Rutherford (ed.), *Identity: Community, Culture, Difference* (London: Lawrence & Wishart, 1990), 210.
19. Wendy Martin, *An American Triptych* (Chapel Hill: University of North Carolina Press, 1984), 20.
20. Ashcroft, Griffiths, and Tiffin, *The Empire Writes Back*, 5.
21. *Works of the Rev. Sydney Smith* (Boston: Phillips, Sampson & Co., 1856), 141.
22. Quoted in Gelpi, *The Tenth Muse*, 57.
23. Quoted in Edmund Wilson, 'Harriet Beecher Stowe,' in Elizabeth Ammons (ed.), *Critical Essays on Harriet Beecher Stowe* (Boston: G. K. Hall, 1980), 120.
24. Caroline Kirkland, 'Novels and Novelists,' *North American Review*, 86 (1853), 111–12.
25. Carroll Smith-Rosenberg's influential essay, 'The Female World of Love and Ritual: Relations between Women in Nineteenth-Century America,' appeared in the first issue of the feminist journal *Signs*, 1 (1975), 1–30. It has been reprinted as part of her book *Disorderly Conduct: Visions of Gender in Victorian America* (New York: Knopf, 1985).
26. 'Separate Spheres, Female Worlds, Woman's Place: The Rhetoric of Women's History,' *Journal of American History*, 75 (June 1988), 14–15.

27. 'Passionlessness: An Interpretation of Victorian Sexual Ideology, 1790–1850,' *Signs*, 4 (1978), 233.

28. Smith-Rosenberg, *Disorderly Conduct*, 69.

29. Sedgwick, quoted in Cott, 'Passionlessness,' 233.

30. Kerber, 'Separate Spheres,' 15.

31. 'Rewriting the Scribbling Women,' *Legacy*, 2 (Fall 1985), 11.

32. See Nancy R. Cott, *The Bonds of Womanhood: 'Woman's Sphere' in New England, 1780–1835* (New Haven, Conn.: Yale University Press, 1977) and Mary P. Ryan, *The Empire of the Mother: American Writing about Domesticity* (New York: Haworth Press, 1982).

33. Harriet Beecher Stowe, quoted in Mary Kelley, *Private Woman, Public Stage: Literary Domesticity in Nineteenth-Century America* (New York: Oxford University Press, 1984), 249.

34. *Womanhood in America from Colonial Times to the Present* (New York: Franklin Watts, 1983), 144.

35. Harriet Beecher Stowe, *My Wife and I*, quoted in Kelley, *Private Woman, Public Stage*, 327.

36. *Woman's Fiction* (Ithaca, NY: Cornell University Press, 1978), 32.

37. The breakdown in women's culture at the turn of the century has been the subject of extensive debate by feminist social historians. See Carroll Smith-Rosenberg and Ellen DuBois in 'Politics and Culture in Women's History: A Symposium,' *Feminist Studies*, 6 (1980); Nancy Sahli, 'Smashing: Women's Relationships before the Fall,' *Chrysalis*, 8 (1979), 17–27; Lillian Faderman, *Surpassing the Love of Men: Romantic Friendships and Love between Women from the Renaissance to the Present* (New York: Morrow, 1981); and Martha Vicinus, 'Sexuality and Power: A Review of Current Work on the History of Sexuality,' *Feminist Studies*, 8 (1982), 133–56.

38. *A History of American Literature, 1607–1765* (2 vols., 1878; repr. Williamstown, Mass.: Corner House Publishers, 1973), ii. 318–19.

39. Charlotte Perkins Gilman, *The Man-Made World* (New York: Charlton Co., 1911), 105.

40. For two different accounts of *The Wide, Wide World*, see Baym, *Woman's Fiction*, 143–50, and Jane Tompkins's introduction to the Feminist Press edition. Joyce Carol Oates introduced me to Warner's *Diana*.

41. *New England Local Color Literature: A Woman's Tradition* (New York: Frederick Ungar, 1983), 119.

42. Paul Lauter, 'Race and Gender in the Shaping of the American Literary Canon,' *Feminist Studies*, 9 (1983), 449.

43. Robert Stepto, 'Afro-American Literature,' in Elliott (ed.), *Columbia Literary History of the United States*, 786.

44. 'The Integrity of Memory,' 293.

45. 'Ideology in American Literary History,' *Critical Inquiry*, 12 (Summer 1986), 652.

46. 'Minority Discourse and the Pitfalls of Canon Formation,' *Yale Journal of Criticism*, 1 (1988), 200.

47. 'Ideology in American Literary History,' 637.

48. Emory Elliott, 'Preface,' *Columbia Literary History of the United States*, xi–xii.

49. 'The Extra,' *American Literature*, 57 (May 1985), 293, 306, 307.

50. The terms here are adapted from Hazel V. Carby, *Reconstructing Womanhood: The Emergence of the Afro-American Woman Novelist* (Oxford: Oxford University Press, 1987), 16–19.

51. These terms are from Denise Riley, *'Am I That Name?' Feminism and the Category of 'Women' in History* (Minneapolis: University of Minnesota Press, 1988).

52. I am indebted to Professor Rámon Saldívar of the University of Texas at Austin for this information.

53. Joe David Bellamy, 'The Dark Lady of American Letters,' *Atlantic Monthly*, 22 (Feb. 1972), 65.

54. Walter Clemons, 'Joyce Carol Oates: Love and Violence,' *Newsweek*, 11 Dec. 1972, 72–7.

55. Alice Walker, *In Search of Our Mothers' Gardens* (New York: Harcourt Brace Jovanovich, 1983), xii.

CHAPTER 2

1. Edwin McDowell, 'Women at PEN Caucus Demand a Greater Role,' *New York Times*, 17 Jan. 1986.

2. *Women Writers at Work: The Paris Review Interviews*, ed. George Plimpton (Harmondsworth: Penguin, 1989), 216.

3. Michiko Kakutani, citing Elizabeth Hardwick, 'Mary McCarthy, 77, is Dead; Novelist, Memoirist and Critic,' *New York Times*, 26 Oct. 1989.

4. Susan P. Conrad, *Perish the Thought: Intellectual Women in Romantic America 1830–1860* (New York: Oxford University Press, 1976), 48.

5. Ibid. 50.

6. 'Margaret Fuller, 1810–1850,' *American Writers* (New York: Charles Scribners and Sons, 1986), 282.

7. *Margaret Fuller: American Romantic* (New York: Doubleday, 1963); quoted in Marie Urbanski, *Margaret Fuller's Woman in the Nineteenth Century* (Westport, Conn.: Greenwood Press, 1980), 38.

8. See Philip Rahv, 'The Dark Lady of Salem,' in *The Blithedale Romance*, Norton Critical Edition (New York: Norton, 1978), 337.

9. *The Letters of Margaret Fuller*, ed. Robert N. Hudspeth (Ithaca, NY: Cornell University Press, 1984), iii. 199 n. 4.

10. Margaret Fuller, *Woman in the Nineteenth Century* (New York: W. W. Norton, 1971), 38–43. While she also wrote about herself as Minerva and Mariana, Fuller's Miranda persona was well known to her

contemporaries. James Russell Lowell caricatured Fuller as 'Miranda' in his *Fable for Critics*: 'Miranda meanwhile has succeeded in driving | Up into a corner, in spite of their striving, | A small flock of terrified victims, and there | with an I-turn-the-crank-of-the-universe air, | And a tone which, at least to *my* fancy appears | Not so much to be entering as boxing your ears | Is unfolding a tale of herself, I surmise, | For 'tis dotted as thick as a peacock's with I's.'

11. George Lamming, *Pleasures of Exile* (London: Michael Joseph, 1960); Octave Mannoni, *Psychologie de la colonisation* (Paris: Seuil, 1950); Philip Mason, *Prospero's Magic: Some Thoughts on Class and Race* (London: Oxford University Press, 1962); Aimé Césaire, *Une Tempête* (Paris: Seuil, 1969); Roberto Fernandez Retamer, 'Caliban: Notes Towards a Discussion of Culture in Our Americas,' in *Caliban and Other Essays* (Minneapolis: University of Minnesota Press, 1989); and Max Dorsinville, *Caliban without Prospero: Quebec and Black Literature* (Erin, Ont.: Press Porcepic, 1974). See e.g. Charlotte H. Bruner, 'The Meaning of Caliban in Black Literature Today,' *Comparative Literature Studies*, 13 (Sept. 1976), 240–53; Thomas A. Hale, 'Sur *Une Tempête* d'Aimé Césaire,' *Études Litteraires*, 6 (1973), 21–34; Marta E. Sanchez, 'Caliban: The New Latin-American Protagonist of *The Tempest*,' *Diacritics*, 6 (Spring 1976), 54–61; Alden T. Vaughan, 'Shakespeare's Indian: The Americanization of Caliban,' *Shakespeare Quarterly*, Summer 1988, 137–53; Alden T. Vaughan, 'Caliban in the "Third World",' *Massachusetts Review*, 29 (Summer 1988), 289–313. Thanks to Gayle Wald and Michael Cadden for their suggestions about this material.

12. 'Caribbean and African Appropriations of *The Tempest*,' *Critical Inquiry*, 13 (Spring 1987), 538.

13. See Trevor R. Griffiths, '"This Island's Mine": Caliban and Colonialism,' *Yearbook of English Studies*, 13 (1983), 159–80.

14. 'Caliban's Triple Play,' *Critical Inquiry*, 13 (Autumn 1986), 182–96.

15. 'Modernism and the Harlem Renaissance,' *American Quarterly*, 39 (Spring 1987), 93.

16. Michael Cadden, 'Shakespeare and Colonialism,' paper presented at the American Shakespeare Association, Spring 1989.

17. 'Caribbean and African Appropriations of *The Tempest*,' 577. An exception to the pattern is the American expatriate novelist Rachel Ingall's sad fable, *Mrs. Caliban* (London: Faber and Faber, 1983).

18. See Barbara Kiefer Lewalski, 'English Literature at the American Moment,' in Elliott (ed.), *Columbia Literary History of the United States*, 25.

19. *The Machine in the Garden* (New York: Oxford University Press, 1964), 72.

20. Raleigh and Hale in Vaughan, 'Shakespeare's Indian,' 141.

21. *Shakespeare's Ghost Writers* (New York: Routledge, 1989), 26.

22. 'Prospero's Wife,' *Representations*, 8 (Fall 1984), 18–19.

23. 'The Genius of Margaret Fuller,' *New York Review of Books*, 10 Apr. 1986, 14.

24. *On Lies, Secrets, and Silence* (New York: W. W. Norton, 1979), 200.

25. Bell Gale Chevigny, *The Woman and the Myth: Margaret Fuller's Life and Writings* (New York: The Feminist Press, 1976), 39.

26. Ibid. 39.

27. Ibid. 42.

28. Quoted in Thomas Wentworth Higginson, *Margaret Fuller Ossoli* (Boston: Houghton Mifflin, 1884), 18.

29. Chevigny, *Woman and the Myth*, 42.

30. Laurence Buell, *Literary Transcendentalism: Style and Vision in the American Renaissance* (Ithaca, NY: Cornell University Press, 1973), 77.

31. Hardwick, *New York Review of Books*, 10 Apr. 1986, 17.

32. Quoted in Urbanski, *Margaret Fuller's Woman in the Nineteenth Century*, 7.

33. *Memoirs of Margaret Fuller Ossoli*, ed. R. W. Emerson, W. H. Channing, and J. F. Clarke (1884), i. 202–3, quoted in Chevigny, *Woman and the Myth*, 91.

34. Quoted in David Leverenz, 'The Politics of Emerson's Man-Making Words,' *PMLA* 101 (Jan. 1986), 39.

35. *Letters of Ralph Waldo Emerson*, ed. Ralph C. Rusk (New York: Columbia University Press, 1939), ii.353.

36. *Woman's Journal*, 15 July 1882, 223.

37. Fuller, quoted in Chevigny, *Woman and the Myth*, 63.

38. See Kolodny, 'The Problem of Persuasion in a Culture of Coercion.' Thanks to Annette Kolodny for sharing this work in progress.

39. See Jeffrey Steele, *The Representation of the Self in the American Renaissance* (Chapel Hill: University of North Carolina Press, 1987), 106 ff.

40. 'The Call of Eurydice: Mourning and Intertextuality in Margaret Fuller's Writing,' 24. Thanks to Professor Steele for sharing this section of his work on Fuller.

41. Quoted in Urbanski, *Margaret Fuller's Woman in the Nineteenth Century*, 147.

42. Quoted in Chevigny, *Woman and the Myth*, 233.

43. Annie Fields, *Life and Letters of Harriet Beecher Stowe* (Boston: Houghton Mifflin, 1897), 27–8.

44. E. Bruce Kirkham, 'Introduction,' *The Pearl of Orr's Island* (Hartford: Stowe Day Foundation, 1979).

45. Quoted in Judith Fetterley, *Provisions* (Bloomington: Indiana University Press, 1985), 381.

46. Ibid. 30–1.

47. Sarah Orne Jewett to Annie Fields, quoted in Fetterley, *Provisions*, 378.

48. Ibid. 379.

49. Sheena McKay, 'Hair-Raising in New England,' *Times Literary Supplement*, 3 Mar. 1989, 332.

50. An exception was the production in the American Theater, San Francisco, in 1855. The playbill headlined 'Laura Keene will appear this evening as MIRANDA in Shakespear's [*sic*] Great Play of THE TEMPEST!' None the less, a reviewer noted, 'Miss Keene's Miranda . . . was not the feature of the evening; it was Caliban who carried off the honors.' See George R. MacMinn, *The Theater of the Golden Era in California* (Caldwell, Ida.: The Caxton Printers Ltd., 1941), 92.

51. Stephen Orgel, 'Introduction,' *The Tempest* (Oxford: Clarendon Press, 1987), 70.

52. See 'A Modern Mephistopheles, or The Long Love Chase,' Alcott Papers, 59M–309, Houghton Library, Harvard University.

53. Joan Givner, *Katherine Anne Porter: A Life* (New York: Simon and Schuster, 1982), 170.

54. Enrique Hank Lopez, *Conversations with Katherine Anne Porter* (Boston: Little Brown, 1981), 203.

55. *Katherine Anne Porter's Women* (Austin: University of Texas Press, 1979), 143.

56. Katherine Anne Porter, 'Afterword,' to Willa Cather, *The Troll Garden* (New York: Signet, 1984), 141.

57. 'Ocean-1212-W,' in Charles Newman, *Sylvia Plath: A Symposium* (Bloomington: Indiana University Press, 1970), 272.

58. For a discussion of this production, which involved heavy cuts in the text, see Mary Nilan, 'The Stage History of *The Tempest*: A Question of Theatricality,' Ph.D. diss. (Northwestern University, 1967), 166–71. Thanks to David Kastan for this and much other information about the stage history of the play.

59. *Sylvia Plath: A Biography* (New York: Simon and Schuster, 1987), 37.

60. Plath, *The Journals of Sylvia Plath*, ed. Ted Hughes and Frances McCullough (New York: Dial Press, 1982), 77.

61. 'Sylvia Plath and Her Journals,' in Paul Alexander (ed.), *Ariel Ascending: Writings about Sylvia Plath* (New York: Harper and Row, 1985), 153.

62. Laura E. Donaldson, 'The Miranda Complex: Colonialism and the Question of Feminist Reading,' *Diacritics* 18 (Fall 1988), 68, 71.

63. 'Foreword,' Patricia Jones-Jackson, *When Roots Die* (Athens: University of Georgia Press, 1987). In the fall of 1989, Hurricane Hugo inflicted severe damage on the Sea Islands.

64. Quoted in Henry Louis Gates, *The Signifying Monkey: A Theory of Afro-American Literary Criticism* (New York: Oxford University Press, 1988), xxiv, 175.

65. 'Re-writing *The Tempest*,' *WLWE* 23 (Winter 1984), 77.

66. Chantal Zabus, 'A Calibanic Tempest in Anglophone and Francophone New World Writing,' *Canadian Literature*, 104 (Spring 1985), 42–3.

67. Nixon, 'Caribbean and African Appropriations of *The Tempest*,' 538.

68. Gates, 'The Master's Pieces: On Canon-Formation and the Afro-

American Tradition,' paper presented at Princeton University, Spring 1989, 32.

CHAPTER 3

1. Madelon Bedell, 'Introduction,' *Little Women* (New York: Modern Library, 1983), ix–lxix.
2. Cynthia Ozick, 'The Making of a Writer,' *New York Times Book Review*, 11 Jan. 1982, 24; 'Governors Recall Books of Their Youth,' *New York Times*, 16 Nov. 1989. The most popular books were *Huckleberry Finn* and *Tom Sawyer*.
3. See Nina Baym, *Woman's Fiction* (Ithaca, NY: Cornell University Press, 1979); Jane Tompkins, *Sensational Designs: The Cultural Work of American Fiction 1790–1860* (New York: Oxford University Press, 1985); Ann Douglas, 'Introduction,' *Little Women* (New York: New American Library, 1983), vii–xxvii; Sarah Elbert, *A Hunger for Home*, rev. ed. (New Brunswick, NJ: Rutgers University Press, 1987); Anne Rose, *Transcendentalism as a Social Movement* (New Haven, Conn.: Yale University Press, 1981); Nina Auerbach, *Committee of Women* (Cambridge, Mass.: Harvard University Press, 1978), and 'Afterword,' *Little Women* (New York: Bantam Books, 1983); and Judith Fetterley, '*Little Women*: Alcott's Civil War,' *Feminist Studies*, 5 (1979), 369–83.
4. *Lies, Secrets, and Silence*, 201. In *Of Woman Born* (1976), Rich compared her parents to Alcott's parents, and described her breaking away from the intellectual influence of her own father.
5. Baym, *Woman's Fiction*, 32–3.
6. *The Selected Letters of Louisa May Alcott*, ed. Joel Myerson and Daniel Shealy, with Madeleine Stern (Boston: Little, Brown, 1987), 60.
7. LaSalle Corbett Pickett, *Across My Path* (New York: Brentano's, 1916), reprinted in Madeleine Stern (ed.), *Critical Essays on Louisa May Alcott* (Boston: G. K. Hall, 1984), 42.
8. Myerson and Shealy (eds.), *Letters*, 12–13.
9. Bronson Alcott, 'Journal,' 9 Sept. 1869.
10. Ibid. 81–2.
11. See Myerson and Shealy (eds.), *Letters*, 90; Ednah Cheney, *Louisa May Alcott: Her Life, Letters and Journals* (Boston: Roberts Bros., 1889), 127; and Helena Michie, *The Word Made Flesh* (New York: Oxford University Press, 1986), 28.
12. Sanford Salyer, *Marmee: The Mother of Little Women* (Norman: University of Oklahoma Press, 1949), 75.
13. *Madwoman in the Attic*, 632.
14. Cheney, *Louisa May Alcott*, 58; Bedell, *The Alcotts*, 238.
15. Ibid. 241.

16. Louisa May Alcott, 'A Memoir of My Childhood,' *The Woman's Journal*, 19 (26 May 1988), 180.

17. Myerson and Shealy (eds.), *Letters*, 1 Apr. 1887, 307.

18. Cheney, *Louisa May Alcott*, 60.

19. See Ann Douglas, 'Introduction,' xvi.

20. Cheney, *Louisa May Alcott*, 69.

21. Louise Chandler Moulton, 'Louisa May Alcott,' in Elizabeth Stuart Phelps (ed.), *Our Famous Women* (1883; repr. Freeport, NY: Books for Libraries Press, 1975), 49.

22. Myerson and Shealy (eds.), *Letters*, 19 Mar. 1865, 109.

23. Cheney, *Louisa May Alcott*, 140.

24. Pickett, in Stern (ed.), *Critical Essays*, 42.

25. Cheney, *Louisa May Alcott*, 198–9.

26. 'What Boys Read,' *Fortnightly Review*, 45 (1886), 248–59.

27. Myerson and Shealy (eds.), *Letters*, 31 July 1865, 111.

28. Cheney, *Louisa May Alcott*, 199.

29. Myerson and Shealy (eds.), *Letters*, 117.

30. 25 July 1868, Alcott Papers, Houghton Library, Harvard University.

31. Cheney, *Louisa May Alcott*, 199.

32. 'The Domestic Drama of Louisa May Alcott,' *Feminist Studies*, 10 (Summer 1984), 233–54.

33. 26 Oct. 1865, Alcott Papers, Houghton Library, Harvard University.

34. Cheney, *Louisa May Alcott*, 201; Myerson and Shealy (eds.), *Letters* 118–19, 124, 121, 120.

35. Myerson and Shealy (eds.), *Letters*, 1 Apr. 1869, 126.

36. Bronson Alcott, *Journal*, December 1869; quoted in Joel Myerson, '"Our Children Are Our Best Work": Bronson and Louisa May Alcott,' in Stern (ed.), *Critical Essays*, 263.

37. Myerson and Shealy (eds.), *Letters*, 21 Aug. 1879, 235.

38. This reference is to Amy's malapropisms; she means Yorick buying gloves, in Sterne's *Sentimental Journey*. The scene was often painted in the nineteenth century by artists including Stuart Newton and Frith. Many thanks to Juliet McMaster, University of Alberta, for this information.

39. Letter from Madeleine Stern, 21 July 1987, and from Daniel Shealy, 14 July 1987.

40. Myerson and Shealy (eds.), *Letters*, 25 Dec. 1878, 232.

41. Martha Saxton, *Louisa May* (New York: Avon, 1977), 9; Halttunen, 'Domestic Drama,' 241; Fetterley, 'Alcott's Civil War,' 382.

42. Bedell, 'Introduction,' *Little Women*, xxiv; Fetterley, 'Alcott's Civil War,' 382. See also Ann B. Murphy, 'The Borders of Ethical, Erotic, and Artistic Possibilities in *Little Women*,' *Signs* 15 (Spring 1990), 578.

43. *Little Women*, script in Special Collections, Baker Library, Dartmouth College.

44. 'Reflections on *Little Women*,' *Children's Literature*, 9 (1980), 128–39.
45. *A Hunger for Home*, 210.
46. Judith Wynne, 'Profile of a Prolific Writer: Joyce Carol Oates,' *Sojourner*, 7 Mar. 1983, 4. For a helpful explication of the novel, see Elizabeth Lennox Keyser, '*A Bloodsmoor Romance*: Joyce Carol Oates's Little Women,' *Women's Studies*, 14 (1988), 211–24.
47. Bedell, 'Introduction,' xxiv.
48. *Memoirs of a Dutiful Daughter*, trans. Janis Kirkup (Harmondsworth: Penguin, 1963), i. 90.
49. Deirdre Bair, *Simone de Beauvoir: A Biography* (London: Jonathan Cape, 1990), 74–5.

CHAPTER 4

1. See the contemporary reviews of *The Awakening* in the Norton Critical Edition, ed. Margaret Culley (New York: Norton, 1976), 145–55.
2. Kate Chopin, 'Confidences,' in *The Complete Works of Kate Chopin*, ed. Per Seyersted (Baton Rouge: Louisiana State University Press, 1969), ii. 701.
3. *The Awakening* (New York: Norton, 1976), section 32. References to *The Awakening* are to the numbered sections of the novel, rather than to page numbers; they are given parenthetically in the text.
4. Guy de Maupassant, 'Solitude,' trans. Kate Chopin, *St. Louis Life* (28 Dec. 1895), 30, quoted in Culley, 'Edna Pontellier: A Solitary Soul,' in Norton Critical Edition, 224.
5. 'Art for Truth's Sake,' in her autobiography, *Chapters from a Life* (Boston: Houghton Mifflin, 1897).
6. Sarah Orne Jewett, *Letters*, ed. Annie Adams Field (Boston: Houghton Mifflin, 1911), 47.
7. 'Homes of Single Women,' 1877, quoted in Carol Farley Kessler, 'Introduction,' to Elizabeth Stuart Phelps, *The Story of Avis* (repr.; New Brunswick, NJ: Rutgers University Press, 1985), xxii.
8. Phelps, *The Story of Avis*, 126, 246.
9. Quoted in Nancy Cott, 'Passionlessness: An Interpretation of Victorian Sexual Ideology, 1790–1850,' *Signs*, 4 (1978), 236, n. 60.
10. 'The Decadent and the New Woman in the 1890s,' *Nineteenth-Century Fiction*, 33 (1979), 441.
11. Frances Porcher, 'Kate Chopin's Novel,' *The Mirror*, 4 May 1899, and 'Books of the Day,' *Chicago Times Herald*, 1 June 1899, in Norton Critical Edition, 145, 149.
12. Martha Vicinus, 'Introduction,' to George Egerton, *Keynotes and Discords* (repr.; London: Virago Books, 1983), xvi.
13. 'A Keynote to *Keynotes*,' in *Ten Contemporaries*, ed. John Gawsworth (London: Ernest Benn, 1932), 60.

14. Per Seyersted, *Kate Chopin: A Critical Biography* (New York: Octagon Books, 1980), 18.
15. Sandra M. Gilbert, 'Introduction,' *The Awakening and Selected Stories* (Harmondsworth: Penguin, 1984), 16.
16. Chopin, 'Confidences,' in *Complete Works*, ii. 700–1.
17. Chopin, 'Crumbling Idols,' in *Complete Works*, ii. 693.
18. Seyersted, *Kate Chopin*, 83.
19. Ibid. 58.
20. Ibid. 209 n. 55.
21. Chopin, 'Confidences,' in *Complete Works*, ii. 702.
22. Quoted in Larzer Ziff, *The American 1890s* (New York: Viking, 1966), 275.
23. Gilbert, 'Introduction,' 25.
24. Thanks to Nancy K. Miller for this phrase from her current work on the development of women's writing in France. I am also indebted to the insights of Cheryl Torsney of the University of West Virginia, and to the comments of the other participants in my NEH Summer Seminar on 'Women's Writing and Women's Culture,' 1984.
25. Thanks to Lynne Rogers, Music Department, Princeton University, for the information about Frédéric Chopin.
26. Gilbert, 'Introduction,' 30.
27. See Gaston Bachelard, *L'eau et les rêves* (Paris: 1942), 109–25.
28. 'Life Without and Life Within,' quoted in Bell Gale Chevigny, *The Woman and the Myth: Margaret Fuller's Life and Writings* (New York: The Feminist Press, 1976), 349. See also Martin, *An American Triptych*, 154–9.
29. 'A New England Nun.' in Michèle Clark (ed.), *The Revolt of Mother* (New York: Feminist Press, 1974), 97.
30. Seyersted, *Kate Chopin*, 196; and Hazel V. Carby, 'Introduction,' to Frances E. W. Harper, *Iola Leroy* (Boston: Beacon Press, 1987), xxv.
31. 'Sibert' [Willa Cather], 'Books and Magazines,' *Pittsburgh Leader*, 8 July 1899, in Norton Critical Edition, 153.
32. Chopin, *Complete Works*, ii. 735.
33. Robert Stone, *Children of Light* (New York: Knopf, 1986), 132.

CHAPTER 5

1. Joy Wittenberg, 'Excerpts from the Diary of Elizabeth Oakes Smith,' *Signs*, 9 (1984), 537. The diary covers the year 1861.
2. 'Femininity,' *The Complete Edition of the Psychological Works of Sigmund Freud*, ed. and trans. Alix and James Strachey (London: Hogarth Press, 1964), xxii. 112–35.
3. Edith Wharton, *The House of Mirth* (New York: Charles Scribners, 1905), 3. All future page references to this work will be included parenthetically in the text.

4. *Edith Wharton's Argument with America* (Athens: University of Georgia Press, 1980), 27. Ammons sees this literature as influenced by such contemporary studies of the economics of marriage as Charlotte Perkins Gilman's *Women and Economics* (1898) and Thorstein Veblen's *Theory of the Leisure Class* (1899).

5. For discussions of these other transitional heroines of women's fiction, see Grace Stewart, *A New Mythos: The Novel of the Artist as Heroine, 1877–1977* (Montreal: Eden Press, 1981), and Ann Douglas, 'The Literature of Impoverishment: The Women Local Colorists in America, 1865–1914,' *Women's Studies*, 1 (1972), 3–45.

6. 'Edith Wharton and Her Works,' in Irving Howe (ed.), *Edith Wharton: A Collection of Critical Essays* (Englewood Cliffs, NJ: Prentice-Hall, 1962), 36.

7. Cynthia Griffin Wolff, *A Feast of Words: The Triumph of Edith Wharton* (New York: Oxford University Press, 1977), 11.

8. 'The "Blank Page" and Female Creativity,' in Elizabeth Abel (ed.), *Writing and Sexual Difference* (Chicago: University of Chicago Press, 1982), 81.

9. See Nina Baym, *Woman's Fiction* (Ithaca, NY: Cornell University Press, 1979), 11–12, 23, 29.

10. 'Justice to Edith Wharton,' in Howe (ed.), *Critical Essays*, 20.

11. *A Feast of Words*, 114–15. Wolff also notes that Wharton herself was called 'Lily' as a girl (p. 110).

12. On *The Lily*, see D. C. Bloomer, *Life and Writings of Amelia Bloomer* (Boston: Arena Publishing Company, 1895), 41–3.

13. Mary Wilkins Freeman repeatedly used the name 'Lily' for the younger woman in a generational transition from women's culture to New Womanhood; see also Lily Almy and Aunt Fidelia in 'A Patient Waiter.' The best recent collection of Freeman's work is *Selected Stories of Mary Wilkins Freeman*, ed. Marjorie Pryse (New York: Norton, 1983).

14. I am indebted for these details to 'A Critical Introduction to *Bertha and Lily*,' an unpublished paper written for my seminar on 'American Women Writers' at Rutgers University in 1984 by Katy Birckmayer, and to Ann Douglas, who first introduced me to the work of Elizabeth Oakes Smith.

15. *The Anglomaniacs* (repr.; New York: Arno Press, 1977). The introduction to this edition is by Elizabeth Hardwick.

16. On H.D. as 'Dryad,' and on her fashionable 'Greekness,' see Barbara Guest, *Herself Defined: The Poet H.D. and Her World* (New York: Doubleday, 1984), 33 ff.

17. See Sheila A. Tully, 'Heroic Failures and the Literary Career of Louise Imogen Guiney,' *American Transcendental Quarterly*, No. 47–8 (Summer–Fall 1980), 178. Cheryl Walker calls Guiney 'the most interesting of the turn-of-the-century [women] poets'; she sees a

commentary on the ambitions and the passions of the New Woman in the final words of Guiney's 'Tarpeia': 'O you that aspire! | Tarpeia the traitor had fill of her woman's desire.' See Cheryl Walker, *The Nightingale's Burden: Women Poets and American Culture before 1900* (Bloomington: Indiana University Press, 1982), 130–3.

18. Ammons, *Edith Wharton's Argument with America*, 39.

19. Joe L. Dubbert, 'Progressivism and the Masculinity Crisis,' in Elizabeth H. Pleck and Joseph H. Pleck (eds.), *The American Man* (Englewood Cliffs, NJ: Prentice-Hall, 1980), 307.

20. 'Justice to Edith Wharton,' in Howe (ed.), *Critical Essays*, 26–7.

21. Elizabeth Ammons points out that Wharton's contemporary readers would have been familiar with the institution of the Working Girls' Club; Wharton's sister-in-law Mary Cadwallader Jones had even written about these clubs in *The Woman's Book* (1894). See *Edith Wharton's Argument with America*, 40–1. A book published the same year as *The House of Mirth*, Dorothy Richardson's *Long Day: The Story of a New York Working Girl* (1905), reprinted in *Women at Work*, ed. William O'Neill (Chicago: University of Chicago Press, 1972), discusses the relationships between factory girls and the leisured ladies who offered them charity and also became the subjects of their fantasies. According to Richardson, working girls even adopted the names of society heroines from the newspapers and from romantic novels.

22. *The Female Imagination* (New York: Knopf, 1975), 241.

23. *A Feast of Words*, 130–1. Wolff maintains that Lily's feelings are narcissistic, whereas I read the conclusion of the novel as a demonstration of her awakened emotional capacities.

24. *Edith Wharton's Argument with America*, 43.

25. Wolff, *A Feast of Words*, 31, 46–7.

26. See Edith Wharton, *A Backward Glance* (New York: Holt, Rinehart and Winston, 1962), chapter 9. Marilyn French, who notes the reference to Burnett, argues that Wharton's writing always remained secretive and in some sense illegitimate. 'Introduction,' *The House of Mirth* (New York: Berkley Books, 1981), xii.

27. Wharton, *A Backward Glance*, 35.

28. Ibid. 207–8.

29. Wolff, *A Feast of Words*, 134–8. Wolff calls *The House of Mirth* a 'momentous' novel.

CHAPTER 6

1. Louise Bogan to Morton Zabel, cited in Elizabeth Frank, *Louise Bogan: A Portrait* (New York: Knopf, 1985), 33.

2. John Aldridge, *After the Lost Generation* (New York: Noonday Press, 1958), 13.

3. See Hermione Lee, *Willa Cather: Double Lives* (New York: Pantheon, 1989), 183.

4. Emily Newell Blair, cited in William H. Chafe, *The American Woman: Her Changing Social, Economic, and Political Role* (New York: Oxford University Press, 1972), 30.

5. Mary Austin, 'The Forward Turn,' *The Nation*, 20 July 1927, 58.

6. Lillian Hellman, *An Unfinished Woman* (New York: Bantam, 1970), 29.

7. Helen L. Horowitz, *Alma Mater: Design and Experience in the Women's Colleges* (New York: Knopf, 1984), 287–8.

8. Theodore Roethke, 'The Poetry of Louise Bogan,' *Selected Prose of Theodore Roethke*, ed. Ralph J. Mills, Jr. (Seattle: University of Washington Press, 1965), 133–4.

9. See William Drake, *Sara Teasdale: Woman and Poet* (San Francisco: Harper & Row, 1979).

10. See Stanley Olson, *Elinor Wylie: A Biography* (New York: Dial Press, 1978).

11. Hugh Kenner, 'More than a Bolus of Idiosyncracies,' *New York Times Book Review*, 17 July 1977, 14.

12. *What the Woman Lived: Selected Letters of Louise Bogan, 1920–1970*, ed. Ruth Limmer (New York: Harcourt Brace Jovanovich, 1973), 86.

13. Frank, *Louise Bogan*, 77.

14. *The Letters of Edna St. Vincent Millay*, ed. Allan Ross Macdougal (New York: Harper, 1952), 173.

15. Katha Pollitt, 'Sleeping Fury,' *The Yale Review* (Summer 1985), 600.

16. See Hortense Flexner King, 'Genevieve Taggard, 1894–1948,' *Sarah Lawrence College Alumnae Magazine*, 14 (Fall 1948), 12; and Genevieve Taggard, 'Children of the Hollow Men,' *Christian Register Unitarian*, 125 (Nov. 1946), 441–2.

17. Elinor Langer, *Josephine Herbst: The Story She Could Never Tell* (Boston: Little, Brown & Co., 1984), 120.

18. Alice Kessler-Harris and Paul Lauter, 'Introduction,' to Tess Slesinger, *The Unpossessed* (New York: Feminist Press, 1984), xi. I am very much indebted to this essay for background material on the Left and fiction in the 1930s.

19. Mary McCarthy, interviewed by Elisabeth Sifton in *Women Writers at Work: The Paris Review Interviews* (New York: Viking Penguin, 1989), 183.

20. Elaine Hedges, 'Introduction,' to Meridel Le Sueur, *Ripening: Selected Work, 1927–1980* (Old Westbury, NY: Feminist Press, 1982), 15. See also Robert Shaffer, 'Women and the Communist Party, USA,' *Socialist Review*, 99 (May–June 1979), 73–118.

21. Hedges, 'Introduction,' 8–11.

22. Deborah Rosenfelt, 'From the Thirties: Tillie Olsen and the Radical Tradition,' *Feminist Studies*, 7 (Fall 1981), 383.

23. See Elinor Langer, 'Afterword,' to Josephine Herbst, *Rope of Gold* (Old Westbury, NY: Feminist Press, 1984), 441.
24. See Janet Sharistanian, 'Afterword,' to Tess Slesinger, *The Unpossessed*, 370–1.
25. See Deborah E. McDowell, 'Introduction,' to Jessie Redmon Fauset, *Plum Bun* (London: Pandora Press, 1985), ix–xxiv.
26. Sandra M. Gilbert and Susan Gubar, *The Norton Anthology of Literature by Women* (New York: W. W. Norton, 1985), 1241–2.

CHAPTER 7

1. *Literary Women: The Great Writers* (New York: Doubleday, 1976), 91–2, 93.
2. Claire Kahane, 'The Gothic Mirror,' in Shirley Nelson Garner, Claire Kahane, and Madelon Sprengnether (eds.), *The (M)other Tongue: Essays in Feminist Psychoanalytic Interpretation* (Ithaca, NY: Cornell University Press, 1985), 335.
3. Ibid. 343.
4. Ibid. 334.
5. *The Coherence of Gothic Conventions* (New York: Methuen, 1986), vi; Mary Jacobus, *Reading Woman: Essays in Feminist Criticism* (New York: Columbia University Press, 1986), 201.
6. Eagleton, *Nationalism: Irony and Commitment* (Belfast: Field Day Theatre Company Limited, 1988), 13–14.
7. Leslie Fiedler, *Love and Death in the American Novel*, rev. edn. (New York: Stein and Day, 1975), 144.
8. Kahane, 'The Gothic Mirror,' 335–6.
9. Fiedler, *Love and Death in the American Novel*, 132.
10. See Jean E. Kennard, 'Convention Coverage or How to Read Your Own Life,' *New Literary History*, 13 (Autumn 1981), 69–88.
11. Diane Price Herndl, 'The Writing Cure: Charlotte Perkins Gilman, Anna O., and "Hysterical" Writing,' *NWSA Journal*, 1 (1988), 68.
12. See Kate Ford, 'Loss and Compensation,' *Times Literary Supplement*, 12–18 Jan. 1990, 46.
13. Thanks to Catherine Gallagher for this perception.
14. Mary A. Hill, *Charlotte Perkins Gilman: The Making of a Radical Feminist* (Philadelphia: Temple University Press, 1980), 152.
15. Gilman, *The Living of Charlotte Perkins Gilman* (New York: D. Appleton–Century Co., 1935), 5–6.
16. Ibid. 98, 100.
17. *The Diary of Alice James*, ed. Leon Edel (New York: Dodd, Mead & Co., 1934), 149.
18. *Reading Woman*, 240.
19. Dr Paula Clayton, quoted in Daniel Goleman, 'Wide Beliefs on Depression in Women Contradicted,' *New York Times*, 9 Jan. 1990.

20. Jeffrey Berman, *The Talking Cure: Literary Representations of Psychoanalysis* (New York: New York University Press, 1985), 54.

21. Jacobus, *Reading Woman*, 233.

22. Patricia Bosworth, *Diane Arbus: A Biography* (New York: Alfred A. Knopf, 1984), 101.

23. Ibid. 132.

24. Arbus's use of the camera had precedent in the early photography of Eudora Welty, and recent parallels in the work of women film directors like Susan Seidelman. In the documentary *Calling the Shots*, shown on British television in Spring 1990, Seidelman and other women filmmakers discussed the way that the camera allowed them access to forbidden turf.

25. Bosworth, *Diane Arbus*, 158.

26. Ibid. 217.

27. *The Journals of Sylvia Plath*, ed. Ted Hughes and Frances McCullough (New York: Dial Press, 1982), 319. An unpublished paper by Jodi Hauptman, 'Mirrors and Pictures: A Comparison of *The Bell Jar* to the Photographs of Diane Arbus,' written for my course on 'American Women Writers' in May 1985, explores similar images of mirrors, shadows, and doubling in Arbus and Plath.

28. Linda Huf, *A Portrait of the Artist as a Young Woman* (New York: Frederick Ungar, 1983), 128.

29. Berman, *Talking Cure*, 127.

30. Judith Walzer Leavitt, 'Birthing and Anesthesia: The Debate over Twilight Sleep,' in *Women and Health in America* (Madison: University of Wisconsin Press, 1984), 181.

31. *Of Woman Born* (New York: W. W. Norton, 1976), 170–1.

32. 'Why Is Your Writing So Violent?' *New York Times Book Review*, 25 Mar. 1981, 10.

33. 'Interview with Joyce Carol Oates,' in John R. Knott, Jr., and Christopher R. Keaske (eds.), *Mirrors: An Introduction to Literature*, 2nd edn. (San Francisco: Canfield Press, 1975), 18–19.

34. Ibid. 19.

35. See Dan Moser, 'The Pied Piper of Tucson,' *Life*, 4 Mar. 1966, 18–24. This source was identified by Tom Quirk, 'A Source for "Where Are You Going, Where Have You Been?"' *Studies in Short Fiction*, 18 (Fall 1981), 413–19.

36. Larry McCaffery, *Anything Can Happen: Interviews with Contemporary American Novelists* (Urbana: University of Illinois Press, 1983), 205.

37. Interview with Diane Johnson, in McCaffery, *Anything Can Happen*, 202.

38. Janet Todd, 'Diane Johnson,' in Janet Todd (ed.), *Women Writers Talking* (New York: Holmes and Meier, 1983), 125.

39. See e.g. Jean Stafford's story, 'The Echo and the Nemesis,' in *Children are Bored on Sunday* (New York: Harcourt, Brace, 1953).
40. Todd, 'Diane Johnson,' 125.
41. McCaffery, *Anything Can Happen*, 213.
42. Diane Johnson, 'The War between Men and Women,' *New York Review of Books*, 11 Dec. 1975.
43. Constance Carey, interview with Diane Johnson, *San Francisco Review of Books*, 1 (Jan. 1976), 17.
44. McCaffery, *Anything Can Happen*, 215.
45. Aljean Harmetz, '"Pet" Film Rights Sold,' *New York Times*, 8 June 1984.
46. Michiko Kakutani, 'Kill! Burn! Eviscerate! Bludgeon! It's Literary Again to Be Horrible,' *New York Times*, 21 Nov. 1989.

CHAPTER 8

1. When Glaspell published the story and also produced it as a one-act play called 'Trifles,' it was taken to refer to the sensational Lizzie Borden case, with its all-male jury. It also served an indirect threat that voteless American women would reject the patriarchal law that had declared their rights and rites to be only trifles. See Susan Gubar and Anne Hedin, 'A Jury of Her Peers,' *College English*, 43 (Dec. 1981), 179–89; Karen Alkaley-Gut, 'Jury of Her Peers: The Importance of Trifles,' *Studies in Short Fiction*, 21 (Winter 1984), 1–10; and Elaine Hedges, 'Small Things Reconsidered: Susan Glaspell's "A Jury of Her Peers,"' *Women's Studies*, 12 (1986), 89–110.
2. See e.g. Patricia Mainardi: 'Women not only made beautiful and functional objects, but expressed their own convictions on a wide variety of subjects in a language for the most part comprehensible only to other women'. 'Quilts: The Great American Art,' *Radical America*, 7 (1973), 56.
3. 'A Map for Rereading: Gender and the Interpretation of Literary Texts,' in Elaine Showalter (ed.), *The New Feminist Criticism* (New York: Pantheon, 1985), 42.
4. Lisa Tickner, 'Feminism, Art History, and Sexual Difference,' *Genders*, 3 (1988), 96.
5. Quoted in Pattie Chase, 'The Quilt as an Art Form in New England,' in *Pilgrims and Pioneers: New England Women in the Arts* (New York: Midmarch Arts, 1987), 81. There is always a great fuss when a man enters a traditionally feminine field, and usually a claim that he has outperformed all the women. In 1886 one Charles Pratt declared himself quilt-making champion of the world. See also the work of Lloyd Blanks, 'He's Raised Needlework to the State of an Art,' *New School Observer*, Mar. 1984. Thanks to Carol Barash for this article.

6. *The Spectacle of Women: Imagery of the Suffrage Campaign 1907–14* (Chicago: University of Chicago Press, 1988), 278 n. 13.

7. *Old Mistresses: Women, Art, and Ideology* (New York: Pantheon, 1981), 78.

8. Elaine Hedges, 'The Nineteenth-Century Diarist and Her Quilts,' *Feminist Studies*, 8 (Summer 1982), 295.

9. For the history of American quilts, see Pat Ferrero, Elaine Hedges, and Julie Silber, *Hearts and Hands: The Influence of Women & Quilts on American Society* (San Francisco: Quilt Digest Press, 1987).

10. See Maude Southwell Wahlman and Ella King Torrey, *Ten Afro-American Quilters* (Center for the Study of Southern Culture, University of Mississippi, 1983).

11. 'Patches, Quilts and Community in Alice Walker's "Everyday Use,"' *Southern Review*, 21 (July 1985), 713.

12. Robert Ferris Thompson, Preface, 'From the First to the Final Thunder: African-American Quilts, Monuments of Cultural Assertion,' in Eli Leon, *Who'd A Thought It: Improvisation in African-American Quiltmaking* (San Francisco Craft & Folk Art Museum, 1987), 17, 21.

13. 'Up, Down, and Across: A New Frame for New Quilts,' in Charlotte Robinson (ed.), *The Artist and the Quilt* (New York: Knopf, 1983), 18.

14. Quoted in Patricia Cooper and Norma Buferd, *The Quilters: Women and Domestic Art* (New York: Doubleday, 1978), 20.

15. Parker and Pollock, *Old Mistresses*, 71.

16. 'Quilts,' 37.

17. Ron Pilling, 'Album Quilts of the Mid-1880s,' *Art & Antiques*, Nov.–Dec. 1982, 72.

18. 'Annette,' 'The Patchwork Quilt,' in Benita Eisler (ed.), *The Lowell Offering* (New York: Harper, 1977), 150–4.

19. Judith Fetterley, *Provisions* (Bloomington: Indiana University Press, 1985), 3.

20. Mary Kelley, *Private Woman, Public Stage: Literary Domesticity in Nineteenth-Century America* (New York: Oxford University Press, 1984), 169.

21. Fetterley, *Provisions*, 14–15.

22. *Emily Dickinson and Her Culture* (Cambridge: Cambridge University Press, 1984), 9, 10.

23. Louisa May Alcott, 'Patty's Patchwork,' in *Aunt Jo's Scrap-Bag* (Boston: Roberts, 1872), i. 193–215. Thanks to Elizabeth Keyser for bringing this story to my attention; my analysis is indebted to her presentation in our NEH Summer Seminar on 'Women's Writing and Women's Culture,' 1984.

24. Ferrero, Hedges and Silber, *Hearts and Hands*, 37.

25. Ibid. 96.

26. Susan R. Finkel, *New Jersey Crazy Quilts 1875–1900* (Trenton, New Jersey State Museum, 19 Nov. 1988–8 Jan. 1989).
27. Ferrero, Hedges, and Silber, *Hearts and Hands*, 87.
28. Ibid. 94.
29. 'The Making of a Militant,' in Elaine Showalter (ed.), *These Modern Women* (New York: Feminist Press, 1989).
30. Ann S. Stephens, 'The Quilting Party,' in John S. Hart (ed.), *The Female Prose Writers of America* (Philadelphia: E. H. Butler, 1857), 204–10; and Mary Wilkins Freeman, 'A Quilting Bee in Our Village,' *The People of Our Neighborhood* (Philadelphia: Curtis, 1898), 113–28.
31. Kate Chopin, 'Elizabeth Stock's One Story,' in Sandra M. Gilbert (ed.), *The Awakening and Selected Stories* (New York: Penguin, 1984), 274–80.
32. Dorothy Canfield Fisher, 'What My Mother Taught Me,' and 'The Bedquilt,' in Susan Cahill (ed.), *Women and Fiction 2* (New York: New American Library, 1978).
33. Quoted in Parker and Pollock, *Old Mistresses*, 68.
34. In Showalter (ed.), *These Modern Women*.
35. Elaine Hedges, 'The Needle or the Pen: The Literary Rediscovery of Women's Textile Work,' in Florence Howe (ed.), *Tradition and the Talents of Women* (Urbana: University of Illinois Press, 1991).
36. 'Up, Down, and Across,' 32.
37. DuPlessis, 'For the Etruscans,' in Showalter (ed.), *The New Feminist Criticism* (London: Virago, 1986), 278.
38. Lynn Miller and Sally Swenson (eds.), in *Lives and Works* (Methuen, NJ: Scarecrow Press, 1981).
39. Donnell-Vogt believes that the basic quilt patterns are archetypal representations of the female body. In her own art, she explains, quilt-making 'was essential in giving me a base for exploring my situation as a woman and as an artist . . . quilts became for me a confirmation and restatement of women's toils in child-raising of the physical labor in the cultural shaping and maintenance of persons. . . . Finally, I saw quilts as the bliss and the threat of the womb made visible, spread out as a separate object shaped by the imaginative wealth of women's work and body experience.' Ibid. 12.
40. 'The Needle and the Pen,' in Howe (ed.), *Tradition and the Talents of Women*. Hedges argues in this essay that needlework and writing are antagonistic in women's literature, but her concern is with sewing as domestic task rather than the quilt metaphor.
41. Baker and Baker, 'Patches,' 706.
42. Ibid. 718.
43. Thompson, in Leon (ed.), *Who'd A Thought It*, 13, 17.
44. See Marie Jean Adams, 'The Harriet Powers Pictorial Quilts,' *Black Art*, 3 (1980), 12–28; Gladys-Marie Fry, 'Harriet Powers: Portrait of a Black Quilter,' in Anna Wadsworth (ed.), *Missing Pieces: Georgia Folk Art*

1770–1976 (Atlanta: Georgia Council for the Arts and Humanities, 1976), 16–23.

45. Baker and Baker, 'Patches,' 716.
46. 'The Integrity of Memory: Creating a New Literary History of the United States,' *American Literature*, 57 (May 1985), 291–2.
47. 'Afterword,' *Ideology and Classic American Literature* (Cambridge: Cambridge University Press, 1986), 438.
48. See ch. 3, 'Melting Pots,' in Werner Sollers, *Beyond Ethnicity: Consent and Descent in American Culture* (New York: Oxford University Press, 1986), 66–101.
49. 'Excerpts from Jackson's Speech: Pushing Party to Find Common Ground,' *New York Times*, 20 July 1988, A18.
50. Cindy Ruskin, *The Quilt: Stories from the NAMES Project* (New York: Pocket Books, 1988), 12.
51. Ibid. 13.
52. Dr Beverly Gordon, quoted in 'When an Object Evolves from an It to a He or She,' *New York Times*, 16 Nov. 1989.
53. 'Notes and Comment,' *The New Yorker*, 5 Oct. 1987, 31.
54. Simon Watney, quoted in John Seabrook, 'The AIDS Philosopher,' *Vanity Fair*, Dec. 1990, 111.
55. See Ellen Carol DuBois and Vicki L. Ruiz, *Unequal Sisters: A Multi-Cultural Reader in U.S. Women's History* (New York: Routledge, 1990).
56. Alice Walker, quoted in Henry Louis Gates, Jr. (ed.), *Reading Black, Reading Feminist* (New York: Meridian, 1990), 11.
57. Robert Phillips, 'Joyce Carol Oates: The Art of Fiction LXXII,' *Paris Review*, Winter 1978, 225–6.
58. Hortense Spillers, 'Cross-currents, Discontinuities: Black Women's Fiction,' in Marjorie Pryse and Hortense Spillers (eds.), *Conjuring: Black Women's Fiction and Literary Tradition* (Bloomington: Indiana University Press, 1985), 250.
59. These are the words of Barbara Christian, writing about Walker in 'The Highs and Lows of Black Feminist Criticism,' in Gates, *Reading Black, Reading Feminist*, 44.

INDEX